AF668427

Rabindranath Tagore

A Pictorial Biography

Rabindranath Tagore

A Pictorial Biography

Nityapriya Ghosh

NIYOGI
BOOKS

Published by

NIYOGI BOOKS
D-78, Okhla Industrial Area, Phase-I
New Delhi-110 020, India
Tel: 91-11-26816301, 49327000
Fax: 91-11-26810483, 26813830
email: niyogibooks@gmail.com
www.niyogibooks.com

Text ©: Nityapriya Ghosh

Editor: Madhuparna
Design: Write Media

ISBN: 978-81-89738-75-4

Year of Publication: 2011
Reprint: 2012

All rights are reserved. No part of the publication may be reproduced or transmitted in any form or by any means, electronic or mechanical, including photocopying, recording or by any information storage and retrieval system without the written permission and consent of the Publisher.

Printed at: Niyogi Offset Pvt. Ltd., New Delhi, India

Contents

The young Poet, Calcutta, c. 1886.

Preface

In June 1901, Rabindranath Tagore wrote a poem and published it in *Bangadarsan*, a magazine he was editing at that time. Later in 1914, he included it in his book of verse, *Utsarga*. The poem has been familiar to biographers of Tagore and often quoted. It begins with the words: '*Bahir haite dekho na eman kare*' and concludes with '*Kabire pabe na tahar jibancharite*'. The Poet pleaded to his readers not to look at him from outside and that one would not find him in the facts of his life. In the long poem, he elaborated on the subject. He specified where the Poet could not be found and where he could be; not in the personal joys and sorrows of the Poet, but in the life of people whom the Poet sought to understand, in the smells, sounds and sights of Nature that shaped their lives, days and nights, in the songs he composed to give a form to the dreams which, however, eluded him.

Rabindranath wrote the poem when he was forty and had published eighteen volumes of poems and songs, fourteen musical and prose plays, two novels, four books of short stories and six books of essays and letters. This work was slender compared with the productions of his next forty years. But his views on biography remained unchanged. He himself made no effort to state the events of his life in his two autobiographical books or in his several essays when he was requested to write about himself. In a characteristic letter to Nirmalkumari Mahalanobis, wife of famous Indian statistician Prasanta Mahalanobis and the Poet's close associate, he mentioned that he himself could never furnish the facts of his life for which one would have to go to Prasanta, the repository of the facts. Prasanta, however, was too busy a man to write the biography of the Poet. In the initial stages, he did, of course, assist E.J. Thompson in providing basic facts and influences on the life of the Poet.

Major biographers of Tagore, mentioned in the Bibliography section of this book, had broadly two approaches. One, analysis of Tagore's works in the light of his life; the other, a chronicle of his time. The present work belongs more to the second category than the first. In the broad sweep of their narration, the biographers of the second type tended to pass by incidents, anecdotes and issues which are no less interesting and significant. This biography seeks to fill some gaps.

An artist's depiction of Chowringhee Road in mid-nineteenth century.

The world of Jorasanko

Rabindranath Tagore was born on 7 May 1861 in Calcutta. In those days, Calcutta had no electricity, gas, underground sewage drains, piped drinking water or public transport, except horse carriages, not to talk of telephones, motor cars or cooking gas. The large mansion built by his ancestors was situated in a narrow lane in north Calcutta, which then was called the 'black' town and was culturally if not physically distinctly distant from the 'white' town where the English settlers lived. Four years before Tagore's birth, Queen Victoria of England had taken over the administration of India from the East India Company under a charter from the Crown of England, which had slowly but steadily spread its tentacles to expropriate the riches of India that had attracted invaders for over ten centuries. The Jorasanko residence of the Tagores was a universe by itself, cut off from mainstream Calcutta for a number of reasons. There is no recorded history of Rabindranath's ancestors prior to the times of his grandfather Dwarkanath Tagore. His ancestors lived in a village in Jessore, now in Bangladesh. They were proud Brahmins, but their reputation in the constricted village society got tarnished by a certain marriage in the family—with a converted Muslim called Pir Ali Khan. The stigma of a Pirali Brahmin was too much for the family, some of whom left the village and settled in a sparsely populated part of Calcutta. However, coming in touch with the East India Company, Panchanan Kushari, one of the ancestors, prospered. He was revered by his lowly neighbours and called 'Thakur', which in Bengali has many meanings—priest, master, Lord. 'Thakur' became Tagore in the English tongue. Two of Panchanan's grandsons—Nilmani and Darpanarayan—having acquired wealth through landed properties and businesses, but for some other reasons, decided to split. Nilmani built the Jorasanko mansion and Darpanarayan the Pathuriaghata mansion. Nilmani's successors chose to live as Pirali Brahmins, shunned by the Bengali upper castes. Darpanarayan's successors managed to shed their dubious caste connection and became prominent members of the Hindu society. The Jorasanko and Pathuriaghata clans lived socially estranged lives. That was one reason why the Jorasanko universe had its constricted social life.

Dwarkanath (1794–1846), the fourth generation successor of Panchanan, was a colossal figure in modern India. Versed in Persian, English and Sanskrit, he extended his financial empire—diverting from ever-expanding landed properties to other business enterprises, such as indigo, coal, shipping and banking—and became the most eminent Indian of his times, whose company was sought after even by the English ruling class. He was warmly welcomed at Queen Victoria's court; the Queen herself having addressed him as Prince. He made friends with literary giants of Europe like Charles Dickens and Max Mueller. Back home he was a follower and patron of Rammohun Roy (1772–1833), who initiated social and religious reforms in India. Dwarkanath sustained the Brahmo Samaj, founded by Rammohun, though keeping himself strictly within orthodox Hindu rites. Strangely enough, Dwarkanath has been rarely mentioned in Rabindranath's memoirs or letters. Rabindranath preferred to be known as Devendranath's son rather than as Dwarkanath's grandson. He never visited Dwarkanath's tomb in England, where the Prince died prematurely.

Devendranath (1817–1905) was an easy-going youth, who was deeply upset at the death of his grandmother. He took to studying

Left: Jorasanko mansion, built by Nilmani Thakur and his successors. Facing page: A portrait of Dwarkanath Tagore by Baron de Schwiter.

philosophy—Indian and Western. His father was vexed at the son's indifference to his many commercial ventures, and created a Trust to manage the landed properties. Within two years of Dwarkanath's death, the bank he had founded failed and all his businesses floundered. The liabilities were more than the assets. Devendranath promised to pay off all the liabilities and even offered to give up the Trust lands. The creditors, overwhelmed at this gesture, settled for instalments and got their money back over a prolonged time.

Devendranath formally adopted the Brahmo religion on 21 December 1843. It was indeed a momentous decision and Rabindranath used to commemorate the day (7 *Paush*, according to the Bengali calendar) till the last year of his life. Devendranath had also founded the Tattabodhini Sabha to discuss and debate philosophy and religion and initiated *Tattabodhini*, a magazine for discourse in social and religious subjects. Both the Sabha and magazine had a long life and Rabindranath became closely associated with them when he came of age. Devendranath had neglected his father's business and land enterprises when the latter was alive, but was compelled in the absence of his father to look after the estates. He not only maintained the estates but also extended the zamindari considerably. The family, that was on the verge of being pauperised, thereby survived and continued to hold a position of esteem financially.

The Jorasanko Tagore family was ostracised because of its Pirali stigma. Devendranath's adoption of the Brahmo religion made it further removed from mainstream Hindu society. Devendranath also eschewed the English society and concentrated on the spread of the Brahmo religion, fighting against those Christian missionaries, who were bent on maligning Indian religions. This made the family more insular.

Rabindranath, however, did not feel the constriction as the Jorasanko Tagores lived in a joint family, and indeed what a huge family that was! Rabindranath was the youngest of the fifteen children of Devendranath—the difference between the eldest and the surviving youngest sibling was as much as twenty-one years. Dwarkanath had built another mansion in the ancestral compound—the original later had the postal address as 6 Dwarkanath Tagore Lane while the latter as 5 Dwarkanath Tagore Lane. One of Rabindranath's surviving uncles, Girindranath, lived in no. 5, and had a large family of his own, and his eldest grandson was only six years younger than Rabindranath. The two families, with handsome earnings from the zamindari, lived with a huge entourage—servants, maids, cooks, doorkeepers, gardeners, palanquin bearers, horse keepers, and all the rest of it.

A mother of fifteen children (four of them died very early) can hardly be expected to look after all of them by herself; nor was it customary in a rich Bengali family for mothers rearing children by themselves. However, it is evident from the accounts of Rabi's childhood memories (his mother died when he was fourteen) that he did not feel neglected by his mother. But for daily chores, the children were each allotted special servants and Rabi's childhood was dominated by his man-servants who kept him on a tight ration of food, clothes and entertainment (which meant recitals of the Ramayana, ghost stories, robbers' adventures, in their own illiterate ways).

The child Rabi was too sensitive, even when he was hungry, to ask for a few more morsels of rice or a cup of milk. That he developed a sense of deprivation is indicated in his letters. In the letters that he wrote from Silaidaha, in north Bengal, on 27 June 1894 to his niece Indira (1873–1960), and during a sea voyage on 29 March 1929 to Nirmalkumari Mahalanobis, he remembered how in his childhood, on winter mornings, he looked longingly at the personal cook of his elder brother, Jyotirindranath (1849–1925), who was married at that time, preparing toasts for his brother and spreading butter on them, while he was left out in the care of self-seeking servants. There was a distinct barrier between the elders and the young ones in the Jorasanko household. There would be *jatras*, plays and music sessions on the spacious compound—the young ones were allowed to see the elaborate preparations made for the show but not to join the session. If a boy was spotted in the adult crowd, he was publicly scorned and quickly carried off by the servants, while the boy remained mortified imagining the delights he had been denied of.

Enough care was, however, taken for the children's education at home. There was a *pathsala* (primary school) in the house itself, where Rabi started his elementary three 'R's. He was admitted to five schools in ten years, along with his immediate elder brother and a cousin. The guardians—Devendranath, who stayed most of the time outside Jorasanko and used to travel all over India by river or to the hills—and his elder brothers found the trio misfits in all the schools. Rabindranath wrote and spoke about his unhappy school life in many of his essays and lectures—the indifferent, sometimes hostile teachers; the harassment of boys when ragged by other schoolmates; the claustrophobic classrooms and the dry lessons. His guardians also did not seem to be too keen on Rabi's pursuit of academic studies. Rabi was taken off to the Himalayas by his father; and then again to Silaidaha,

Above: Sarada Sundari, wedded at the age of six, who bore fifteen children, and died at the age of fifty.
Below: Rabindranath Tagore at the age of five.
Facing page: Devendranath Tagore, called Maharshi (the great sage), by Brahmos.

one of the zamindari estates, by Jyotirindranath right in the midst of his academic sessions. His classmate-brother developed insanity during school life; his cousin passed the entrance examination but Rabi dropped out of St. Xavier's School at the age of fifteen.

Above: Rabi, his brother Somendranath, cousin Satyaprasad with family friend Srikantha Sinha; photographed c. 1873–74. Top right: St. Xavier's School, where young Rabi studied for a brief period.

Rabi's futile school education was more than compensated by his home tutors, who taught him languages and science. Even in his old age, he remembered the names of his tutors and the subjects taught by them. He had a sound foundation in Bengali; he overcame the fear of an alien language like English; and developed an emotional attachment with Sanskrit. Children of the house received lessons in physical training from skilled wrestlers. Rabi had such a well-developed body that an English surgeon, who was given a call to treat Rabindranath when he fell unconscious at the age of seventy-nine had exclaimed in surprise: 'What a splendid body!' Reputable musicians of the time gave the children lessons in Bengali and classical Indian music. Rabi never liked systematic training in music, but the musical environment of the Jorasanko house had ingrained in him the fine intricacies of the *ragas* (musical modes in Indian classical music expressing different moods in their characteristic way of progression). He ended up writing some 2,000 songs, which even today, seventy years after his death, mesmerise millions. Professional classical musicians never cease to wonder at the bold experiments Rabindranath had made with the *ragas*, which demonstrate his total command over them.

Rabi's First Train Journey

Our first halt was to be for a few days at Bolpur. Satya had been there a short time before with his parents. [Satyaprasad Gangopadhyay (1859–1933), son of Rabi's eldest sister, and one of the trio—Satya, Somendra and Rabindra—who were schoolmates. Satya was around fourteen and Rabi twelve, when Rabi had his first train journey.] No self-respecting nineteenth-century infant would have credited the account of his travels which he gave us on his return. But we were different, and had had no opportunity of learning to determine the line between the possible and the impossible. Our Mahabharata and Ramayana gave us no clue to it. Nor had we then any children's illustrated books to guide us in the way a child should go. All the hard-and-fast laws which govern the world we learnt by knocking up against them.

Satya had told us that, unless one was very very expert, getting into a railway carriage was a terribly dangerous affair—the least slip, and it was all up. Then, again, a fellow had to hold on to his seat with all his might, otherwise the jolt at starting was so tremendous there was no telling where one would get thrown off to. So when we got to the railway station, I was all a-quiver. So easily did we get into our compartment, however, that I felt sure the worst was yet to come. And when, at length, we made an absolutely smooth start, without any semblance of adventure, I felt woefully disappointed.

(From *Jibansmriti*, translated by
Surendranath Tagore as *My Reminiscences*)

Rabi, at the age of fourteen.

Out in the open world

Rabi broke away from the small world of Jorasanko when he was sent to England at the age of seventeen to sit for the Indian Civil Services (ICS) examinations. His second elder brother, Satyendranath Tagore (1842–1923) was the first Indian to join the ICS in 1864 when Rabi was only three. Staying as paying guests in English households for about a year, Rabi joined University College, London, but after three months or so he was called back home. He jocularly said in his old age that his father feared that he might marry a white girl, hence the order to come back. While in London, he had been writing open letters to his relations in Jorasanko, and those letters with descriptions and comments on the English lifestyle and the West's liberal view of women were being serially published in a magazine which was edited by his eldest brother, a philosopher-poet. The letters were light and witty, bearing signs of the young man's growing maturity.

This is not to say that Rabi was immature before he crossed the seas for the first time. He had the distinction of writing a poem, at the age of sixteen, which could not be published possibly because of the Vernacular Press Act, 1878. The poem 'Dilli Darbar' was written on the misfortunes of the country when the Viceroy of India, Lord Lytton, held the Delhi Durbar to commemorate Queen Victoria's assumption of the title: 'Empress of India'. Rabi recited the poem at the Mela ground after the annual session of the Hindu Mela had been roughed up by the administration. The Mela was initiated ten years ago by the Jorasanko Tagores and a few nationalist intellectuals of Calcutta to promote a sense of Indianness in literature, music and handicrafts.

Even earlier, at the age of thirteen, one of Rabi's poems, 'Hindu Melay Upahar', got published in *Amrita Bazar Patrika*, then a bilingual newspaper. By the time he left for England, one of his long narrative poems 'Kabikahini' was published in a literary magazine; he had also written book reviews, literary criticisms, short stories, as well as a novel. He was inspired by Thomas Chatterton, a young eighteenth-century poet, who had invented a fictional fourteenth-century poet under whose name he used to publish his poems. Rabi also invented Bhanusimha Thakur, supposed to be a Vaishnava lyricist of the Middle Ages, and published poems under his name. Rabi was flattered to learn later, though mistakenly, that far away in Germany, a Bengali scholar had written a PhD treatise on Bhanusimha Thakur, a poet of the Middle Ages! The poems were set to tune by him at a later stage and continue to be hugely popular, with their lilting tunes and pseudo-Brajabuli dialect (a Maithili dialect).

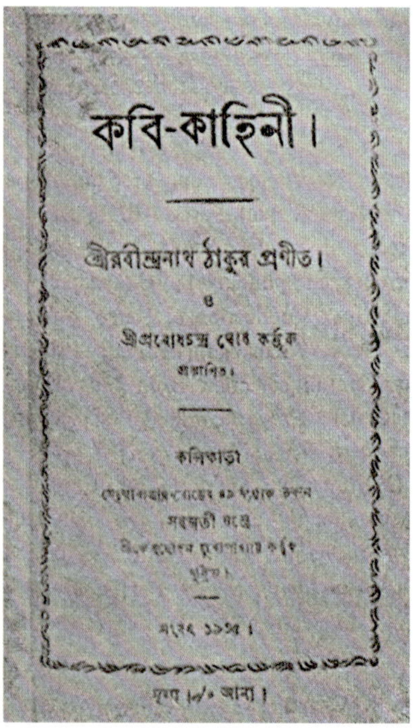

Above: The cover of Kabikahini, *Rabi's first book of verse, published in 1878.*
Facing page: In England, c. 1878-79.

When Rabi came back to Calcutta, he had two books of verse to his credit, and two more were to be published shortly. Years later, however, he dismissed these verses as artificial products of fervid imagination fed on English romantic poetry. The language, he felt, was stilted; the metrical styles were borrowed from contemporary Bengali poetry; and the contents were utterly unreal. He struck his own chord after a strange experience. In the 1930 Hibbert Lectures in London, he spoke about the moment:

> When I was eighteen, a sudden spring breeze of religious experience for the first time came to my life and passed away leaving in my memory a direct message of a spiritual reality. One day while I stood watching in early dawn the sun sending out its rays from behind the trees, I suddenly felt as if some ancient mist had in a moment lifted from my sight and the morning light on the face of the world revealed an inner radiance of joy. The invisible screen of the commonplace was removed from all things and all men, and their ultimate significance was intensified in my mind which is the

> definition of beauty. That which was memorable in this experience was its human message, the sudden expansion of my consciousness in the superpersonal world of men. The poem that I wrote on the first day of my surprise was named 'The Awakening of the Waterfall'. The waterfall, whose spirit lay dormant in its ice-bound isolation, was touched by the sun and bursting in a cataract of freedom, it found its finality in an unending sacrifice, in continual union, with the sea.

Rabindranath had written about this moment of revelation in his *Jibansmriti* (My Reminiscences) in 1911 and some other essays but never translated the long poem. The passage quoted is an extract from *The Religion of Man*, which he delivered over three days as Hibbert Lectures. Hindusthan Musical Products recorded the passage in the Poet's voice in 1939 and Akashvani re-recorded it for a cassette in 1999, called *Facets of a Genius*.

Rabindranath's stay in England exposed him to Western music. He had heard European music in his own household, even Chopin and others, before he came to England, as he had mentioned to Albert Einstein in 1930. He had tried to understand its spirit and structure, but as he had confessed to Einstein, who invited him to his house at Berlin, Indian music touched him more deeply than European. European music, he admitted, was epic in character, with a broad background and Gothic structure, but the fundamental lyrical quality of Indian music appealed to him even more.

The Plight of a Singer

During the whole period of my stay in England (1878–79) I was mixed up in a farcical comedy which I had to play out from start to finish. I happened to get acquainted with the widow of some departed high Anglo-Indian official. She was good enough to call me by the pet name Ruby. Some Indian friend of hers had composed a doleful poem in English in memory of her husband. It is needless to expatiate on its poetic merit or felicity of diction. As my ill luck would have it, the composer had indicated that the dirge was to be chanted to the mode *Behaga*. So the widow one day entreated me to sing it to her thus. Like the silly innocent that I was, I weakly acceded. There was fortunately no one there but I who could realise the atrociously ludicrous way in which the *Behaga* mode combined with those absurd verses. The widow seemed intensely touched to hear the Indian's lament for her husband sung to its native melody. I thought that there the matter ended, but that was not to be...

She was in a suburban locality some distance away from London, and though I frequently got letters from her inviting me there, my dread of that dirge kept me from accepting those invitations. At length I got a pressing telegram from her. I was on my way to college when this telegram reached me, and my stay in England was then about to come to its close. I thought to myself I ought to see the widow once more before my departure, and so yielded to her importunity. Instead of coming home from college, I went straight to the railway station. It was a horrible day, bitterly cold, snowing and foggy. The station I was bound for was a terminus for the line. So I felt quite easy in mind and did not think it worthwhile to inquire about the time of arrival.

All the station platforms were coming on the right-hand side, and in the right-hand corner seat I had ensconced myself reading a book. It had already become so dark that nothing was visible outside. One by one the other passengers got down at their destinations. We reached and left the station just before the last one. Then the train stopped again, but there was nobody to be seen, nor any lights on platform. The mere passenger has no means of divining why trains should sometimes stop at the wrong times and places, so, giving up the attempt, I went on with my reading. Then the train began to move backwards. There seems to be no accounting for railway eccentricity, thought I as I once more returned to my book. But when we came right back to the previous station, I could remain indifferent no longer. 'When are we getting to—?' I inquired at the station. 'You are just coming from there' was the reply. 'Where are we going now, then?' I asked, thoroughly flurried. 'To London.' I thereupon understood that this was a shuttle train. On inquiring about the next train to—, I was informed that there were no more trains that night. And in reply to my next question I gathered that there was no inn within five miles.

I had left home after breakfast at ten in the morning, and had had nothing since. When abstinence is the only choice, an ascetic frame of mind comes easy. I buttoned up my thick overcoat to the neck and, seating myself under a platform lamp, went on with my reading. The book I had with me was Spencer's *Data of Ethics*, then recently published. I consoled myself with the thought that I might never get another such opportunity of concentrating my whole attention on such a subject. After a short time, a porter came and informed me that a special train was running and would be in in half an hour. I felt so cheered up by the news that I could not go on any longer with the *Data of Ethics*. Where I was due at seven I arrived at nine. 'What is this, Ruby?' asked my hostess. 'Whatever have you been doing with yourself?' I was unable to take much pride in the account of my wonderful adventures which I gave her. Dinner was over; nevertheless, as my misfortune was hardly my fault, I did not expect condign punishment, especially as the dispenser was a woman. But all that the widow of the high Anglo-Indian official said to me was: 'Come along, Ruby, have a cup of tea.'

I never was a tea-drinker, but in the hope that it might be of some assistance in allaying my consuming hunger I managed to swallow a cup of strong decoction with a couple of dry biscuits. When I at length reached the drawing room I found a gathering of elderly ladies, and among them one pretty young American who was engaged to a nephew of my hostess and seemed busy going through the usual pre-marital love passages.

'Let's have some dancing,' said my hostess. I was neither in mood nor bodily condition for that exercise. But it is the docile who achieve the most impossible things in this world; so, though the dance was primarily got up for the benefit of the engaged couple, I had to dance with the ladies of considerably advanced age, with only the tea and biscuits between myself and starvation.

But my sorrows did not end there. 'Where are you putting up for the night?' asked my hostess. This was a question for which I was not prepared. While I stared at her, speechless, she explained that as the local inn would close at midnight I had better betake myself thither without further delay. Hospitality, however, was not entirely wanting, for I had not to find the inn unaided, a servant showing me the way there with a lantern. At first I thought this might prove a blessing in disguise, and at once proceeded to make enquiries for food: flesh, fish or vegetable, hot or cold, anything. I was told that drinks I could have in any variety but nothing to eat. Then I looked to slumber for forgetfulness, but there seemed to be no room even in her world-embracing lap. The bedroom with its sandstone floor was icy cold, an old bedstead and worn-out washstand being its only furniture.

In the morning the Anglo-Indian widow sent for me to breakfast. I found a cold repast spread out, evidently the remnants of last night's dinner. A small portion of this, lukewarm or cold, offered to me last night could not have hurt any one, while my dancing might then have less like the agonised wrigglings of a landed carp.

After breakfast my hostess informed me that the lady for whose delectation I had been invited to sing was ill in bed, and that I would have to serenade her from her bedroom door. I was made to stand up on the staircase landing. Pointing to a closed door, the widow said: 'That's where she is.' And I gave voice to that *Behaga* dirge, facing the mysterious unknown on the other side. Of what happened to the invalid as a result I have yet received no news...

(From *Jibansmriti*, translated by
Surendranath Tagore as *My Reminiscences*)

The Poet and his admirer, Virchandra Manikya, at Kurseong, 1896.

Back home, a writer with promise

However, in the first flush of excitement after his return from England, Rabindranath wrote two music dramas—*Valmikipratibha* (The Genius of Valmiki, 1881) and *Kalmrigaya* (The Fatal Hunt, 1882)—which were instant hits with the cultural elite of Calcutta. He had used some ten Irish and Scottish tunes for the songs he composed; the rest of the tunes were derived from traditional Indian songs and a few were composed by Jyotirindranath. His exposure to the English opera must have inspired Tagore to write music dramas based on the Ramayana, but he could not sustain his interest in European music, even though in the first public lecture he had delivered at the age of twenty, he had disparaged Indian music and extolled the Western.

Meanwhile, young Rabindranath's fame as poet was on the rise. Virchandra Manikya (1839–96), Maharaja of the princely state of Tripura, was so impressed with his poems that he sent an emissary to Jorasanko to inform the Poet of his deep appreciation of Tagore's new volume of verse, *Bhagnahriday* (The Broken Heart, 1881). Bankimchandra Chattopadhyay (1838–94), the first novelist in India and the then reigning monarch of Bengali literature, publicly garlanded the twenty-one-year-old Poet, complimenting him on his new book of verse, *Sandhya-Sangit* (The Evening Song, 1882).

One of the principal vehicles of young Rabindranath's prolific writings was the magazine *Bharati*, which had a very long life from 1877 to 1923—edited by various members of the Jorasanko Tagore family. Around the magazine gathered notable writers of the time who had affinity with the Jorasanko culture. *Bharati*, with Dwijendranath Tagore (1840–1926), the eldest brother of Rabindranath, as its first editor, broke away from its predecessor *Tattabodhini Patrika* which was religion-oriented to focus on literature, science and society. Rabindranath's contribution to *Bharati* was substantial. His prose pieces on various subjects, not necessarily literary, were surprisingly more mature than his verses written so far.

In another short-lived magazine called *Balak*, edited by the women of Jorasanko, Rabindranath's novel *Rajarshi* (The Sage King, 1887) appeared, which he had written after much research on the history of the royal dynasty of Tripura. This was not his first novel. Earlier, *Bauthakuranir Hat* (The Marketplace of *Bauthakurani*, 1883) and *Karuna* had appeared in *Bharati*. *Karuna* (1877–78) was his first attempt in novel-writing. Based on contemporary life, it is notable only because it was his first attempt in the novel genre but *Bauthakuranir Hat* was based on the history of Bengal in later Middle Ages, featuring Pratapaditya, a big landlord, who dared to defy the Moghul rule. The novel did not stress on the political history but the tragic drama in the family of Pratapaditya. Rabindranath had absolutely no sympathy for Pratapaditya, though his niece Sarala Devi (1872–1945) would subsequently glorify the landlord as a great patriot, in the heyday of Bengal's nationalist upsurges in 1904–05, much to the annoyance of her uncle.

Rabindranath, at the age of twenty-three, was married off to a village girl of ten. Child marriage was the custom of the day. Dwarkanath and Devendranath were married off at the age of fifteen and seventeen; their brides were only six. Eighteen-year-old Dwijendranath had a bride of ten. Similarly, fifteen-year-old Satyendranath married a girl of eight, nineteen-year-old Jyotirindranath married a girl of nine. Devendranath's daughters were also married off at a tender age—the eldest at nine, the three others at twelve, eleven and twelve, respectively. Rabindranath's other less known brothers also married young, though the exact ages of their brides are not known.

In his public address—'Hindu Bibaha' (Hindu Marriage)—in 1887, Rabindranath must have had at the back of his mind the tradition of child marriage in his family. Although he pleaded that girls should not be married before their puberty, preferably after their child-bearing age, he justified child marriage in affluent joint families, where tender girls could be looked after by their elders, hence healthy mothers could bear healthy children. Grown-up girls might find it difficult to adjust in a new family—young girls might not face such problems. Much later, in 1925, when Count Keyserling (1880–1946) asked Rabindranath to contribute an essay on the Indian system of marriage for his *The Book of Marriage*, he observed (in the translation of Surendranath Tagore [1872–1940], his nephew):

The Poet and his bride, Mrinalini.

> The 'desire' (attraction between sexes) however, against which India's solution of the marriage problem declared war, is one of Nature's most powerful fighters; consequently, the question of how to overcome it was not an easy one. There is a particular age, said India, at which this attraction between the sexes reaches its height, so if marriage is to be regulated according to the social will, it must be finished with before such age. Hence the Indian custom of early marriage.

This passage in 'The Indian Ideal of Marriage' was picked up by the editor of a magazine in London called *The New Statesman* to support Catherine Mayo's lurid descriptions of the Indian society where licentious men were described roaming around while women were afraid to freely move, and where child marriage seemed to be the custom, as was even in the Tagore family. Although Tagore protested against Miss Mayo's deliberate distortions of the other aspects of Indian social life (the English papers refused to publish numerous protest letters from Indians against Miss Mayo's book but *The Manchester Guardian* did publish Tagore's long letter), he had little to defend against the case of child marriage. He himself married off his daughters at a tender age—Renuka at the age of ten, Mira at the age of twelve, though efforts to marry her off began when she was ten. Madhurilata's age at marriage was an exception from the rule; she was married at fifteen. Of course, in 1927, when Miss Mayo's book was published, the social scene of Calcutta had radically changed and child marriage was unthinkable in Bengali middle-class society.

Kadambari, literary companion of the young Poet.

Four months after Rabindranath's marriage, there was a traumatic incident in the Tagore family. Jyotirindranath's wife Kadambari committed suicide at the age of twenty-five. She featured prominently in Rabindranath's *Jibansmriti* and *Chhelebela* (My Childhood Days), mostly as a surrogate mother—although Rabi was fourteen and Kadambari sixteen when Rabi's mother died.

Kadambari came to the Tagore family as a bride, aged nine, illiterate, unaccustomed to the environment of a rich landlord family. Her husband was ten years older than she, the most handsome man in the household and most accomplished amongst the Tagores (the civilian elder Satyendranath was away from the family). He was a singer, composer, painter and playwright.

The bride was groomed according to the Tagore tradition. After his wife's death, Devendranath lived away from Jorasanko—leaving the household at the care of Jyotirindranath, who dropped out of Presidency College, Calcutta, to look after the estates, from his Jorasanko office. The elder Dwijendranath was indifferent to household affairs. Kadambari played the principal role in *Manmayi* when she was twenty-one—singing a year earlier in the music drama by Svarnakumari Devi (1855–1932), her second eldest sister-in-law. She was referred to as the queen bee in the literary club informally run by Jyotirindranath, where the famous poets of the time, Biharilal Chakrabarti, Akshay Chandra Chaudhuri and his wife Saratkumari—both enthusiasts in literary matters—gathered in the evening.

When Rabi came back from London, he added verve to the club. Kadambari has been referred to as one of the participants who discussed and planned issues of *Bharati*. There was no indication that Kadambari was neglected by the family or her husband. Jyotirindranath, of course, was a busy man. He acted as the secretary of Adi Brahmo Samaj, founded by his father, for a long eighteen years till the death of Kadambari. He was a successful playwright for the commercial theatre; *Puruvikram* (The Might of Puru, 1874), *Sarojini* (1876), *Asrumati* (1880) and *Swapnamayi* (1883) are some of his works. Apart from looking after the already vast zamindari, he attempted business in jute, indigo and shipping. A fine linguist, he translated plays from French—one of which was *Alikbabu*, adapted from a Moliere play, in which Kadambari played the role of Hemangini.

There is no reason to imagine that Kadambari felt lonely in such a big household. She was childless and looked after a daughter of Svarnakumari as her own; unfortunately the five-year-old girl died after a fall from the stairs. Jyotirindranath often took his wife on long vacations, away from the daily chores at Jorasanko, to riversides, hills, as well as to workplaces of Satyendranath. He had become the talk of the town when he took his wife on horse rides to the Calcutta Maidan, at a time when women of the Tagore family were always a subject for gossip, even if they were spotted walking on their own roof-tops!

Barring a few exceptions, Rabindranath used to customarily dedicate his published books. All the books, seemingly dedicated to Kadambari, were ambiguously worded. The first one, *Bhagnahriday* was dedicated to '*Srimati Hey*'. *Bibidha Prasanga* (1883), a collection of short prose pieces, was not dedicated specifically, but one piece, 'Samapan', has been interpreted as being a dedication to Kadambari. In between these two, Rabindranath had dedicated two books to Jyotirindranath: one to Saudamini, his eldest sister, and one to Indira, his niece. *Chhabi O Gaan* (1884), a book of poems, was dedicated to (in Author's translation): '... the feet of one, the light of whose eyes used to bear out the flowers every day in the morning, the flowers that blossomed last spring forming the garland this year'. This, again, is assumed to be a dedication to Kadambari. *Prakritir Pratisodh*, a dramatic book of verse, and *Saisab Sangit*, again another book of verse, were published after the death of Kadambari, in 1884, and dedicated to 'You'. *Bhanusimha Thakurer Padabali*, also in 1884, was dedicated to (in Author's translation): 'You had asked me many times to publish Bhanusimha poems. I did not pay heed to your request. Now I publish the poems, but you are no more to see the publication.'

The dedications are enough indications of Rabindranath's affection and admiration for his '*Natun Bouthakrun*'. But the first dedication—'*Srimati Hey*'—has proved to be intriguing. That the person to whom the dedication is offered is a woman cannot be questioned because it is a *Srimati*. But whom did '*Hey*' refer to? Was it Hemangini, a character in *Alikbabu* who was enacted on one occasion by Kadambari? Sajanikanta Das (1900–62), renowned for his research in Bengali literature and a close associate of Rabindranath, claims that Rabindranath, in his last years, had smilingly nodded in affirmation when asked if '*Hey*' was the initial of Hemangini. Prabhat Kumar Mukhopadhyay (1892–1985), the first major biographer of Rabindranath, claims that Indira Devi, the Poet's niece, had told him that '*Hey*' was the shortened version of Hecate, a nickname for Kadambari in the Tagore household. Hecate is the Greek goddess with three heads—the three being Biharilal Chakrabarti whom Kadambari adored, her own husband and her dear brother-in-law. Prasantakumar Pal (1938–2007), another biographer, did find Rabindranath scribbling 'Hecate Thacroon' three times on Tagore's earliest extant manuscript. It is quite possible that young Rabi, who translated *Macbeth* with the help of a tutor, was acquainted with the goddess and teased his sister-in-law with the nickname. But Prasantachandra Mahalanobis (1893–1972), the most dependable associate of Rabindranath, confounds us with an entry in his diary. In 1928, he asked the Poet, what '*Hey*' stood for? The Poet gave it a thought and replied that he could not remember. This is quite intriguing—how could he forget if '*Hey*' meant Kadambari?

Equally intriguing is the source of the poem, 'Chhabi' (The Picture) in the book of verse named *Balaka* (The Flight of Cranes, 1916). The poem was inspired by a photograph or a painting which the Poet saw in a relative's house in Allahabad, in 1914. Charuchandra Bandyopadhyay (1877–1938) and Kshitimohan Sen (1880–1960) believed it was a picture of his wife, while Prasantachandra believed it was Kadambari's. All three are authorities on the Poet's life! Charuchandra was with Rabindranath, travelling to Allahabad. Those who get elated to find Kadambari in as many Tagore poems as possible will not, however, accept Charuchandra's view.

There was reportedly a suicide note by Kadambari which was allegedly destroyed at the explicit command of the grand patriarch, Devendranath. There was no ripple in newspapers or magazines; supposedly they had been induced not to publish the news. Even today, speculations over the suicide are rampant—that she was a neurotic, susceptible to be easily hurt; that she was neglected by her husband; that she was jealous of an actress who supposedly was intimate with her husband; that she was devastated by the marriage of Rabindranath whom she loved so dearly; and so on.

Above: Jnanadanandini, Satyendranath, Kadambari (standing from left) and Jyotirindranath (seated). Facing page: Jyotirindranath (right), in whose shadow the Poet grew up in his youth.

The Poet preferred to stay in small rooms.

Meditating on the Infinite Being

Rabindranath was appointed the secretary of Adi Brahmo Samaj (the Brahmo Samaj created by Rammohun Roy and Dwarkanath Tagore in 1828 subsequently split into Adi Brahmo Samaj led by Devendranath; Bharatbarshiya Brahmo Samaj led by Keshab Chandra Sen from 1866 onwards and Sadharan Brahmo Samaj by Sibnath Shastri from 1878) in 1884, when Jyotirindranath vacated the post after the death of his wife. He accepted the task earnestly. In a chapter titled 'The Vision' from *The Religion of Man*, he explains how he viewed religion:

> I was born in a family which, at that time, was earnestly developing a monotheistic religion based upon the philosophy of the Upanishad. Somehow my mind at first remained coldly aloof, absolutely uninfluenced by any religion whatever. It was through an idiosyncrasy of my temperament that I refused to accept any religious teaching merely because people in my surroundings believed it to be true...
>
> Then came my initiation ceremony of Brahmanhood (at the age of nearly twelve) when the Gayatri verse of meditation was given to me, whose meaning, according to the explanation I had, runs as follows:

> Let me contemplate the adorable splendour of Him who created the earth, the air and the starry spheres, and sends the power of comprehension within our minds.
>
> This produced a sense of serene exaltation in me, the daily meditation upon the Infinite Being which unites in one stream of creation my mind and the outer world. Though today I find no difficulty in realising this Being as an infinite personality in whom the subject and object are perfectly reconciled, at that time the idea to me was vague. Therefore the current of feeling that it aroused in my mind was indefinite, like circulation of air—an atmosphere which needed a definite world to complete itself and satisfy me. For it was evident that my religion is a poet's religion, and neither that of an orthodox man of piety nor that of a theologian. Its touch comes to me through the same unseen and trackless channel as does the inspiration of my songs. My religious life has followed the mysterious line of growth as has my poetic life. Somehow they are wedded to each other and, their betrothal had a long period of ceremony, it was kept secret to me.

As an ardent Brahmo, Rabindranath pitted himself against two major adversaries—Chandranath Basu (1844–1910) and Bankimchandra Chattopadhyay—both of whom young Rabi had deeply regarded and who in their turn held the young Poet in warm affection. Chandranath Basu, an essayist in religious and educational matters, was a conservative in social outlook. He was made a butt of ridicule in one of Rabindranath's satirical poems where Chamu Basu, a character in the poem, was a covert sketch of Chandranath, and another character, Damu Basu, was of Jogendrachandra Basu (1854–1905), the editor of an anti-Brahmo magazine. The poem featured in *Kadi O Komal*, a book of verse published in 1886. The poem raised such a furore that Rabindranath dropped the poem in subsequent editions of the book. Chandranath was again attacked in a poem 'Hing Ting Chhat' (included in the book of verse, *Sonar Tari*, 1894).

Rabindranath at this time had a spat with Bankimchandra on the interpretation of Krishna in the Mahabharat. Bankimchandra asserted that Truth was relative and Untruth could be justified if it was good for the people. Young Rabi protested in a public address which he named 'Ekti Puratan Kahini' (An Old Story, 1884). He said that Truth was

With leaders of the Indian National Congress in Calcutta, 1890: (standing from left) Nalinibihari Sarkar, Manmohan Ghosh, Rabindranath, Hemchandra Mallik and Shelley Bandypadhyay, W.C. Bonnerjee (seated left) and Ferojshah Mehta (seated right).

absolute and could not be compromised at any cost. The address caused irritation among not only the devout Hindus but also the Brahmos. A vexed Bankim, however, did not bear any grudge against Rabi. The latter's exasperation was mainly caused by the appearance of two magazines initiated by Bankimchandra—*Nabajiban* and *Prachar*—which championed orthodox Hindu religion. As the newly appointed secretary of Adi Brahmo Samaj, Rabindranath went all out against this orthodoxy and wrote farces and poems, making fun with the concept of Arya—the pure Hindu.

Bankimchandra was an icon for young Rabi, who used to eagerly wait for issues of *Bangadarshan*—the magazine edited by Bankimchandra—and who regularly read out his novel *Bishbriksha* (The Poison Tree) to his sister-in-law, Kadambari, as it was serialised in the magazine. Rabi was barely in his teens then. But he was not that impressed by Bankim's *Anandamath*, the novel that aroused intense patriotic fervour among Bengalees. In his letters to Chandranath Basu, young Rabi pointed out the deficiencies of the novel with its cardboard characters. *Anandamath* was fiercely debated by the Muslims and its copies burnt. They thought that the author was biased against Muslims. 'Vande Mataram', the rallying song of the sanyasis in the novel, was particularly disliked by Muslims. The first two stanzas of the song were, however, set to tune by Rabindranath to the satisfaction of the novelist and sung by him at the sixth session of the Indian National Congress (INC) in Calcutta (December 1890). The Bengal Partition days (1904–08) reverberated with the song sung by young protestors against Lord Curzon's Divide and Rule policy. Rabindranath was in a piquant situation when the INC Working Committee, in 1937, was debating if 'Vande Mataram' should be adopted as the national anthem of the country, and Jawaharlal Nehru referred the problem to Rabindranath. Most Bengali intellectuals demanded the acceptance of the song which had been the war-cry of freedom fighters throughout India. Rabindranath suggested a compromise—acceptance of the first two stanzas which were free of Hindu religious associations. The Working Committee accepted Rabindranath's advice. But the Constituent Assembly resolved in 1950 that 'Janaganamana' composed by Rabindranath would be the national anthem of India and 'Vande Mataram' was honoured with an equal status.

'Janaganamana' was composed in 1911 and was first sung in the 27th session of the INC in Calcutta that year. The song has a strange history. Rabindranath was approached by a friend/relative with a request to compose a song for the Delhi Durbar in honour of Emperor George V. The request was spurned and the Poet composed a song not in honour of an English king but as a homage to 'the ruler of the minds of all people'. The rumour created by the Anglo-Indian Press that the song was an ode to King George seemed to have a long life—from the time when Ezra Pound had mentioned it in a letter to his father in 1913, ridiculing W.B. Yeats (1865–1939), who seemed to have been taken in by the rumour, down to these days when somebody or the other questions Tagore's love for his country, citing this alleged ode to George V.

William Rothenstein (1872–1945), the painter, recounts an amusing story in his *Men and Memories*. Sometime in 1912–13, at a gathering in his house in London, when the general conversation seemed to have sagged, Rothenstein sought to enliven the mood by asking everybody to sing their national anthems. W.B. Yeats, the ardent Irish nationalist, stood up and after reciting a few lines he abruptly sat down; he had forgotten the words. Ernest Rhys (1859–1946), the editor of *Everyman* Library series, stood up next to sing his Welsh national song and gave up for the same reason. Next was Rabindranath, who stood up to sing 'Vande Mataram' but sat down without finishing the song, having forgotten the words. It was now the turn of the host, who stood up and sang 'God Save the King' from start to finish. But he had also stumbled!

Left: Prayer hall of the Adi Brahmo Samaj. Facing page: The Poet's portrait painted by William Rothenstein.

As the secretary of the Adi Brahmo Samaj, Tagore delivered a lecture on Rammohun in 1885 during *Maghotsava* of the Sadharan Brahmo Samaj. *Maghotsava* was the annual ceremony of the Brahmos; 11 *Magh* in the Bengali calendar being the foundation day of the Brahmo Mandir established in 1830. Rabindranath made no distinction between the Adi and Sadharan Brahmo Samaj. In course of time, the enfeebled Brahmo Samaj with its three formations would have only nominal existence. *Maghotsava* constituted a major celebration time for which Rabindranath would contribute numerous Brahma songs, prayers and sermons throughout his life.

Rammohun Roy was the strongest influence in shaping Rabindranath's religious, philosophical as well as social ideas, perhaps more than Devendranath. Rabindranath wrote essays in Bengali and English, and lectured in the country and abroad on Rammohun's contribution to the creation of modern India. His numerous references to Rammohun can be summed up in his strong reaction to a preposterous statement made by M.K. Gandhi (1869–1948) in Cuttack on 24 March 1921 and subsequently published in *Young India*. Gandhi had commented that Tilak and Rammohun Roy would have accomplished greater heights if they had not been so greatly influenced by English learning. This was what Gandhi had said:

> Rammohun and Tilak (leave aside my case) were so many pygmies who had no hold upon the people compared with Chaitanya, Sankar, Kabir and Nanak. Rammohun, Tilak were pygmies before these saints.

Then clarifying that he had high regards for Tilak and Rammohun Roy, Gandhi observed, 'It is my conviction that if Rammohun and Tilak had not received this education but had their national training they would have done greater things like Chaitanya.'

Learning this Rabindranath shot back on 10 May 1921 from near Zurich to C.F. Andrews (who published this letter in *Letters to a Friend*, 1928):

> So long as our intellectual attainments were solely dependent on an alien giver, we have been accepting and not acquiring. Therefore these attainments have mostly been barren of production, as I have discussed in my pamphlet on Education. But it would be wrong to blame the Western culture itself for such futility. The blame lies in our not using our receptacle for this culture. Intellectual parasitism causes degeneracy in the intellectual organs of the mind. It is not the food, but the parasitism, that has to be avoided.
>
> At the same time, I strongly protest Mahatma Gandhi's depreciation of such great personalities of modern India as Rammohun Roy in his zeal for declaiming against our modern education. Every Indian ought to be proud of the fact that, in spite of immense disadvantages, India still has been able to produce greatness of personality in her children, such as we find in Rammohun Roy. Mahatmaji has quoted the instances of Nanak, Kabir and other saints of medieval India. They were great because in their life and teaching they made organic union of the Hindu and Muhammedan culture—and such realisation of the spiritual unity through all differences of appearance is truly Indian.

Facing page: Rammohun Roy, as painted by H.P. Briggs—preserved in Bristol Museum.

In the modern age, Rammohun Roy had that comprehensiveness of mind to be able to realise the fundamental unity of spirit

> in the Hindu, Muhammedan and Christian cultures. Therefore he represented India in the fullness of truth; and this truth is based, not upon rejection, but on perfect comprehension. Rammohun Roy could be perfectly natural in his acceptance of the West, only because his education had been perfectly Eastern—he had the full inheritance of the Indian wisdom. He was never a schoolboy of the West, and therefore he had the dignity to be a friend of the West. If he is not understood by modern India, this only shows that the pure light of her own truth has been obscured for the moment by the storm-clouds of passion.

The use of the word, 'pygmy', to describe Rammohun stung Rabindranath beyond endurance. On 17 May 1921, he again wrote a note to Andrews from Hamburg, explaining Rammohun's contribution:

> In the time of Rammohun Roy the West had come to the East with a shock that caused panic in the heart of India. The natural cry was exclusion. But this was the cry of fear, the cry of weakness, the cry of the dwarf. Through the great mind of Rammohun Roy the true spirit of India asserted itself and accepted the West, not by the rejection of the soul of India, but by the comprehension of the soul of the West.

On 29 August 1921, Rabindranath had strongly condemned the Non-Cooperation movement at a public lecture, which was published as 'The Call of Truth' (in Rabindranath's own translation) in *The Modern Review* in its October 1921 issue. Gandhi explained his stand, seeking to clarify the

At the age of twenty-one.

political issues in his 'The Great Sentinel', in the October 1921 issue of *Young India*. Gandhi had even called on Rabindranath at his Jorasanko house on 6 September 1921 and had spent some four hours in debating the issues, in the presence of Andrews, to explain the aim and method of the Non-Cooperation movement. The berating of Rammohun by Gandhi rankled in his mind to such an extent that during the meeting, as Rabindranath himself had reported it later to L.K. Elmhirst, Rabindranath had said, 'And Gandhiji, why do you allow followers to call you Mahatma? Are you a Mahatma?' Gandhi had reportedly answered that common people in India were used to worshipping a symbol and that was why he did not object to being addressed as a Mahatma.

There is no truth in the popular notion perpetuated by biographers of Gandhi and Tagore that it was Tagore who had conferred the title of Mahatma on Gandhi and it was Gandhi who conferred the title of Gurudev on Tagore. Gandhi was addressed as Mahatma in public receptions at Durban, South Africa, in July 1914. And Tagore was called Gurudev (an epithet that stuck to Tagore for ever) by Brahmabandhab Upadhyay (1861–1907), the famous Vedantist turned revolutionary, who was invited to start the school at Bolpur in 1901, that was later known as the Santiniketan school.

While Rammohun was the strongest intellectual influence on Rabindranath, Devendranath was the strongest emotional influence on him. Rabindranath did not study the ancient Indian scriptures as a scholar would. He learnt these largely through his father and other scholars who formally or informally deliberated on interpretations of the Vedas and the Upanishad. Devendranath never accepted the Vedas in their entirety. In the volumes of *Brahmodharma,* he collected *slokas* (verses) from the Vedas, Mahabharat, Gita, Manusamhita and Purans which he considered appropriate for his monotheistic Brahmo religion. The *slokas* Rabindranath used in the first part of his life were primarily derived from *Brahmodharma*. These were used in his essays, lectures and sermons delivered as the proponent of Adi Brahmo Samaj.

In the latter part of his life, he consulted two Sanskrit scholars of his school—Kshitimohan Sen and Bidhusekhar Shastri (1878–1957) for the *slokas* he used. In a Bengali essay (contained in the collection of essays, *Pather Sanchay*), written in 1912, in England, we find Rabindranath mentioning an occidental scholar, who wished to hear him recite from the Vedas. Rabindranath has written that he recited from whatever he knew of the Vedas and the scholar at once identified the source of the *slokas*. One month before his death, he had told Rani Chanda (the wife of one of his secretaries; she attended him when he was in his sick bed and used to note down the stray comments the Poet made) that people thought that he was a great Sanskrit scholar when, in fact, he used to intersperse his talks with Vedic *slokas* to impress upon his listeners with a meagre stock of the *slokas*!

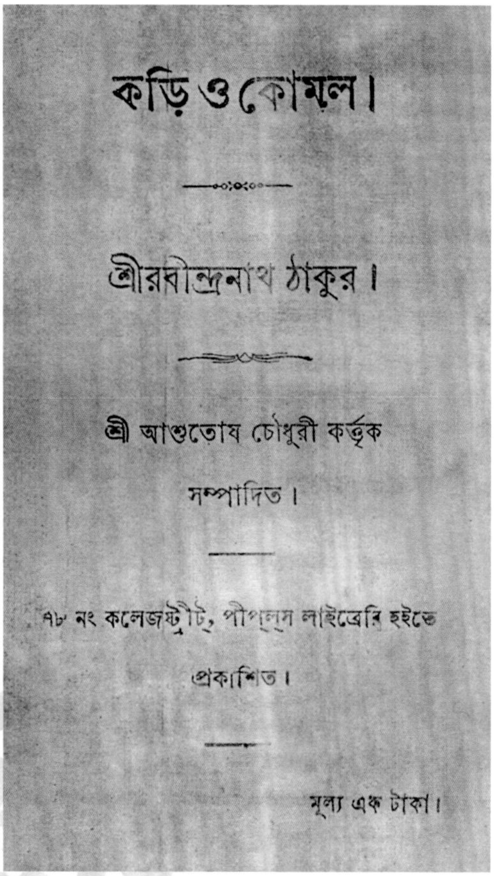
কড়ি ও কোমল।

শ্রীরবীন্দ্রনাথ ঠাকুর।

শ্রী আশুতোষ চৌধুরী কর্ত্তৃক
সম্পাদিত।

৭৮ নং কলেজষ্ট্রীট্, পীপ্‌লস্ লাইব্রেরি হইতে
প্রকাশিত।

মূল্য এক টাকা।

Cover of Kadi O Komal,
published in 1886.

At the crossroads

Rabindranath, at twenty-seven, was at the crossroads of his literary career. *Kadi O Komal* (The Sharp and the Flat) was a collection of sonnets and sonnet-like poems on themes of death, love and country, away from the fanciful flights of his earlier poems. His innovations in language and metrical measures were beginning to crystallise and he had a band of young followers who not only imitated his verses but also his dress and looks. Rabi of that time has been described by a contemporary poet in glowing words: he looked just like poet Milton, a tall and slim physique, complexion fairest of fair, with an oval face, his nose, eyes and brows perfect as if drawn with a brush of paints, his long curls reaching the shoulders. Milton at the college was addressed as Lady by classmates, Rabi also could be called a lady, with a soft woman-like voice, wrote that poet.

Kadi O Komal, however, spawned severe criticism. One of the critics, Kaliprasanna Kavyavisharad (1861–1907), had a love–hate relationship with Rabi. A poet and a journalist, who dared brave cultural policing and courted arrest for a poem printed in his magazine, whose songs would be inspiring in the Bengal Partition days, came out with a parody of *Kadi O Komal*. Kaliprasanna was a scholar and produced an authentic compilation of Vidyapati's lyrics. Rabi also was engaged in the same exercise and he had handed over his ten-year-research on Vidyapati, a celebrated lyricist of Mithila of the later Middle Ages, to Kaliprasanna earlier, who eventually, however, did acknowledge this help. But he did not like the love poems that Rabi was writing, as he thought that the poems were sensuous and indistinct at the same time. Kaliprasanna would be remembered by Rabindranath in his old age as one of his earliest foes.

Rabindranath had a major break in his life when his father sent him to north-east Bengal to manage the family's landed properties. He had been there earlier but only on holidays. In 1876, he was there to see Jyotirindranath hunting tigers; in 1888, he went with his own family for a pleasure trip; and then in 1890 he joined the Punyaha celebrations—the first day of the year when the landlord meets the tenants, who voluntarily pay rent as much or as little as they like and their payments are not counted by clerks. On his first visit for Punyaha, Rabindranath, as the young landlord, remitted Rs 100,000 as rent. Whether this huge remission earned him the gratitude of his tenants or was it a diplomatic move on his part to earn their loyalty is an open question. However, another gesture of the young landlord was wholly welcomed by Muslim tenants (who constituted the bulk of north-east Bengal's population)—Rabindranath ordered all tenants, Muslims and Hindus, to be given equal seating honour as guests. From 1891, Rabindranath settled down, not as an occasional visitor but as a resident landlord.

There were several teething troubles—complicated system of accounts keeping; arcane language to couch those accounts; questionable conduct of clerks and officers who till then had a free hand in management; and the quarrelsome character of the poor tenants. The Permanent Settlement of land executed by Lord Cornwallis, in 1793, was essentially an extortionist method to fleece the toiling peasants. Landlords were free to impose levies and collect rent as much as they wanted as long as they paid up government dues on time. It took nearly one hundred years and a half to abolish the zamindari system in Bengal, with minor changes in the Tenancy Act, in favour of tenants' rights, attempted in the later years. The system itself was exploitative, however benevolent the zamindar might have been.

Rabindranath was a benevolent zamindar par excellence. L.S.S. O'Malley, the district magistrate of Rajshahi, wrote in the *Bengal District Gazetteers*, in 1916:

The estate house at Silaidaha.

It must not be imagined that a powerful landlord is always oppressive and uncharitable. A striking instance to the contrary is given in the Settlement Officer's account of the estate of Rabindranath Tagore, the Bengali poet, whose fame is worldwide. It is clear that to poetical genius he adds practical and beneficial ideas of estate management, which should be an example to the local zamindars.

A very favourable example of estate government is shown in the property of the poet, Sir Rabindranath Tagore. The properties brook no rivals. Sub-infeudation within the estate is forbidden, *raiyats* (tenants) are not allowed to sublet on pain of ejectment. There are three divisions of the estate, each under a sub-manager with a staff of *tehsildars* (revenue collectors), whose accounts are strictly supervised. Half of the *dakhilas* (receipts) are checked by an officer of the head office. Employees are expected to deal fairly with the *raiyats* and unpopularity earns dismissal. Registration of transfer is granted on a fixed fee, but is refused in the case of an undesirable transferee. Remissions of rent are granted when inability to pay is proved. In 1312 (AD 1905), it is said that the amount remitted was Rs 57,595. There are Lower Primary Schools in each division, and at Patisar, the centre of management, there is a High English School with 250 students and a charitable dispensary. These are

> maintained out of a fund to which the Estate contributes annually Rs 1,250 and the *raiyats* 6 pies to rupee in their rent (a pie was 1/192 of a rupee). There is an annual grant of Rs 240 for the relief of cripples and the blind. An agricultural bank advances loans to *raiyats* at 12% per annum. The depositors are chiefly Calcutta-friends of the poet, who get interest at 7%. The bank has about Rs 90,000 invested in loans.

This was a report on Kaligram Pargana of Rajshahi District with the headquarters at Patisar. More familiar names to the readers of Tagore are those of Silaidaha, the headquarters of Birahimpur Pargana of Nadea (now Kushthia) District and Sajadpur, the headquarters of Sajadpur Pargana of Pabna District. All these were situated in East Pakistan after the Partition of India.

It took time for the urbane Poet to adjust himself with the countryside. In December 1890, he wrote to his wife:

> I have reached Kaligram today. It took me three days. I had to cut across a diverse terrain. First, a big river—then a small river, trees and plants on both sides, quite nice to see, then the river got narrower, almost a canal, with tall banks—I felt quite confined. Then, at one spot water flew at a fierce speed and it took twenty to twenty-five men to drag the boat...I cannot reconcile myself that I have to take the same route to go back to Birahimpur. There is no current at all in this river. Water-hyacinths float, there are jungles at places, there is a smell of stench that usually comes off village ponds—and I am afraid there will be swarms of mosquitoes at night. If it gets more intolerable I will retreat to Calcutta from here itself (in Author's translation).

Between November 1889 and December 1895, Rabindranath wrote some 250 letters to his niece Indira from the zamindari estates. These humorous, often lyrical letters reflect the thoughts of Rabindranath on a wide range of subjects. Indira was of almost the same age as his wife. That he chose to write these letters to a niece and not to his wife indicates that intellectually Indira was closer to him than his wife. Some of these letters were collected, after deletion of personal references, and published in 1911 as *Chhinnapatra* (Torn Letters, 1912) and were later translated by his nephew Surendranath Tagore, the principal and his most trusted translator in English, and published as *Glimpses of Bengal* in 1921.

Facing page: At Silaidaha, 1890.

The keynote of these letters is evident in a letter written on 22 September 1894 when Rabindranath was reading a biography of Goethe and sharing his thoughts with Indira, who was also reading it at the same time. Rabindranath wrote:

> Goethe on his death-bed wanted 'more light'. If I have any desire left at all at such a time, it will be for 'more space' as well; for I dearly love both light and space. Many look down on Bengal as being only a flat country, but that is just what makes me revel in its scenery all the more. Its unobstructed sky is filled to the brim, like an amethyst cup, with the descending twilight and peace of the evening; and the golden skirt of the still, silent noonday spreads over the whole of it without let or hindrance.

The houseboat called Padma *on River Padma and its tributaries, made famous by its references in* Chhinnapatra.

A story-writer

In the introduction to *Glimpses of Bengal*, Rabindranath wrote, 'The letters translated in this book span the most productive period of my literary life, when owing to great good fortune, I was young and less known.' He was not, of course, confined within his estates all that time—Silaidaha, the nearest of the estates from Calcutta, was half-a-day's journey by train and boat. He was fully abreast of the educational, political and social scenes of the metropolis. He was writing poems, plays, essays, songs throughout, but the genre to which he seriously gave thought at this period was short stories. He was the first Indian to give the short story its formal structure. He wrote 95 short stories—the first in 1877, the last in 1941—and thought in his ripe old age that his stories were never appreciated in Bengal. He was pleased when in 1940, a post-graduate student wrote an essay in a literary periodical on his short stories. Earlier, he was surprised to know that the Marxists of Bengal considered him a bourgeois writer. He almost thundered in a letter to Amiya Chakrabarti (1901–86; a poet and his secretary for some years) that those critics should not gloss over his short stories which centred around simple men and women of the countryside. The Marxists later countered that Rabindranath knew the common man, but from the regal perch of his luxurious houseboat, *Padma*—he might not have looked down on the species known as *praja* (tenant) but he looked at them

Right: At the age of twenty-five.
Facing page: The Poet and C.F. Andrews at Santiniketan, in 1918.

from a distance; *prajas* would never dare come close to the zamindar or confide in him their innermost thoughts.

Rabindranath must have been shocked when the management of a magazine, of which he was the literary editor, asked him to write stories lighter than what he had been contributing. The weekly magazine, *Hitabadi*, was a commercial venture, capital for which was raised by a number of notable literary, social and political figures of Calcutta, Rabindranath himself being one. Six stories were supposed to have been contributed by Rabindranath in 1891 (though the relevant issues of the periodical could not be determined, as the files were incomplete), after which he disassociated himself from the periodical. One of the stories, 'The Postmaster', was framed on a real-life character of Sajadpur, as mentioned in *Chhinnapatra*. Translated and published in *The Modern Review* (January 1911), the story attracted the notice of William Rothenstein, an artist, who was interested in Indian culture and was visiting India at that time, and who continued to ask Rabindranath for stories. Rabindranath had no time or inclination to translate his own stories or novels. Translations by others were considered by Rothenstein, 'too monstrously ill done for words' and *Glimpses of Bengal Life*, a collection of stories translated by Rajaniranjan Sen, June 1913, 'too bad to pass on to anyone'.'The Postmaster', one of the finest stories Rabindranath wrote, had to wait till 1918 to be included in the second collection of Tagore stories published by Macmillan, the first having come out in 1916.

Macmillan, finding Tagore a veritable mine after the Nobel Prize award in 1913, went on a publishing spree of Tagore's works. It published *Hungry Stones and Other Stories* which contained thirteen stories. The preface to the book was misleading; it said:

> The stories contained in this volume were translated by different hands. The version of 'The Victory' is the author's own work. The seven stories which follow it were translated by Mr C.F. Andrews with the author's help. Assistance has also been given by the Rev. E.J. Thompson, Panna Lal Basu, Prabhat Kumar Mukherji and Sister Nivedita.

Among the 'assistants', Andrews knew no Bengali. Tagore used to freely dictate translations of his stories and essays to Andrews who prepared the typescripts. Tagore was too civilised to deny Andrews the translator's credit. Sister Nivedita needed no help from Tagore; in fact, he never knew that she had translated 'Kabuliwala' till the manuscript was discovered among her papers after her death in 1911. The three

As editor of Sadhana.

others were already published in *The Modern Review*; these were edited by Macmillan's editors, who might have also edited E.J. Thompson's translation. Thompson needed no assistance from Tagore—he knew Bengali well. He was furious with Macmillan and vexed with Tagore for such a cavalier way of book publishing. He refused to translate any more stories by Tagore, apart from one more—'Subha'—which he had already done. The second book of stories, *Mashi and Other Stories*, was preposterous. A collection of fourteen stories, it never acknowledged that these were all translations and that too by various persons. The same lack of editorial judgement (no introductions, no notes, nothing about the chronology of the original stories, not to speak of any statement on selection criteria) was manifest in the third (1918) and fourth (1925) collections by Macmillan.

Even though the translation quality was uneven, country-specific details were dropped in the translations for fear of incomprehensibility to non-Bengali readers. Ernest Rhys was ecstatic about Tagore, the short-story writer. In *Rabindranath Tagore, a Biographical Study* (1915), he devoted a whole chapter on Tagore's stories, even though he had only *Glimpses of Bengal Life* to judge from. Tagore had permitted Rajaniranjan Sen to translate his stories in 1909 and later tried to revoke his permission without success. On the basis of Sen's thirteen imperfect translations, Rhys placed Tagore amongst the frontline story writers of the world. In creation of atmosphere, Tagore, he said, was comparable with only Flaubert, and much better than Turgenev or George Sand. 'The House of Barich' (*Hungry Stones*) would be, Rhys averred, as famous as Axel's 'Villiers de L'Isle-Adam's Hall', Balzac's 'Flemish House', Scott's 'House of Lammermoor', Edgar Poe's 'House of Usher' and Childe Roland's 'Dark Tower'. The characteristics that marked out Tagore stories, as Rhys said, were: 'It is as if a folktale method were elaborated with literary art, inclined to the imaginative side of everyday life, yet dwelling fondly on the human folk it portrayed.'

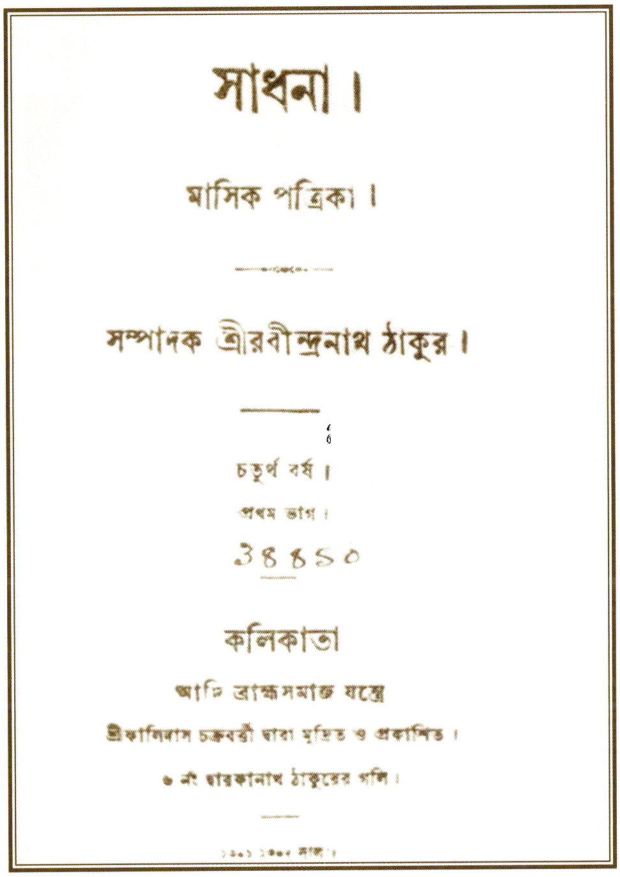
সাধনা।

মাসিক পত্রিকা।

সম্পাদক শ্রীরবীন্দ্রনাথ ঠাকুর।

চতুর্থ বর্ষ।

প্রথম ভাগ।

কলিকাতা

আদি ব্রাহ্মসমাজ যন্ত্রে

শ্রীকালিদাস চক্রবর্ত্তী দ্বারা মুদ্রিত ও প্রকাশিত।

৬ নং দ্বারকানাথ ঠাকুরের গলি।

Cover page of Sadhana.

Breaking away from the weekly *Hitabadi*, Rabindranath began to write short stories from December 1891 to December 1893 for each issue of *Sadhana*, a magazine edited by one of his nephews, and continued to contribute, after a break of seven months, in all the issues from August 1894 to September 1895 when he himself edited *Sadhana*. When in May 1898, he took up the editorship of the Tagore's family magazine—*Bharati*—he contributed seven stories in one year, after which he gave up the editorship. This was the period Tagore described as the most productive years. He would be writing some thirty more stories, but there was a difference between the early and late years. In an interview, on 23 February 1936 to an English daily called *Forward*, he said:

> Being a landlord I had to go to villages and then I came in touch with the village people and their simple modes of life...At first I was quite unfamiliar with the village life as I was born in Calcutta

and so there was an element of mystery for me...My earlier stories have this background and they describe this contact of mine with the village people. They have the freshness of youth. Before I had written these stories, there was not anything of that type in Bengali literature...My later stories have not got that freshness, though they have greater psychological value and they deal with problems. Happily I had no social or political problems before my mind when I was quite young...During my youth whatever I saw appealed to me with pathos quite strong, and, therefore, my earlier stories have a greater literary value because of their spontaneity. But now it is different. My stories have got the necessary technique but I wish I could go back once more to my former life.

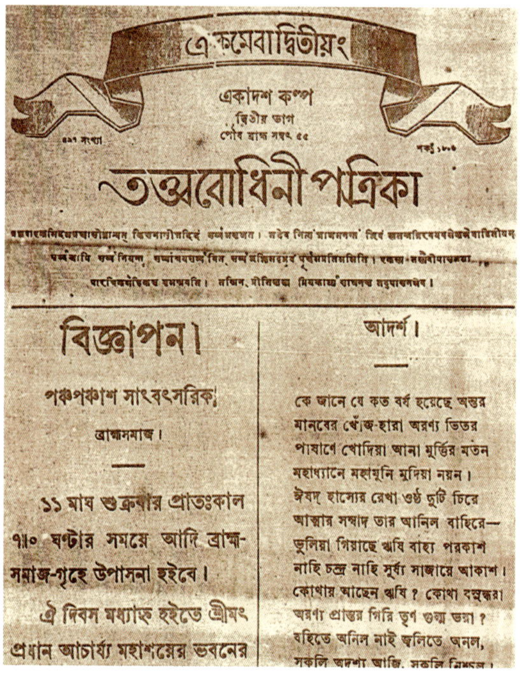
একমেবাদ্বিতীয়ং

একাদশ কল্প
দ্বিতীয় ভাগ

তত্ত্ববোধিনী পত্রিকা

বিজ্ঞাপন।

পঞ্চপঞ্চাশ সাংবৎসরিক

ব্রাহ্মসমাজ।

১১ মাঘ শুক্রবার প্রাতঃকাল ৭।৷০ ঘণ্টার সময়ে আদি ব্রাহ্ম-সমাজ-গৃহে উপাসনা হইবে।

ঐ দিবস মধ্যাহ্ন হইতে শ্রীমৎ প্রধান আচার্য্য মহাশয়ের ভবনের

আদর্শ।

কে জানে যে কত বর্ষ হয়েছে অন্তর
মানবের খোঁজ-হারা অরণ্য ভিতর
পাষাণে খোদিয়া আনা মুর্ত্তির মতন
মহাধ্যানে মহামুনি মুদিয়া নয়ন।
ঈষদ্ হাস্যের রেখা ওষ্ঠ দুটি চিরে
আত্মার সম্বাদ তার আনিল বাহিরে—
ভুলিয়া গিয়াছে ঋষি বাহ্য পরকাশ
নাহি চন্দ্র নাহি সূর্য্য সাজায়ে আকাশ।
কোথায় আছেন ঋষি? কোথা বসুন্ধরা
অরণ্য প্রান্তর গিরি তৃণ গুল্ম ভরা?
বহিতে অনিল নাই জ্বলিতে অনল,

Tattabodhini Patrika, *one of the magazines edited by Rabindranath between May 1911–April 1912. Facing page: Goethe, German poet.*

As an editor the achievement of Rabindranath was not much. A successful editor must assemble a number of good writers around him, bring out the paper on time, see that the paper is financially viable, and have the stamina to give the paper a long life. None of the magazines Rabindranath edited were launched by him. The editorship was thrust upon him when the magazines, except one, all initiated by the Jorasanko Tagores, began to flounder. Briefly, the magazines Rabindranath edited were: *Sadhana* (December 1894–November 1895); *Bharati* (May 1898–April 1899); *Bangadarshan*, re-started (May 1901–April 1905); *Bhandar* (May 1905–July 1907); and *Tattabodhini Patrika* (May 1911–April 1912). Editing and proofreading, for a perfectionist like Rabindranath, who was extremely insistent on correct printing, soon became a telling task on his nerves. Soliciting writers, getting copy on time, supervision of the printing press became a drudgery for him. He chose to fill the pages of the magazines by his own writing because it was easier than correcting others' copies. When he edited others' manuscripts, he had to extensively delete, add and correct. Even as big a writer as Ramendrasundar Trivedi (1864–1919) did not escape his revisions. The magazines edited by him, after all the pain Rabindranath took, did set the benchmark for Bengali magazines, particularly *Sadhana*.

Goethe and Rabindranath

A precocious Rabindranath, who at the age of seventeen wrote for the family magazine *Bharati* about the love affairs of Goethe, not at all approving of the fickleness of the great poet's heart, hardly knew that he would be frequently bracketed with Goethe—of course, not in matters of love or romance, but for poetic qualities and other common features. The first important person who invoked Goethe while writing about Tagore's poetry was Verner Von Heidenstam whose lobbying for Tagore won the unknown Bengali the Nobel Prize. He wrote a letter to the secretary of the Nobel Committee of the Swedish Academy:

> Just as a selection of Goethe's poems could well convince us of Goethe's greatness, even if we were unfamiliar with his other writings, so we can say quite definitely of these poems by Tagore, which we have had in our hands this summer, that through them we have come to know one of the very greatest poets of our age.

In the first decade of the Nobel Awards for literature, Goethe was the touchstone to determine the worthiness of the candidates. Tagore in 1928 at Santiniketan reminded a German physicist of Goethe. Arnold Sommerfeld (1868–1951), professor of physics in Munich, came to Santiniketan during a world lecture tour. Krishna Dutta and Andrew Robinson quoted in their biography of Tagore this impression of Sommerfeld:

> He is to India perhaps the same as old Goethe was to the Germany of his time. Like Goethe he is infinitely diligent: he works from early in the morning till night. Even his interest in craftwork was shared by Goethe. His image is known to all, but actual appearance is much more beautiful than his picture, a pure type of Aryan stock, with a lightness in the colour of the skin resembling that of an elephant's tusk. With his patriarchal beard he looks older then his sixty-eight years. His English is like music. The evening on the upper terrace of his house next to his studio is unforgettable.

At a dinner with scholars in China, in 1924, Tagore confessed that he tried to read Goethe in German but his little knowledge of German was a barrier:

> I also wanted to learn German, and by reading Heine in translation, I thought I had caught a glimpse of the beauty there. Fortunately I met a missionary lady from Germany and asked her help. I worked hard for some months, but being rather quick-witted, which is not a good quality, I was not persevering. I had the dangerous facility which helps one to guess the meaning too easily. My teacher thought that I had almost mastered the language—which was not true. I succeeded, however, in getting through Heine, like a man walking in sleep crossing unknown paths with ease, and I found immense pleasure. Then I tried Goethe. But that was too ambitious. With the help of the little German I had learnt, I did go through Faust. I believe I found my entrance to the palace, not like an inmate who has keys for all the doors, but a casual visitor who is tolerated in some general guest room, comfortable but not intimate. Properly speaking, I do not know my Goethe.

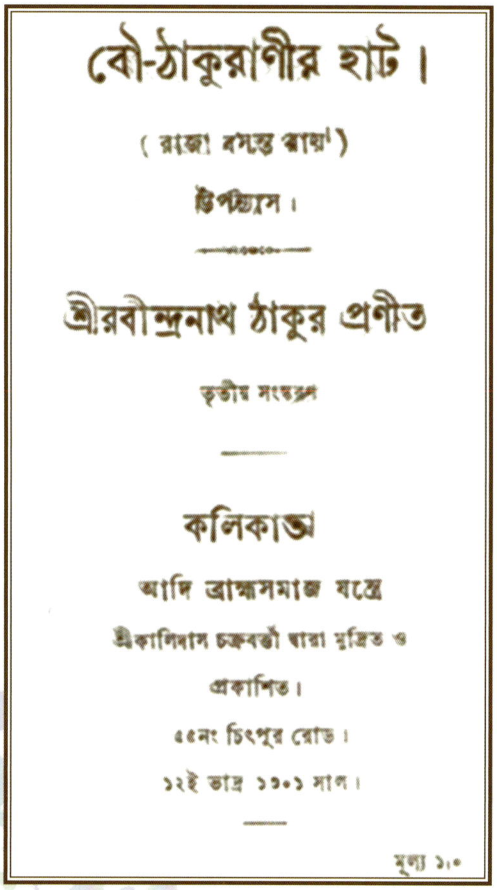

বৌ-ঠাকুরাণীর হাট।

(রাজা বসন্ত রায়)

উপন্যাস।

শ্রীরবীন্দ্রনাথ ঠাকুর প্রণীত

তৃতীয় সংস্করণ

কলিকাতা

আদি ব্রাহ্মসমাজ যন্ত্রে

শ্রীকালিদাস চক্রবর্ত্তী দ্বারা মুদ্রিত ও

প্রকাশিত।

৫৫নং চিৎপুর রোড।

১২ই ভাদ্র ১৩০১ সাল।

মূল্য ১৷০

Cover of Bouthakuranir Hat, *a novel, later adapted as* Raja Basanta Ray, *a play.*

A playwright and an actor

Before Rabindranath firmly settled down in north-east Bengal, he spent one month in Solapur in Bombay Presidency (where his civilian brother was posted), writing a play, *Raja O Rani* (The King and the Queen, 1889). Haraprasad Sastri (1853 1931), veteran scholar and then librarian of the Bengal Library, reported on this play in the annual official report on Bengali publications. Chandranath Basu, earlier in the same post and in similar reports, had appreciated Rabindranath's *Valmikipratibha, Rudrachanda* (1881) and *Bhagnahriday*. Haraprasad wrote:

> His dramas when performed before a select audience by the members of his own family produce a powerful effect, but they are generally meant for the cultured few. They are never enacted in public theatres, and are not likely to be appreciated by their audience.

Haraprasad was prophetic. Rabindranath's plays were not popular in the public theatres of Calcutta. The public theatre is considered to have run for the first time in 1872; earlier Bengali plays were staged in private houses to which only the invitees had access. Jyotirindranath's plays were commercially produced and had moderate success. Rabindranath's presence in the public theatres is not recorded anywhere and it is presumed he shunned the glitter and glamour of the commercial stage. But *Raja O Rani* was an exception. It was a hit at the Emerald Theatre, which staged the play nineteen nights in 1890, ten nights in 1891, five nights in 1892 and several nights till 1900. Funnily enough, when in 1929 Tagore revised *Raja O Rani*, considering it too long and replete with irrelevances, into *Tapati* and permitted Sisir Kumar Bhaduri (1889–1959), the doyen of Bengali commercial theatre, to stage it; it fell flat.

Raja O Rani was Rabindranath's attempt to write a five-act play, what was then considered a Shakespearean model. The model would be discarded soon and Rabindranath would forge his own format for his plays, which were however not tried on public boards. Earlier, *Raja Basanta Ray*, a play adapted for the commercial stage in 1886 from *Bauthakuranir Hat*, was a hit on public boards, although Rabindranath had nothing to do with it. His attitude to the Bengali commercial stage was expressed in 1895 as a comic indictment in a short story 'Manbhanjan' (Appeasement), which was made into a silent film in 1923 and again in 1930—the first one was a flop, the second a hit.

Several members of the Jorasanko Tagore household were good actors, the pick of them, of course, being Rabindranath. But they acted before the family and the town's elite were also invited on such occasions. Abanindranath Tagore (1871–1951), Rabindranath's nephew and a great painter, was a good actor. In his memoirs, he remembered that several actors from the public theatre sneaked into one such private staging of *Raja O Rani*, to watch how the Tagores acted and immaculately replicated the Tagores on public stage. Thus, in 1897, Girischandra Ghosh (1844–1912), the reigning playwright and actor, who had no love for the Tagores, grudgingly admitted after witnessing a private enactment of a farce by Rabindranath, *Baikunther Khata* (The Account Books of Baikuntha), that the Tagores were truly born actors.

One of the major creations in Rabindranath's early zamindari years was a play, *Bisarjan* (1890). With the same material as he had used in his novel *Rajarshi*, he had drafted this play but it was never staged outside the family premises till 1923. Perhaps the public theatre might have avoided staging it for the anti-Kali sentiments it expressed. Haraprasad Sastri had remarked in the official report in 1890 that the play was a clever ploy to spread Brahmoism. The novel *Rajarshi*, the writer remembered in his *Jibansmriti*, was inspired by a dream in which a young girl had exclaimed: 'Why so much blood on the steps of the temple?' Tagore expressed his strong sentiments against Kali-worship to Romain Rolland (1866–1944) who took notes for his diary later collected in his French *Inde*. Tagore was well aware that Rolland had the deepest regard for Ramkrishna Paramhansa (1836–86) and Swami Vivekananda (1863–1902), devotees of Goddess Kali, and consciously spoke against Kali worship in strong terms. Rolland had never seen in Tagore such an intense emotion of hatred earlier. Tagore explained that in his childhood days once while passing by the bigger Kali temple in Calcutta (possibly meaning Kalighat Kali Temple), he had noticed a stream of blood surging above the temple threshold and a woman passing by, dipped her finger in the blood and smeared the blood on her child's forehead. Tagore would tremble in anger and aversion recounting such baneful acts and describing a wretched priest shaking a young goat before immolating it before Kali. Such bloody practices, Tagore believed, had perpetuated violence and wars, aroused the excitement of killer nations—their thirst for blood. He could not reconcile himself with such practices, even metaphysically. He believed that Kali worshippers were not in a healthy or honest state of mind and wanted to destroy this image of Kali. He welcomed the rational atheism of the West to wash out these monstrosities that had gained ground over the centuries in his country.

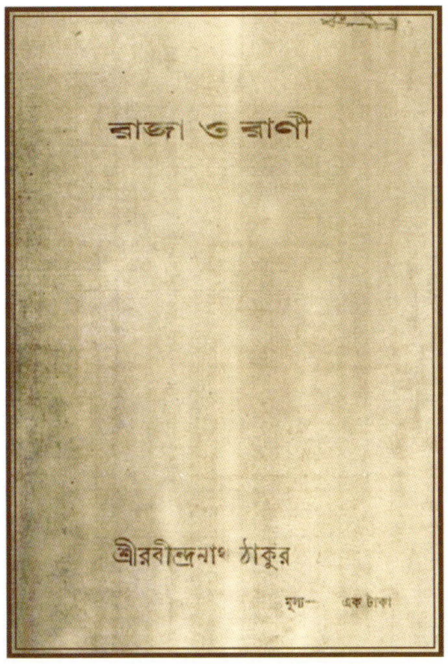

Left: Raja O Rani, *a five-act play, staged at the Emerald Theatre between 1890–1900. Right: Gaganendranath Tagore, nephew of the Poet, associated with many of the Poet's theatrical performances. Facing page: With nephew Abanindranath, c. 1888 89.*

Rolland in his notes, in August 1930, wrote that he did not argue with Tagore because he was more interested in drawing out Tagore's thoughts; but he could not but point out that such instances of blood-thirstiness were plentiful in Western religions and as a child Rolland himself reacted in similar ways to the Bible. In 1913, Tagore himself had expressed to an interviewer in London his aversion to the Old Testament's violent scenes.

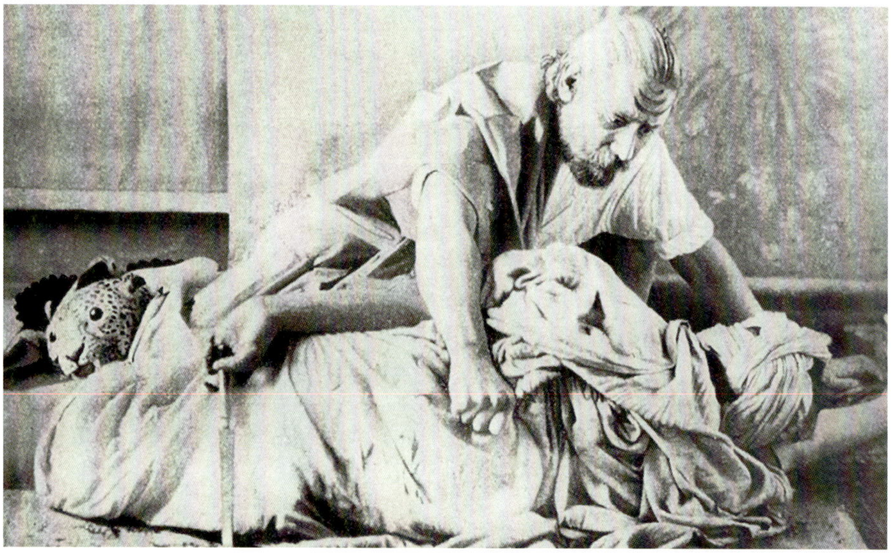

As Raghupati in Bisarjan, *1893, at Jorasanko.*

Rabindranath played the crucial role of Raghupati, the orthodox Brahmin priest pitted against the king, Govindamanikya, who forbade animal sacrifices in Kali temples. In the final scene, when his young disciple Jayasimha sacrificed himself before Kali because he had promised royal blood as offering to the deity, a shocked Raghupati lost his faith in Kali and threw away the idol. Eyewitnesses report that on the stage, Rabindranath was so engrossed in play acting that he physically lifted the heavy clay idol on the stage and was about to throw it on the audience before he recollected himself. His co-actors were shocked to see Rabindranath lifting the image, although there were stage arrangements for dragging it off the wings. As a result, the playwright-actor had to take a month's rest because he had sprained himself with the effort to destroy the idol. That was in 1890. In 1923, the play was staged four times consecutively on the Empire stage in Calcutta with huge success. Rabindranath this time played the role of Jayasimha. The audience was astounded to see the sixty-two-year-old Poet in the role of the young disciple. This time again, on one occasion, the actor in the role of Raghupati found to his consternation that Rabindranath, as Jayasimha, fell down in distress and despair and never, according to the cue, stood up. The actor improvised some words and pulled Jayasimha on his feet. Jayasimha thanked Raghupati off the stage, because he had a muscle sprain when he fell and was in no condition to stand up on his own.

Amritalal Basu (1853–1929), who once dominated the Bengali stage as an actor and playwright, wrote a very long letter in the Letters' column in

The Indian Daily News. After describing the performance of *Bisarjan*, which he saw on 25 August 1923, as an unqualified success, he commented on Tagore's acting:

> The great Poet is a great actor, almost a master of the technique of stagecraft. But, young aspirants to histrionic fame, beware of the great master! As in poetry one must drink at the fountain of Rabindranath's mind and not simply borrow his words, so, on the stage, one should imbibe the spirit of his acting and not imitate him in action, attitude, gesture or pose. They are all his own, and the copyright is not to be infringed.

Tagore was not pleased with the encomium—all the actors whom Basu praised and whom he advised not to imitate Tagore were trained by Tagore himself.

The sixty-two-year-old Poet acting as young Jayasimha in Bisarjan, *1923, Calcutta.*

In one of his letters from Silaidaha, the lonely Poet remembered that Goethe might have been essentially an introvert, nonetheless had Herder, Schlegel, Humboldt, Schiller, Kantall, who created a pervasive intellectual climate from which a creative writer like him could imbibe ideas. However, Bengal's literary climate was so barren! The vast sky and bright light on the Padma River overwhelmed the mind of the Poet but he at times pined for company and implored friends to visit him. Dwijendralal Ray (1863–1913) and Jagadis Chandra Bose (1858–1937) were frequent visitors. Ray, who studied agricultural development in England, was enthusiastic in potato growing in Silaidaha but both the playwright (as Ray would be one) and the Poet were frustrated that the seeds sown refused to grow into potatoes. It was Jagadis Chandra, who insisted that each evening that he spent on the Padma, the host must tell him a new story. Many Tagore stories were fruits of the scientist's appreciation. When friends failed to come, the young landlord would fall back on his civilian friend, Lokendranath Palit (1865–1915) who was posted in north-east Bengal. The literary debates between the civilian and the Poet formed a few chapters of *Panchabhuut* (Five Elements, 1897); one of the elements was imagined to have been Loken (Lokendranath Palit), the others the Poet's nieces—Indira and Sarala, and Pramathanath Chaudhuri, as well as the Poet himself. Pramathanath (1868–1946), who married Indira, became famous for his French orientation and for creating a Bengali prose style, writing

Above: Family lunch at Silaidaha, with niece Indira serving food. Below: The Poet at Silaidaha with Jagadis Chandra Bose, Lokendranath Palit (seated from left), Rathindranath, Mahim Devvarma and Surendranath (standing from left).

short stories and belles-lettres and for editing *Sabuj Patra* (Green Leaves, 1914), a literary magazine, which was highly regarded but one that did not have a long life. *Panchabhuut* was dedicated to Jagadindranath Ray (1868–1926), the Maharaja of Natore, to whom the young landlord paid visits. The Maharaja would continue to be a close friend of Rabindranath and later even edited *Manasi* and *Manasi O Marmabani*. *Prabasi*, the most influential Bengali monthly edited by Ramananda Chattopadhyay (1865–1943), with a varied range of interests, had Rabindranath as its principal writer. *Manasi* was also greatly patronised by Rabindranath, who was described as having two shes—*Prabasi* and *Manasi*!

With his friend, Loken Palit.

During the Silaidaha–Sajadpur–Patisar years, several volumes of verses were published: *Manasi* (1890), *Chitrangada* (1892), *Sonar Tari* (1894), *Chitra* (1896), *Kanika* (1899), *Katha* (1900), *Kahini* (1900), *Kalpana* (1900), *Kshanika* (1900). The poems in *Manasi*, which was considered by the Poet as his first major book of verse, were written before he settled in the zamindari. The poems were a break from the poems in *Kadi O Komal*, a break from fancy to imagination, a break from expressions of love and beauty in their poetic outbursts to an artistic condensation, from love to despair and resignation, a break from confinement within sonnets to an expansive metrical style.

Udayan, Santiniketan.

A difficult Poet

The first poem, 'Sonar Tari' (The Golden Boat), after which the book of verse *Sonar Tari* was named, proved to be the epicentre of a storm that would fiercely blow almost ten years after the publication of the poem. The Poet would have to explain the poem a number of times when readers and critics, not necessarily hostile, asked what the boat stood for, why it was golden, who the boatman (or boatwoman) was, what the harvest really implied. The poem has proved to be one of the most popular poems for recitation in Bengal for more than a century and equally intractable to teachers of poetry. The poem had six stanzas of five lines each, rhymed on the pattern aabaa, with long-drawn vowels, conveying a sense of utter loneliness, expectation and ultimate emptiness and is difficult to be translated.

Apart from the fact that all translations are shadows of the original, it is interesting to see how the Poet translated it and let it be included in *The Fugitive* (1921), his seventh volume of verse published by Macmillan.

> The rain fell fast. The river rushed and hissed. It licked up and swallowed the island, while I waited alone on the lessening bank with my sheaves of corn in a heap.

> From the shadows of the opposite shore the boat crosses with a woman at the helm.
>
> I cry to her, 'Come to my island coiled around with hungry water, and take away my year's harvest.'
>
> She comes and takes all that I have to the last grain, I ask her to take me.
>
> But she says, 'No'—the boat is laden with my gift and no room is left for me.

It is not known when the poem was translated but it could not have been before 1911–12 when Rabindranath began to translate his poems in right earnest. The storm, referred earlier, raged in 1906 when Dwijendralal Ray made a parody of the poem: 'A song by an old boatman'. To Ray, 'Sonar Tari' was not only abstruse but meaningless and contradictory. An agricultural expert, he asked how could paddy be harvested in the rainy season and how could a small island grow so much paddy? This criticism called forth a defence of the poem by the reputable professor of history, Jadunath Sircar (1870–1958), and others. An exchange of bitter letters between Tagore and Ray also occurred on a number of issues, including this poem. It is to be noted that the Poet dropped the 'golden' motif in the translation and clearly identified the figure at the helm of the boat as a woman. He would be explaining and expanding the idea of the poem on a number of occasions and also exclaiming why readers could not simply see the image of a cloudy day in the rainy season.

Facing page: At the age of thirty.

One interesting incident can be recalled here, as narrated by Amita Sen, daughter of Kshitimohan Sen. In 1928, when she was a student of class IX at the Santiniketan school, one evening, she and some of her classmates were summoned by Gurudev. When they reached the first floor of Udayan, where Gurudev stayed those days, they found a few distinguished guests talking to Gurudev. They were told to sit around Gurudev who straightaway asked them, 'Have you read my poem "Sonar Tari"?' They yelled and said yes. 'Have you understood it?' Again they yelled and said yes. 'What have you understood?' The most articulate of the students, Amita Sen (known as Khuku, to clear the confusion of two identical names), Tagore's most favourite singer, later said, 'It is a rainy day. The cultivator has reaped his corn and waited at the river bank for a boat. The cultivator saw a boat and called the boatman and requested to take the harvest on the boat. The boatman anchored the boat and collected the harvested corn. The cultivator said, "Please take me along too." But the boatman could not accommodate the harvester, who was left alone.' Gurudev smiled and told the gentlemen, 'Look, my school children have got it so easily—why do the learned people find it so difficult?' The students sat proudly and were told by Gurudev, 'Get lost quickly. Otherwise you will get befuddled.' The students came away from Udayan as a victorious team.

'Sonar Tari', the poem, was recorded in the Poet's voice by Hindusthan Musical Records for a gramophone disc in 1936. Much earlier, Hemendramohan Basu recorded 'Sonar Tari' in 1906, for Pathephone. The tenor of young Rabi's musical voice has been, of course, lost in the later recording. On the other side of the Pathe disc was recorded Rabindranath singing 'Vande Mataram' in the classical *Des raga*. People attending his lectures in Calcutta often used to ask Rabindranath to sing for them, taking no consideration of whether the occasion was appropriate or not. Even Bankimchandra had joined the crowd when Rabindranath delivered his one-and-a-half-hour-long lecture 'Ingrej O Bharatbasi' (The English and the Indians) and sat down after the strenuous exercise. A reluctant Rabindranath had to oblige. That was in 1893. Next year, at the commemorative lecture on Bankimchandra, a similar demand for a song was made. This time, however, Sir Gurudas Banerji (1844–1918), the first Indian vice-chancellor of Calcutta University who presided over the meeting, had to sharply rebuke the public for such an untimely request.

What kind of voice did Rabindranath have? There are so many conflicting reports from contemporaries that it is hard to form an opinion. In the Radio biography on Tagore in 1961 made by Satyajit Ray (1921–92), we hear Yuliana Schwartz who was a fifteen-year-old girl in 1930, a member of the Children's Commune in Moscow, recalling Tagore after three decades: 'Then we asked Tagore to recite some of his poems for us. He gladly consented. He had a rich baritone voice and instead of reciting his poems the way we do, he chanted them. As I remember, there were some children's poems and another called "Forward". One of my girlfriends,

The Poet with niece Indira and nephew Surendranath, c. 1886.

Era, presented him with a bouquet of flowers from her own garden. She wanted to thank him for the wonderful musical poetry, but being still under the impression she could say nothing and started to cry.'

Baritone? Indira, his niece, remembered the tenor pitch of her uncle who used to impress listeners with singing English songs, and that was in 1879–80. Dineshcharan Basu wrote about Rabi babu's soft, feminine voice. Kalidas Nag (1891–1966), the historian, used to keep notes on his conversations with the Poet. He wrote that the Poet told him that his voice was severely strained when he sang to an (790-strong) assembly in the 1896 Congress session in Calcutta. There was no microphone those days but the 'Vande Mataram' the Poet sang reached the farthest man in Beadon Square, Calcutta. The strained voice was never restored to its earlier tone and pitch, he said. Not only his songs, his recitations also used to equally impress the listeners, even if they did not know Bengali or English. This was what the poet-translator Dezso Kosztolanyi (1885–1936) wrote about Tagore's recitation. He was not impressed by Tagore's views on the East and the West, which he heard during Tagore's visit to Hungary in 1926, but he added (in Gyula Wojtilla's English translation):

> I no more ponder about these things. I am attentive and open-mouthed. Rabindranath Tagore is reciting one of his poems in his mother tongue...I hear the Bengali language, the offspring of that Sanskrit which was called 'the language of gods', the neo-Sanskrit derived from the Prakrit, which is an all used melody, all deep rhythm and all melting softness, the one-time lullaby of mankind. How much emotional charm this unknown language has! On the stage the Poet is talking with two small birds with a smiling face and a mood of ecstasy. He is chatting with the free bird and the caged bird with such tenderness and so amiably that these small birds will alight on his shoulder...Once I wrote that the verse first pleases us and then we understand it through our very pleasure. Already this pleases me, only still I do not understand its meaning. But suddenly I have an intimation which is more than knowledge: how great a man must be, how great a poet.

Evidently, Tagore was reciting 'Dui Pakhi' (Two Birds) from *Sonar Tari*, which won over the sceptic Kosztolanyi. This brings us to a fascinating chapter in Rabindranath's early life.

Clara Butt on Tagore's Songs

Dame Clara Butt (1873–1936), the English singer who was made a Dame of the British Empire on account of her donations from the proceeds of her many concerts, visited Santiniketan in 1927. She recounted her experience in *My Life of Song* thus:

> In India I met three of the most wonderful personalities of that wonderful country, Mrs Annie Besant, Gandhi and Sir Rabindranath Tagore. The last named lent me his villa, where he wrote many of those wonderful poems, which rank among the great classics of all literature.
>
> I have heard that he sometimes sang and once when he was complimenting me after hearing me sing, I said, 'But you too are a singer; I should so much like to hear you.' He made excuses, deprecating any claim to having a voice, but said at last, 'I have had such pleasure from listening to your wonderful voice that since you wish it, I will sing to you.'
>
> With me alone for an audience, and without any accompaniment of any kind, he then sang two or three songs of his own composition. Rarely have I been so moved by anybody's singing as by that of the stately and venerable Poet; he sang with exquisite feeling and his voice, though quite untrained, had a natural silvery sweetness.

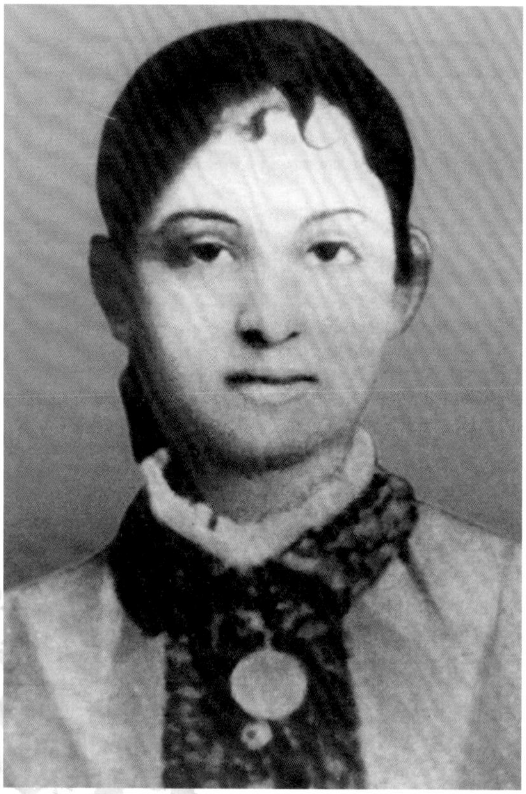

Ana Turkhud was given the task of preparing young Rabi for his first European venture in 1878–79.

A girl remembered

Sajanikanta Das discovered, in 1939, a letter tucked in a book, which was an English translation of Devendranath's autobiography by Satyendranath Tagore. Sajanikanta bought the book from an old book shop. The letter was written by one Ana Turkhud to Jyotirindranath Tagore. The letter is reproduced below:

65, Bombay, Kandevadi
November 26th [1878]

Dear Sir,
I have to apologise to you for having kept your kind letter of the 11th inst., with a copy of 'Kabikahini', unacknowledged so long; but various causes, in the shape of illness, have combined to hinder me from doing so till the present moment, and even as I write this, I have fever upon me.

Thank you very much indeed for sending me the entire publication of 'Kabikahini' though I have the poem myself in the numbers of *Bharati*, in which it was first published, and which Mr Tagore was good enough to give me before going away: and have had it read and translated to me, till I know the poem almost by heart. You are under a misapprehension when you suppose that I have 'learnt' Bengali. I was only a beginner, for ill-health has come in the way of my studies, and I have had to cease continuing them. Believe me.

Yours sincerely

Ana Turkhud

Sajanikanta took the letter to the Poet. Sajanikanta recalls, the letter seemed to have brought the morning brilliance to the Poet's face in that dim evening. The Poet called his son Rathindranath and told him to give the letter the pride of place in the Tagore museum, if they ever planned it.

Ana was one of the three daughters of Dr Atmaram Pandurang, the sheriff of Bombay. Satyendranath Tagore knew the family during his stay at Ahmedabad and Bombay. The family had a leading role in social and religious reforms of the Marathi society. Ana and her sisters were educated in England. Ana (1855–91) was married in 1879 to Harold Littledale, vice-principal of Baroda High School and College. Ana met the Scottish professor during her studies abroad. The marriage took place in Bombay and the married couple left for Edinburgh where Ana died of tuberculosis. Ana used to contribute essays and poems in English and Indian journals under the pseudonym, Nalini.

Rabindranath stayed with the Pandurang family some time during August and September 1878 and on 20 September 1878 left for England. In *Jibansmriti,* he made no mention of Ana but in *Chhelebela,* Ana was fondly and reverentially remembered. In the penultimate chapter of his childhood memories, Rabindranath wrote that his brother Satyendranath placed him with the Marathi family which was abreast of the English way of living, so that the young boy could have a bit of training in living according to the Western style.

> There was a girl in that family who was educated abroad. She sparkled in sophistication. I had little education myself and she could not have been faulted if she ignored me. But she did not. I could not flaunt any academic worth but at the slightest opportunity I let her know that I could write poems. That was my only capital to draw out a favour. She took my poetic capability at face value, without trying to weigh its merit. She asked for a pet name and I provided it, which she liked. I wanted to associate the name with my poems. I wove the name in a poem, and she heard it in *Bhairabi raga.* She said, 'Poet, I may rise up from my death-bed if I hear your song.' This shows that women, when they want to please somebody, exaggerate to spread a little more joy.
>
> I remember she was the first to appreciate my appearance. And that appreciation had a few detailed points. For example, she specially

> said, 'You have to give me word, you shall never grow a beard, you must never cover the contours of your face.' Everybody knows that I did not keep her words. She died before disobedience manifested on my face.
>
> In that banyan tree of ours, in some years, birds from foreign lands come and build nests. Before the rhythm of their wings is identified, they fly away. They bring unfamiliar tunes from distant forests. In the same way messengers of our own come in the midst of our life from unknown worlds and expand their command on our hearts. They come without our call but they do not respond at the end. While they pass along they weave a border of flowers on the wrapper of life and enhance forever the value of days and nights (Author's translation).

With wife Mrinalini and eldest daughter Madhurilata.

One would think that the letter from Ana revived the Poet's memory of that girl. But on 1 January 1927, he had remembered her during a conversation with two major composer-singers of the time—Atulprasad Sen (1871–1934) and Dilip Kumar Ray (1897–1980). He remembered her as a girl of sixteen while he too was sixteen—educated, clever, companionable, as he remembered her. He recalled a few gestures of the girl which might have been distinctly erotic overtures, but being the young shy lad as he was, he had never thought of reciprocating.

It is not known if Rabindranath followed Ana's life or writings or knew that Ana died in 1891. He grew his beard before he was thirty. But he was never sure of the dates of his life, causing frequent problems for his biographers. It was his perception of Ana, not dates that matter. He was never so frank about a girl who loved him as he was about Ana. The pet name he gave Ana must have been Nalini, a name frequently used in his early poems.

Chitra, a collection of poems, written between 1894–96, is considered by many Bengali critics as the finest fruition of his poetical genius. The

The Poet with daughter Madhurilata and son Rathi, 1889.

poems at the same time address *Jibandevata,* the interpretation of which has been varied, both by the Poet and his critics; 'Lord' sometimes is the Lady of his life or the Muse. E.J. Thompson thought,

The Poet's nephews—Surendranath (right) and Balendranath (left).

> ...without some knowledge of the doctrine many of the poems of this period must seem the vaguest gibberish. It is partly because such poems have been translated and printed in the West, without a word of any kind, that so widespread a belief has sprung up that Rabindranath is a weaver of beautiful but meaningless words and images...But the book merits its simple, inclusive title. In no other book has he attained to more single-minded adoration and celebration of Beauty...The greatest poem of all, 'Urbasi', is perhaps the greatest lyric in all Bengali literature, and probably the most unalloyed and perfect worship of Beauty which the world's literature contains.

Rabindranath brought his wife and children to Silaidaha in 1898 for a stable family life. Earlier his family visited him for temporary stays. The big joint family set-up at Jorasanko gave little privacy to the married couple. Earlier he took Mrinalini to Gazipur in the United Provinces in 1888, where Mrinalini had the Poet all to herself. *Manasi* poems were mostly written there and the book was dedicated to his wife through a poem, not by name. Keeping his family at Jorasanko was financially comfortable for him; he used to get allowances for supervising the estates while his family expenses were defrayed by the estate. However, Rabindranath decided to suffer minor losses and brought his wife and five children (Madhurilata twelve years, Rathindranath ten, Renuka seven, Mira four and Sami two) to Silaidaha.

The River Padma and the houseboat named *Padma* dominated the Poet's life in Silaidaha. He was an expert swimmer. Rathi remembered his father once jumping into the swelling river to rescue his own slippers which were salvaged but had become useless for future use. On another occasion, the Poet saw a woman drowning; he asked the boatman to pull her up immediately. The surging waters frightened even the expert swimmers who hesitated. The zamindar leaped overboard and swimming across currents clutched the hair of the woman, who however, refused to be rescued—she, a neglected wife of a tenant wanted to commit suicide. The zamindar forcibly took her up on the boat. The tenant was summoned and Rathi reported that the reconciled couple was not heard quarrelling again. The simple life on the Padma—a naked boy squatting on the ground, a listless girl looking vacantly, a buffalo wallowing in shallow water—all these formed the staple of *Chaitali* which was included in his first anthology of poems, *Kabyagranthabali* (1896), and later published as a book in 1912. One of the poems of *Chaitali* is familiar even to the non-Bengali readers of Tagore; known as 'Karma' in others' translation, Rabindranath himself had translated it in English:

> The morning came, but my servant appeared not.
>
> Doors were wide open, the water was not drawn from the well, the man had been out all night.
>
> As the hours passed my anger grew, and I devised punishments for him.
>
> At last he came and bowed to me with joined hands.
>
> I shouted angrily, 'Go out! I never want to see you again!'
>
> He looked blankly and remained silent for a minute! Then said in a whisper, 'My little daughter died last night,' and without another word, duster in hand, he went to his daily task.

The English Writings of Rabindranath Tagore, Vol. IV.

The placid life on the river and the river bank was, however, disturbed by business worries. His two nephews—Surendranath and

At the age of thirty-five.

Balendranath (1870–99)—had opened a business company, Tagore & Co., in Kushthia, a town near Silaidaha. The businesses—mostly village industries like storage of grain, bailing of jute, sugarcane-crushing—were running well. But Surendranath could not stick to one objective—he was contemplating cooperative societies and insurance business for which he used to stay away from Kushthia. Balendranath was an image of his uncle, more interested in literature than in business. Rabindranath took active interest in the nephew's businesses as a partner which sank because the manager of the company misappropriated a huge sum of money throwing Rabindranath heavily in debt. Akshay Kumar Maitreya (1861–1930), the historian, was a frequent visitor to Silaidaha. He had resolved to revive the dying silk industry of Bengal. Rabindranath patronised the silk industrial house which Maitreya had founded at Rajshahi to encourage the historian-industrialist. He experimented with silkworms in his estate, which caused immense headache to the amateur entrepreneur. However, in one year, he grew a huge and unmanageable amount of silk.

Open-air classes at Santiniketan school.

A school in the lap of nature

Mrinalini, though coming from a village, was nurtured at Jorasanko, hence, she could not adjust herself to the lonely life at the estates. Children's education was another worry. Rabindranath sought permission from his father to start a school at Santiniketan. Devendranath had bought land near Bolpur in 1863. Over some time, a building was constructed there called Santiniketan.

The land later came to be known after the building. A Brahmo temple was built in 1891. Family members used to come and go but it was Rabindranath who made the place distinctive, founding a boarding school in 1901. In a lecture in Moscow in 1930, Tagore said what he wanted to do of Santiniketan but could not do. The lecture was published in *The Modern Review* of January 1931 as 'My School':

> I selected a beautiful place, far away from the contamination of town life...I knew that the mind has its hunger for the ministration of nature, mother-nature, and so I selected this spot where the sky is unobstructed to the verge of the horizon. There the mind could have its own dreams and the seasons could come with all their colours and movements and beauty into the very heart of the human dwelling.

And there I got a few children around me and I taught them. I was their companion. I sang to them. I composed some musical pieces, some operas and plays and they took part in those plays. I had only five or six students at that time.

People did not have any confidence in a poet and they had the right to doubt my confidence in bringing up their children and truly educating them in their orthodox fashion. And so I had very few students to begin with.

My idea was that education should be a part of life and must not be detached from it and be made into something abstract. And so when I brought these children around me, I allowed them to live a complete life. They had perfect freedom to do what they wished, as much liberty as was possible for me to give them. And in all their activities I tried to put before them something which would be interesting to them. I tried to arouse their interests in all things, in nature's beauty and the surrounding villages and also in literature, through play-acting, through listening to music in a natural manner, not through merely class teaching.

They knew when I was employed in writing some drama and they took an interest as it went on and developed, and in the process of their rehearsal they got through a great deal more of reading of

Samindranath, the Poet's youngest son, was among the first batch of students of Santiniketan school. The Poet with Sami and other students.

literature than they could through grammar and class-teaching. And this was my method. I knew the children's mind. Their subconscious mind is more active than the conscious one, and therefore, the important thing is to surround them with all kinds of activities which could stimulate their minds and gradually arouse their interests.

I had musical evenings—not merely music classes, and those boys who at first did not have any special love for music, would, out of curiosity, listen to our songs outside of the room, and gradually they too were drawn into the room and their taste for music developed. I had some of the very great artists of our land and while they went on with their work, the boys could watch them and saw day by day how those works developed.

An atmosphere was created and what was important, this atmosphere had provided the students with a natural impulse to live in harmony with it. In the beginning it was easier to feel this, when I had only a few students; I was then almost their only companion and teacher and it was truly [the] golden age of our school. I know that the boys who had then the privilege of attending that institution look back on those days with much love and longing. But as the number grew it became more and more expensive for me to carry on the school in my own way. In the first place, we in our country have the tradition that it is the teacher who has the responsibility to give education to those who come to him to be taught, and in our country there were students who used to have free tuition, also their lodging free in their teachers' house. It was the teachers who acknowledged their own responsibility. They had the privilege of being educated, and they owed it to society that they should help their students and in return should not claim anything in the shape of fees or remuneration.

And this was our custom from the olden days and I began like that. Free tuition, lodging and boarding and all necessities of life, I supplied to my students out of my own poor resources. But you can imagine with the modern condition of life it was not possible to continue like this, because now you have to get the help of teachers whose salaries are high and there are other expenses which daily seem to increase. I find it impossible now to keep that idea in the heart of the institution that teaching should be a duty of the teacher to impart to the students and that it should not have the atmosphere of a shop where you can buy commodities with money. I was compelled to give up this idea and now gradually it has taken the shape of the ordinary school.

Only I tried my best to have some aspect in the school which they did not have in their orthodox schools. The teachers shared the common life with the boys, it was a community life. In the sports and festivals the teachers and the students fully co-operated with each other. It was not like a cage in which the birds are fed from the outside, but it was like a nest which students themselves co-operated in building up their own life, with their love, with their daily work and their plays.

I believe that we still have this true to a great extent. It is difficult owing to the fact that my colleagues with whom I have to work are brought up in a different manner, not having the same chance as I had to play truant when they were young and give up their school days. They have their own ideas about education and it is difficult wholly to get rid of them. And so something alien to the central ideal does creep into this institution through those who are there to help me. I had in the beginning to struggle very hard with my teachers, not with the students, as very often happens in other schools. But I had to take sides with the boys when they were punished for no fault of their own, but that of their teachers. I had to be firm and defend the boys, which offended my teachers. I remember one day a new teacher came and when he found that some of the boys were doing their lessons up on the tree, he was furious because of this want of discipline on their part. I had then to protect the boys from the schoolmaster. I told him that when these boys grow up to his age they will not have the great privilege of climbing up to the trees to do their lessons. They would become more respectable and keep away from mother-nature.

But I believe that the atmosphere has been created and it is going on. Now it has grown. The number of the students is increasing year by year, which is not always an advantage. But it cannot be helped.

Left: The Poet along the famous rows of sal trees at Santiniketan. Facing page: Learning amidst nature at Santiniketan school.

Another aspect which is of later growth is that the number of girls has been increasing. The co-education system is quite a new thing in India. But it has been working perfectly. We have had no cause for complaint. And very often the boys and girls go together on excursions; the boys help the girls in bringing fuel and fetching water and the girls cook the dinners for the boys and everything is managed by mutual help. That is a great education in itself.

There is another factor which I consider to be important. I always try to get from outside of India, from Europe and from the Far East, lecturers who come to the school to teach and also share the simple life of the school with our students. This is another factor creating the atmosphere of this place. Our boys are very natural in their relationship with those foreigners, guests and visitors. My idea is that the mind should find its freedom in every respect, and I am sure that our children have through their early training freedom from the barriers of the country and race and creeds and prejudices. And it is always difficult to get rid of those when we grow up and even if it is sedulously cultivated in our school-books and also by the people who wish the boys to be proud of their own exploits and running down other countries. And this is really clinging to certain prejudices which are considered nationalistic. And with the help of these visitors I have tried my best to make the minds of our boys more hospitable to the guests who come to us and I think I have been successful.

Then there are other activities. We have in the neighbouring villages some primitive people who need our help and we have started some night-schools and our boys go there and teach them. Then you have the village work in connection with our institutions and those boys who have the opportunity to study the conditions of our village life and to know how to help them efficiently through scientific and up-to-date methods of cultivation and fighting diseases. To impart not merely academic information, but how to live a complete life is, according to me, the purpose of education.

The only thing I have not been able to provide our boys with is science, owing to the enormous expense it would entail, which in a poor country like ours, is difficult to meet. I have not yet been able to arrange for it. Our students and I hope some day it will be possible for me to fill up that deficiency...

From the conversational tone of Tagore, it is clear that he was not delivering a lecture but answering a question raised by a student in Moscow who wished to know how his school combined its life and work with its surroundings. Shorn of dates and names, the answer gives the essence of the Santiniketan school.

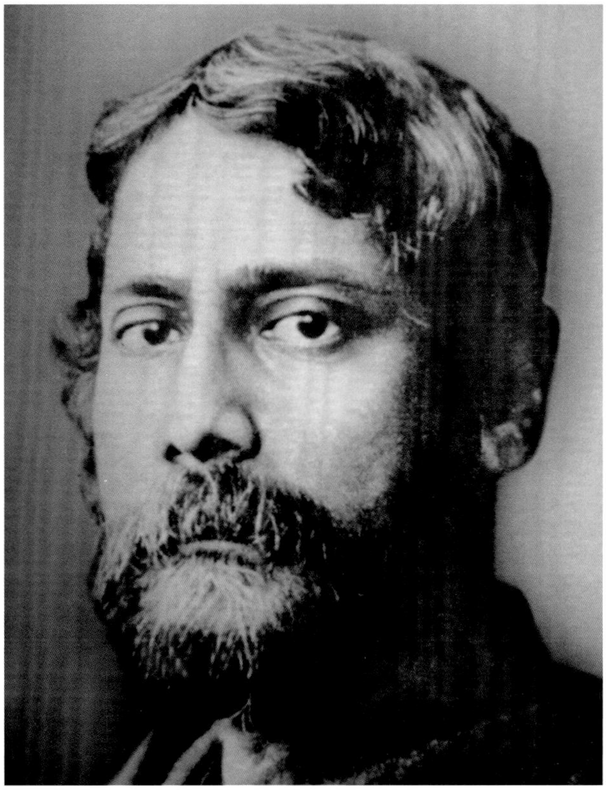

The Poet in 1905; photographed by Sukumar Ray.

The first of Rabindranath's 'musical pieces, some operas and plays' as mentioned in the Moscow lecture was *Saradotsav*, 1908, which the Poet translated in 1912–13 as the *Autumn Festival*. The numerous songs of the prose-play were written by Rabindranath particularly to engage the restive students readying themselves to go home for the Puja holidays. Teachers joined students—by 1907 Santiniketan had twelve teachers and eighty students—for stage performances, with Gurudev as a prompter at the wings. At the second performance, Gurudev appeared himself as the Sanyasi, who, in one scene, was about to take an unwarranted exit, when a smart boy-actor held him back saying, 'Where are you going, Sanyasi, I have some words to tell you'!

The other plays Rabindranath wrote for the boys and girls of the school were: *Mukut*, 1908 (adapted from his story with the same name); *Malini*, 1909 (written originally in 1896 but not staged earlier); *Prayaschitta*, 1910 (adapted from *Bauthakuranir Hat*); *Lakshmir Pariksha*, 1910; *Raja*, 1910 (translated as *The King of the Dark Chamber* in 1913 and thoroughly revised by Rabindranath; also abridged as *Arupratan*, 1919); *Achalayatan*, 1911 (abridged as *Guru*, 1918); *Dakghar*, 1911; *Falguni*, 1915 (translated by the Poet as *The Cycle of Spring*, 1917); *Varshamangal*, 1921 with its variants as *Seshvarshan, Sravangatha* and *Gitotsava*; *Muktadhara*, 1922 (translated by the Poet as *The Waterfall*, 1922); *Vasanta*, 1923 and its variant *Navin*, 1931; *Natir Puja*, 1926 (translated by the Poet as *The Dancing Girl's Worship*, 1927); *Nataraj*, 1927; *Tapati*, 1929; *Sapmochan*, 1931; *Chandalika*, 1933; *Tasher Des*, 1933; *Chitrangada*, 1936; *Muktir Upay*, 1938; *Syama*, 1939. The only plays which were never staged in Santiniketan during Rabindranath's lifetime were *Muktadhara* and *Raktakarabi*, 1924, nor was *Chirakumar Sabha*, 1925, a comedy that laughed at youths bent on staying as bachelors, which was perhaps not meant for boys and girls.

The forty-year-old Santiniketan, when its founder died, predictably had its hiccups, minor and major, some overcome, some the founder could not forget ever. The 'Ashram', as Santiniketan was called by students and teachers, was suspected to harbour terrorists during the

Swadesi movement that was sparked off by the Partition of Bengal, 1905. Rabindranath himself was a suspect for a long time although the Poet laughed at the idea. In 1911, guardians, especially government employees, were scared by a secret circular published in a newspaper forbidding studies at Santiniketan. The lieutenant-governor of Bengal, at the request of the Poet, intervened and the circular was withdrawn. But the Poet was shocked when Jagadis Chandra Bose and his wife, whom the Poet respected, hinted that Aurobindo Mohan Bose (1892–1977; a major translator of Rabindranath's poems and his life-long devotee; Jagadis' nephew; and a student of Santiniketan) did not grow up to their expectations and that they did not like that Aurobindo neglected his college studies and frequently visited Santiniketan. That meant that the Boses had no faith in Tagore's educational methods and ideals. The Boses never realised that they had hurt Tagore, who could never recover from the shock. Even in an obituary article on Jagadis, Rabindranath was tongue-in-cheek in his estimation of the scientist. Not that he doubted the extraordinary achievements of the scientist, but he remembered that when the scientist was about to give up his experiments in Europe for lack of funds, Rabindranath had secured a grant of Rs 15,000 from the Maharaja of Tripura—at a time when he himself was under a heavy debt as he was winding up Tagore & Co., and was about to start his Santiniketan school. He had to beg, borrow and travel on lecture tours all over the world throughout his life to sustain Santiniketan, while funds were never a problem when Jagadis founded Basu Vignan Mandir, his laboratory in Calcutta in 1917.

Rabindranath needed funds all the time, to build classrooms, hostels for the boys and girls, teachers' quarters, guest houses for visitors, for laying out and maintaining the infrastructure, namely, roads, drains, tubewells, various Bhavans, and so on. He took his students all over India and beyond who performed in plays, musical sessions and dances to raise funds. The first performance outside Santiniketan was the staging of *Falguni* at Jorasanko in January 1916. The funds raised in the first night were in aid of the famine-stricken people of Bankura. The play was staged for three nights. And the last time Rabindranath took his students to raise funds was in January–February 1939, when

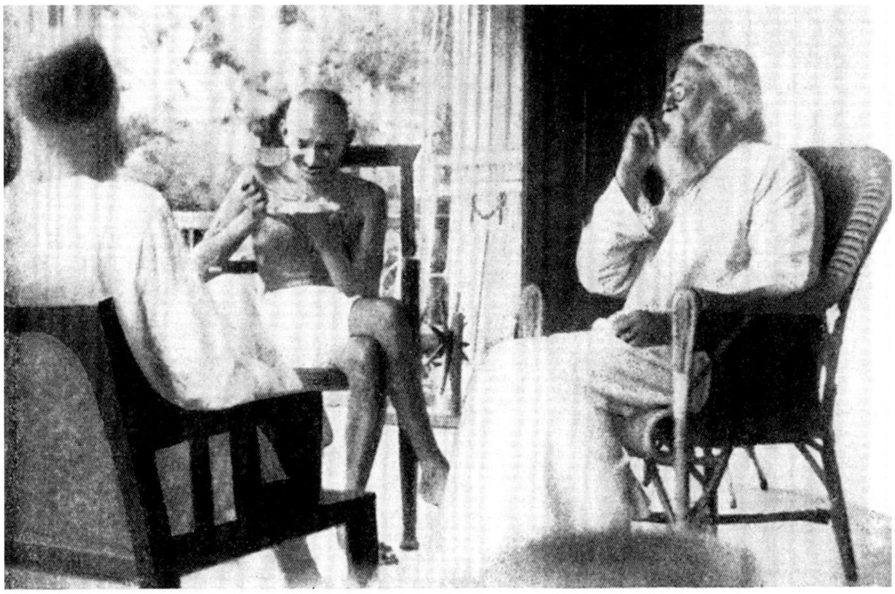

Left: With C.F. Andrews and M.K. Gandhi, at Santiniketan, 1925.
Facing page: Jagadis Chandra Bose, the eminent scientist, who sought to acquaint the West with Tagore's works as early as 1901.

his students presented three dance-dramas—*Tasher Desh, Chandalika* and *Syama* in Sree Cinema in Calcutta. The most strenuous adventure Rabindranath undertook was in 1936, when he took his students to Patna, Allahabad, Lahore and Delhi. In Delhi, Gandhi met the seventy-five-year-old Poet on 25 March and requested him to desist from such an arduous task. The Poet replied that he had to because Visva-Bharati was heavily in debt. Gandhi wanted to know the amount. Sixty thousand rupees, the Poet had replied. On 27 March, the Poet received a draft of Rs 60,000 from 'Your Humble Countrymen', who wrote that they felt humiliated that the Poet at such an advanced age had to exhibit his art from place to place to raise funds for his school and University. It is believed that it was G.D. Birla who had made the payment at the request from Gandhi.

Gandhi first came to Santiniketan on 17 February 1915 with his boys from Phoenix School. After leaving South Africa, he was perplexed with the problem of accommodating the pupils in India. C.F. Andrews mediated and the Phoenix boys stayed in Santiniketan for five months. Gandhi's last visit to Santiniketan was in March 1940. In 1939, *Prabasi* reported a conversation between T. Kagawa (1888–1960), a Japanese pacifist and river activist, and Gandhi. Kagawa told Gandhi that he was going to visit Gosaba in the Sunderbans in Bengal. 'Wasn't he visiting Santiniketan?' asked Gandhi. When Kagawa replied in the negative, Gandhi said, 'Well, Gosaba is Gosaba, but Santiniketan is India.'

With Albert Einstein,
Berlin, 1930.

Indian quietude and European restiveness

Throughout his entire lifespan, there was an undercurrent of conflicting moods in him changing abruptly—a trait Rabindranath himself explained jocularly in a letter to Pramathanath Chaudhuri from Sajadpur (the date characteristically a cross between the English and Bengali calendar: 17 *Magh* 1891, which ought to have been 17 *Magh* 1297 or 29 January 1891):

> Now sometimes I think, two opposite forces are coming in conflict with each other. One is constantly beckoning me to rest and cessation and the other never allowing me to take rest. My Indian quietude constantly clashes with European restiveness—hence pain on one side, detachment on the other. Poetry on one side, philosophy on the other. Love for the country on one side, booing patriotism on the other. An attachment to action on one side, attraction to thoughts on the other. The two are jumbled up thus into fruitlessness and detachment. How do you take it? Please write me how you look at it—I wish to see myself objectively through your eyes (Author's translation).

The period between 1900–01 illustrates this conflict or rather juxtaposition of moods that produced as diverse works as *Naivedya, Chirakumar*

Sabha, Nashtanir, Chokher Bali, and Rabindranath is seen in his myriad roles—as the zamindar hopelessly mired in Tagore & Co.; as the father worrying over children's education and the fruition of his idea of a Brahmacharyasram; and as the editor of *Bangadarshan* pondering the essence of 'nation', raising funds for a scientist who was frustrated in the West for lack of funds, debating with scholars over the independence of Bengali grammar and marrying off his two daughters.

The transition to gay abandon manifest in the earlier book of verse *Kshanika,* to total surrender to God in *Naivedya* (1901) might have been caused by a renewed interest in the Upanishads. The core poems of *Naivedya,* were as Brahmabandhav Upadhyay wrote under a pseudonym in *The Twentieth Century*:

> In all places of worship, be they Christian, Muhamedan, or Hindu, the hundred sonnets can be recited or sung without scruple...The Poet has sung again the old song of the Upanishads in a new strain and let it rise as a cry, of our people to heaven as a memorial for Divine grace.

Quoting this, the biographer Prabhat Kumar Mukhopadhyay commented that this was the first time the Poet expressed himself in the simplest words and the Poet would not care if people did not understand and could not enjoy the poems. Devendranath, to whom the book was dedicated, was so pleased to listen to the devotional poems read out to him from the manuscript that he rewarded the Poet with a handsome purse. The Poet who surrendered totally to God was startled to hear a question from John W. Rattray, a *Friend of India* enthusiast, in 1938, if the question mark was correct in: 'Day after day, O Lord of my Life, / Shall I stand before thee face to face?' It was the first poem in *Naivedya* and the English translation by the Poet formed the no. LXXVI in *Gitanjali*. The Poet read again and again and was so pained by the question mark that Rattray was a bit frightened. The Poet said it was unimaginable that none had pointed out the printing error though the *Gitanjali* was being printed in millions of copies since 1913; of course, he clarified, there would be no question mark. He said, 'I am saying "Shall I stand before thee face to face: I shall stand before thee face to face".' He deleted in the copy of the *Gitanjali* of Rattray, all the three question marks by his own hand and initialed them. Amiya Chakrabarti, the Poet's secretary, was with Rattray and was told to note the corrections.

Unfortunately, to this day, the question mark in the poem remains in many reprints where it should have been a full stop.

Facing page: Back from Europe, 1913, honoured at Bangiya Sahitya Parishad.

The writer who was dedicating a poem every day to his God was not writing in splendid isolation; he was in the midst of all sorts of domestic and business problems and at the same time writing the first psychological novel in Indian literature, *Chokher Bali* (The Eyesore), which was serialised in *Bangadarshan* from April 1901 to March 1903. The novel depicts the yearnings and inhibitions of a young beautiful widow who retires from life, disconsolate because she had wrecked the life of an innocent wife. Alongside with *Chokher Bali*, he was writing *Nashtanir* (The Broken Nest), which was also being serialised in *Bharati* from April 1901 to December 1901. It is tempting to imagine that the manager of Tagore & Co. who swindled a huge amount of money and vanished into the air was reflected in the character who misappropriated funds of the newspaper editor who is the principal character of *Nashtanir*. The editor, an English-educated affluent man, a loving husband, could not, being busy with his newspaper, provide adequate company to his young wife, who built up a nest of her own and developed a possessiveness over her husband's cousin. In the delicate situation, the cousin, who wanted to be a writer and who was slighted by the superior writings of the editor's wife whom he himself tutored to write, was frightened by the possessiveness of the wife and went away to England. The wife found her nest broken; the husband also found his nest broken as he lost the attention of his wife, as well as the newspaper, defrauded by his wife's brother. Before Rabindranath plumbed the depths of women's minds, he had had a dig at shallow young men pledged to bachelorhood—*Chirakumar Sabha* (The Bachelors' Club).

Rabindranath, himself a loving husband and a caring father, had an unfortunate family life. His wife died in 1902. She came to Jorasanko, a slip of a girl from a village, and grew up as the pivot in the big joint family in Calcutta. For the last four years of her life, she reared her five children while her husband was busy with his diverse work. Unfortunately, Rabindranath lost Renuka, his second daughter, an intelligent but ailing girl, who died of tuberculosis when she was twelve, in 1903. Her husband, who was sent to the USA to study homeopathy—he was already an allopath—came back before completing his study

Right: The Poet's children—(from left) Samindranath, Renuka, Madhurilata and Mira. The second son, Rathindranath, not in the picture. Facing page: At the age of thirty-six, at Jorasanko.

and joined the Santiniketan school. When Renuka died, Rabindranath arranged a marriage for him. But he also died after four months of his second marriage, in 1908.

Rabindranath's second son, Sami, a promising boy of eleven, died of cholera in 1907—he had gone to a friend's house for his Puja holidays. Madhuri, the eldest daughter, was married to Sarat, a lawyer, son of poet Biharilal Chakrabarti. Sarat was a busy practising lawyer in Bihar, went abroad to become a barrister at his father-in-law's expense and came back to Calcutta in 1909, staying in Jorasanko. But he left Jorasanko with his wife under unexplained circumstances in 1915, never to come back and keeping no contact with the father-in-law thereafter. Madhuri died of tuberculosis in 1918, away from her father's house. Her father used to visit his daughter, ignoring the misbehaviour deliberately meted out to him by his son-in-law, and gave the dying daughter the much-sought company.

Mira, Rabindranath's third daughter, was married to a promising young man who was also sent abroad by the father-in-law to study agriculture. Nagendranath Gangopadhyay (1889–1954), Mira's husband, came back with the necessary degree in 1911.

Nagendranath had an independent mind but he never had an easy relation with his father-in-law, who wanted to keep Mira under his tutelage. Nagendranath's marriage never worked. His wife was terrified by his presence but his two children, Nitindranath and Nandita, loved him.

The Tagore biographers invariably mention Nagendranath in deprecatory terms, referring to his arrogance, fickleness of mind and his habit of spending money, but never accounting for the money spent. Nevertheless, Nagendranath was entrusted by Rabindranath with the management of estates, the agricultural bank of Patisar and also the management of the family when he went on a long tour to England and the USA in 1912–13. He was also appointed as the secretary of the Adi Brahmo Samaj by the trustee of the Samaj. But for unexplained reasons, he gave up all Tagore-related jobs and joined a mercantile firm. During the Non-Cooperation movement, he courted a jail-term. Coming out of jail, he joined Calcutta University as a professor of agriculture and was sent to England for higher studies. His relation with the wife, already strained, took a critical turn and divorce proceedings were contemplated. Despite all these twists and turns, Rabindranath indulged the capricious behaviour of this talented son-in-law, and sheltered his daughter in Santiniketan.

In 1926, Nagendranath came back to join Calcutta University, after getting the PhD degree. He was a member of the Royal

Agricultural Commission (1926) and Imperial Council of Agricultural Research (1929–30). He contributed a number of articles to the *Visva-Bharati Quarterly* and other journals. After 1932, he settled in England. When his son Nitindranath (1911–32) died in Germany, Nagendranath published an anthology on death, with an introduction by T.S. Eliot, published by Faber & Faber, *The Testament of Immortality*. He had another publication to his credit, *Thoughts of Meditation*. Curiously Krishna Kripalani (1907–92) who married Mira's daughter Nandita in 1936 and taught at Visva-Bharati (1933–46), never mentioned his father-in-law, Nagendranath, in his biography of Tagore. Rabindranath could reconcile himself with the early deaths of Renuka and Sami but he had to put up with the troubled lives of Madhuri and Mira for a long time.

The ailment of which Mrinalini died is not exactly known, but there have been eyewitness reports on how the Poet nursed her for days and nights, staying awake beside his wife, seeking to soothe the ailing patient with a palm-leaf fan in the hot and humid room at Jorasanko. He went up to the roof when his wife died, requesting others to leave him alone. Poem no. 45 in *Fruit-Gathering* conveys the picture of the bereaving man:

Samindranath, who died in 1907 at the age of eleven, is believed to have staged songs and dances to celebrate various seasons of a year in 1906.

> My night has passed on the bed of sorrow, and my eyes are tired.
>
> My heavy heart is not yet ready to meet morning with its crowded joys.
>
> Draw a veil over this naked light, beckon aside from me this glaring flash and dance of life.
>
> Let thy mantle of tender darkness cover me in its folds, and cover my pain awhile from the pressure of the world.

Mrinalini, who died in 1902, at the age of twenty-nine, leaving five children to the Poet's care.

This is the Poet's own translation of the first poem of *Smaran*, the book of verse written in memory of his wife. This was his innermost wish. However, as his son writes of his mother's death—he was fourteen then—'Father met calmly numerous relations and friends the whole day and when everybody was gone, he gave me the slippers my mother wore and told me, keep these with you, and retired to his room.'

The Poet left no stone unturned to restore his second daughter, Renuka, back to health. He went to Hazaribagh and then to Almorah all alone, the son-in-law missing without trace at crucial moments. He flitted from Almorah to Santiniketan, which demanded his presence, and back to Almorah. His daughter was sinking every day, not responding to any kind of treatment. He came back with the ailing child, trudging hill tracks at places where conveyance was blocked owing to landslides. But the frail child could not be revived; his dying daughter asked him to chant the *sloka* from the Yajurveda—*Pita nohsi pita no bodhi*—which seemed to embalm her.

Sami, a mirror image of the father, exceedingly handsome, with a very musical voice, eager to help his classmates (though he did not inherit the father's health) in the boarding house of Santiniketan, carrying the medicine box when his father went to the nearby villages to treat the

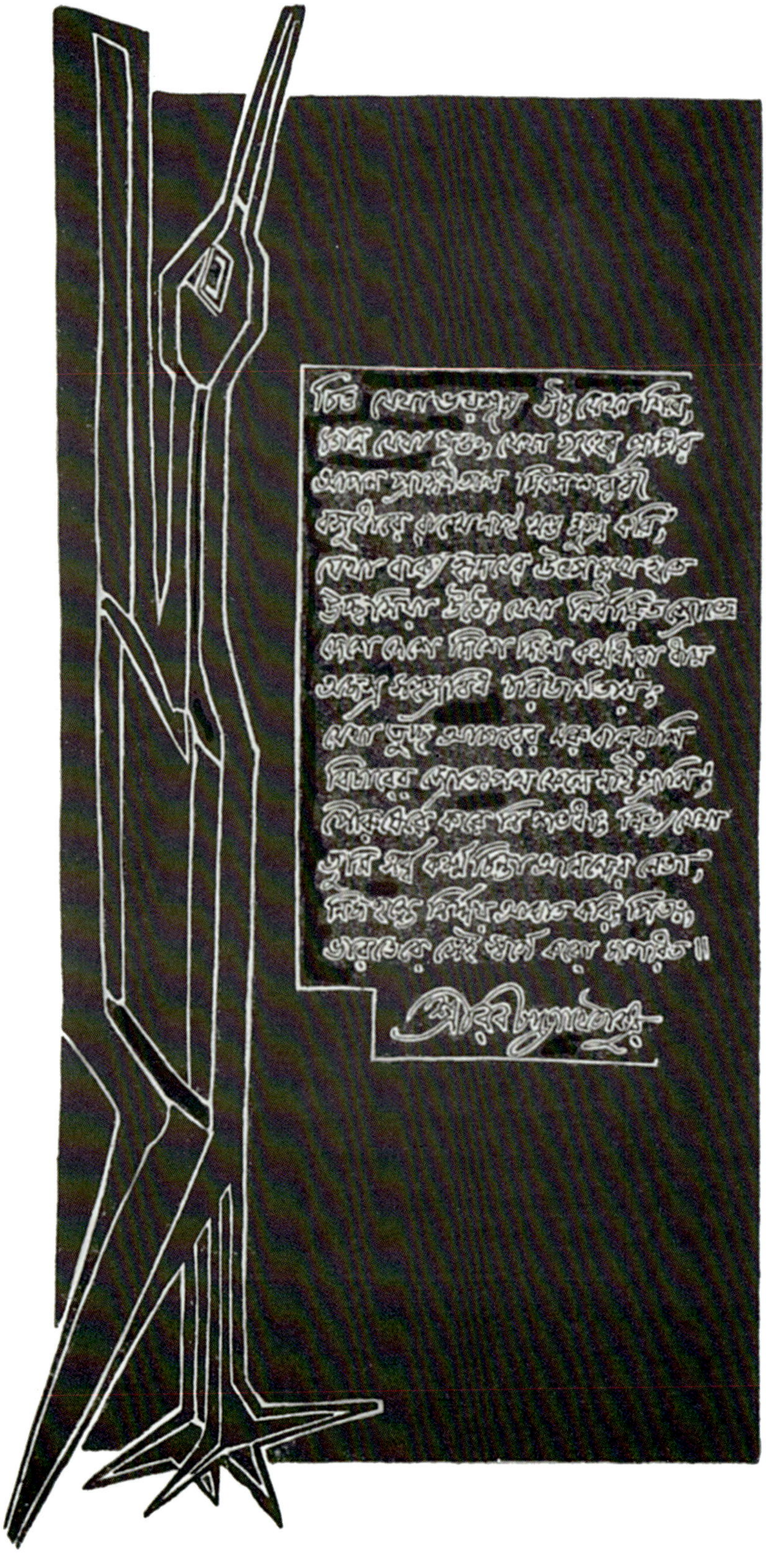

The Bengali version of 'Where the mind is without fear', in the Poet's own writing and illustration.

poor villagers, never came back from Mungher where he had gone for a holiday. Sami was in good care of doctors but who were of little help, because the boy was stricken with an acute case of cholera. Learning of the illness of his son, Rabindranath rushed to Mungher from Santiniketan. When his son died, he sat like a stone while friends cried unceasingly. Rabindranath remembered the day when his grandson Nitindra died in Germany. He wrote to his daughter Mira:

> The night after Sami died I found the sky bathed in moonlight when I was on a railway carriage—there was no hint anywhere that something was missing. My heart told me, there's nothing amiss, everything is embedded in everything and that includes me. I have my work for others unfinished. As long as I exist the workflow will continue. I must gather courage, I must not be weighed down by depression, no connectivity can be lost anywhere—I must naturally adjust whatever happens and there must not be any deficiency in simple acceptance of whatever remains (Author's translation).

In *Naivedya*, love of God and love of the country reinforced each other. The original of the most known poem of Rabindranath is contained in this book: 'Where the mind is without fear' (poem no. 35, *Gitanjali: Song Offerings*). This book also contains the original five poems which constitute the last chapter of his *Nationalism: The Sunset of the Century* (1917).

With Mahatma Gandhi,
Santiniketan, 1940.

His political thoughts

The political thoughts of Rabindranath had several strains. First was his faith in the dual character of Englishmen—small and great. This found expression in his first political speech in 1890 in protest against the British Government's denial of the right of Indians to choose their members in the legislative council. The INC was then into its fifth year. From the very first year of its inception, it was demanding representatives in legislative councils introduced by Lord Canning after the 1857 sepoy mutiny. Lord Cross, secretary of state for India, had introduced a bill in the House of Lords which had no accommodation for the Congress demand. A protest meeting was organised at the Emerald Theatre at Beadon Street with Dwijendranath Tagore in the chair (not a usual role for the poet-philosopher). Among the many speakers were Rabindranath and Kaliprasanna Kavyavisharad—the two would be seen together on many political platforms. Rabindranath's targets of attack were editors of English newspapers, especially *The Pioneer,* which said that Orientals had no maturity to handle the election of representatives and Indians would be better off when left in British care. Rabindranath drew a line between what he would in future call the 'great' and 'small' English. It may be interesting to note whom Rabindranath considered 'great' in his 1890 speech, 'Mantri Abhishek' (Enthroning Ministers): A.O. Hume (the retired ICS officer who conceived the INC); George Yule (the Bengal Chamber of Commerce official and the fourth president of the INC, 1888); Sir William Wedderburn (the fifth INC president, 1889); Thomas Carlyle, Mathew Arnold and John Ruskin (famous English thinkers); Lord Northbrooke, Lord Ripon, Lord Dufferin, Sir Richard Temple (Indian viceroys and lieutenant-governors). The 'small' English were not named but they were obviously Lord Cross and Lord Salisbury, the then prime minister of Britain who endorsed the bill brought by Lord Cross, and, of course, the anti-Indian editors of English newspapers.

In his next political speech, 'Ingrej O Bharatbashi' (The English and the Indians), 1893, he mentioned Edwin Arnold (for *The Light of Asia*) and Alfred Tennyson (for his poem on Akbar) as 'great' Englishmen and ridiculed Rudyard Kipling and Edmund Gosse who appreciated Kipling. In his novels and stories, Kipling was painting India as an arid land, the only oasis being the cantonments. It may be mentioned that Edmund Gosse rejected in 1912 W.B. Yeats' proposal to nominate Tagore as a member of the academic committee of the Royal Society of Literature.

Rabindranath's acknowledgement of the liberal British thinkers as great Englishmen and condemnation of the bureaucrats who lacked the vision of a statesmen continued as long as he lived till he unambiguously denounced the British rule in India in 1941 in his last lecture, 'The Crisis in Civilisation'. When he criticised British legislators in 1890, he did not counter many instances of injustice; however as time passed, instances of deliberate maladministration continued to pile up; hence when in 1917 he was asked to write an article on the current situation in India by *The Manchester Guardian*, his contained anger burst forth in the lecture, 'Chhoto O Baro' (translated by Surendranath Tagore as 'The Small and the Great'). The lecture was long but well structured. He started with the Hindu–Muslim clashes, blaming the Indians for suicidal infights but at the same time pointing out that the partisan rulers were playing the Muslims against Hindus. The second part of the lecture was addressed to those Indian leaders who expected too much from the forthcoming visit of the secretary of state for India, Edwin Montagu. All the proposals made by the liberal Montagu were sure to be sabotaged by the petty local bureaucrats in India. The third part of the lecture expressed the anguish of the speaker at the torture of innocent Bengalis, imprisoned or interned under the Defence of India Act, 1915. He warned the British that the more they treated the subjects unfairly, the more undermined would be the foundation of their existence in India. Rabindranath did

Facing page: As President of Bengal Provincial Congress, Pabna, 1908.

not stop with just delivering lectures. Frequently he intervened in cases of obvious injustice—by that time he was an international celebrity and his admonitions carried weight. In 1917, he wrote to the governor of Bengal to enquire into the ill-treatment of a professor who was kept in a solitary cell and was being driven to insanity. The letter forced the government to take remedial action.

Rabindranath was critical, at a very early age, of the Bengali political leaders who did little except deliver lectures (that too in English). When the INC was formed, he had little faith in the efficacy of agitational politics but was not inimical to the organisation. At Jorasanko, in 1889, he was among the young Tagores who felicitated George Yule, the fourth INC president as well as the English barrister, E. Norton, who was sympathetic to the rights and demands of Indians. He sang 'Vande Mataram' in the 1890 INC session in Calcutta. There is, however, a difference of opinion among the biographers—some say, he sang 'Vande Mataram' in the 1896 INC session in Calcutta. In 1897, he attended the Bengal Provincial Conference (a provincial adjunct of INC) at Natore and next year at Dacca. Nonetheless, Rabindranath had been losing faith in Congress politics, which was termed by Asvinikumar Datta (1856–1923) as a three-day *tamasa*. Aswinikumar, the saintly teacher of Barisal, like Tagore, believed more in social organisation than in agitation and petitions. Rabindranath did take part in the Swadesi movement in 1904–06 in Bengal, which was a spontaneous movement independent of the INC, to protest against the Partition of Bengal. But he retreated in 1906; he thought that the boycott programme was a negative approach to the problem, more important was self-regeneration. Even then, he agreed to preside over the Bengal Provincial Conference at Pabna, 1908, to help the delegates who were divided in their nomination of the president—Rabindranath was the compromise choice. Similarly, in 1917, when the Bengali leaders were in two minds in choosing the chairman of

the reception committee for the INC session in Calcutta, Rabindranath agreed to be the chairman to help organisers tide over the imbroglio; at the end he did not have to.

Rabindranath increasingly criticised agitational politics of the INC and made his famous speech, 'Swadesi Samaj' (self-governing society), 1904, which presented the blueprint of his constructional programme. Self-empowerment, he observed, was the key to nationhood, not begging for crumbs of administrative reforms. All his political speeches would be henceforward hinged on to self-empowerment—a parallel civil society to manage all vital issues—education, health, sanitation, legal settlements through self-appointed arbitration court and generation of income. This is the second and most important strain of his political thoughts.

However, the third strain that got almost everybody's hackles, in his own country and abroad, was the distinction Rabindranath made between patriotism and nationalism. As he explained to the students in Moscow in his talk, 'My School', referred earlier, he fostered love of one's own country but not at the cost of another.

In an early essay in *Bangadarshan* in 1901, when he edited the paper, he sought to define 'nation' in course of a discussion of the term as defined by the French historian Ernest Renan (1823–92). Rabindranath wrote that there was no Bengali or Indian equivalent of the expression 'nation', which was essentially a European concept; the nearest equivalent of it in India was *samaj* or community. The European nations were vibrant but the Indian nation was dormant, with blind habits deadening its spirit. It was essential to revive in the Indian nation a reawakened consciousness of its ancient unity of spirit.

Rabindranath's rosy idea of 'vibrant' European nations was rudely shaken by the South African Boer War (1899–1902) in which British atrocities got wide publicity. The British aggrandisement provoked four poems of *Naivedya*. Rabindranath had been an admirer of Japan's self-reliance in the teeth of Western aggression. When Count Okakura Kakuzo (1862–1913), known in India for his *Ideals of the East*, was visiting India in 1901–02, the Japanese artist was invited by Rabindranath to Santiniketan. His friendship with the Japanese artist was bolstered by Okakura's intimacy with Surendranath and Sarala, Rabindranath's nephew and niece. Okakura's doctrine, 'Asia is One', was appreciated

The Poet with his intellectual friends—(from left) Asutosh Chaudhuri, Ramananda Chatterjee, Trailokyanath Sanyal and Saileschandra Majumdar, 1911.

by Rabindranath but when Japan converted Okakura's cultural Pan-Asianism into a militant political ideal, Rabindranath condemned it right on the soil of Japan in 1916. The First World War put Rabindranath strongly against aggressive nationalism and his lectures on the subject were enough to make enemies of friends in the USA (1916), China (1924), Italy (1926) and Hungary (1926). The Second World War put paid to his idea of dynamic West, as pronounced in his last lecture, 'Crisis in Civilisation'.

Rabindranath's conception of Indian history was the fourth strain of his political thoughts. Since he was not a historian by profession, his history of India was not concerned with events and dates or the rise and fall of ruling dynasties; his history was derived from the Indian epics and Purans, Buddhist *dohas* and tales, classical dramas and poetry, sayings of Indian sages of various centuries.

He sought unity in Indian diversity and he thought that India was spiritually one in the Vedic ages and that oneness was lost more through inter-community strifes than foreign aggressions. It is interesting to note that Jadunath Sircar translated Rabindranath's essay 'Bharatbarsher Itihaser Dhara' (The Course of Indian History), 1912, as 'My Interpretation of Indian History'. Jadunath was an admirer of Rabindranath. He was one of the members of the large team which visited Bodh Gaya in 1904—among others were Rabindranath, Sister Nivedita and Jagadis Chandra Bose. Occasionally, he taught students of Santiniketan, and had even translated four stories of Rabindranath in *The Modern Review*. However, the friendship was marred when Rabindranath asked Jadunath to be a member of the governing body of Visva-Bharati, which was being formed in 1922, and Jadunath refused to be a part of the institution. In a long letter he expressed his admiration of the Santiniketan school but said the proposed college lacked the infrastructure necessary for higher education, that mental discipline and academic grinding were sadly lacking in Santiniketan. Rabindranath was stung by the rude letter and sent out a rejoinder equally stern. Later, in another letter to Ramananda Chattopadhyay, Rabindranath ridiculed Jadunath, who was considered one of the greatest Indian historians, saying that Jadunath might have been good in unearthing dead facts and figures of the past but had no experience of dealing with living processes of the present. A couple of years earlier, Jadunath had embarrassed Rabindranath by suggesting that Sandip, a revolutionary but not a very endearing character in Rabindranath's novel *Ghare-Baire* (*The Home and the World*, translated by Surendranath Tagore, 1919), 1916, reflected the politics of Aurobindo Ghosh (1872–1950), the leading revolutionary theoretician in Bengal, 1904–09. Jadunath had watched the politics of those days and his judgement as a historian carried weight. Rabindranath categorically denied that he caricatured Aurobindo, whom he greatly respected as a revolutionary and later as a man of wisdom.

However, there can be an element of doubt about the sincerity in the statement that Rabindranath respected Aurobindo as a revolutionary. Aurobindo was the undeclared editor and principal writer of the English newspaper *Bande Mataram*, which along with *Sandhya* and *Yugantar*, the two Bengali papers, were launched in the wake of militant Bengali nationalism to fight Lord Curzon's arbitrary decision to partition Bengal in 1905.

Bhupendranath Datta (1880–1961), the young editor of *Yugantar* was sentenced to imprisonment for his seditious articles. Aurobindo translated the two allegedly seditious articles by Bhupendranath and wrote an editorial in *Bande Mataram* protesting government action. He also was arrested on 16 August 1907 but released on bail. On 24 August 1907 Rabindranath paid homage to Aurobindo through a very long poem. Aurobindo, on the other hand, had written a series of articles

The Poet in Calcutta, c. 1915; photographed at Johnston and Hoffmann.

criticising Rabindranath's abjuration of political fights and stress on self-empowerment and his abhorrence of the boycott programme launched by the political agitators.

Bhupendranath, brother of Swami Vivekananda, had approached Rabindranath to seek advice on the resistance programme against the government's divide and rule policy. Rabindranath told him that he would talk about it; he had been observing the excitement caused by the revelation in newspapers of the plan to partition Bengal.

The talk titled 'Swadesi Samaj' was delivered on 22 July 1904 at the Minerva Theatre Board. Many missed the lecture for lack of accommodation and the talk was repeated on 31 July at Curzon Theatre Board, where admission was granted only to ticket-holders, and tickets were again exhausted and many had to be refused admission. Rabindranath's self-empowerment theory, as elaborated in the talk, was welcomed but his aversion to political struggles caused widespread attacks, some of which were later made by Aurobindo.

Howevermuch Rabindranath opposed petition politics, he was drawn into the vortex of public protests and memorials to the secretary of state for India and street processions in 1905. Twenty-three patriotic songs were composed in September–October 1905, set to tunes which the composer taught a few disciples in a friend's house and which were picked up by others and sung on street processions. He himself joined the famous procession on 16 October 1905, the day on which the Partition of Bengal was officially effected, which terminated at the banks of River Ganga, and processionists exchanged *rakhis*—bonds of fraternity—among themselves. The idea of *rakhi* has been generally credited to Rabindranath. It was however mooted in a meeting of many leading political and cultural leaders on 27 September 1905, and the meeting was chaired by Rabindranath.

It has been a matter of intense speculation why Rabindranath retracted from active participation in Swadesi politics. Bipin Chandra Pal (1858–1932), the fiery orator and active political leader much later described Rabindranath as 'a democrat by education but really an aristocrat by nature in the highest sense of the term'. Probably Rabindranath could not stand political polemics and compromises. He had been promoting constructional actions on the ground instead of appeals to the government. He was also firmly against forcible enforcement of the boycott of British goods. An uncharitable view of Rabindranath's retreat from the 1905–06 protests is that bombings and robberies, which freedom fighters resorted to after infructuous public protests, frightened Rabindranath and he withdrew into himself. Leonard Elmhirst (1893–1974) who came to Santiniketan to build up the agricultural infrastructure at Sriniketan had noted in his diary on 15 March 1922 (incorporated in Elmhirst's *Poet and Plowman*): '"My father was," Rathi told Elmhirst, "warned by the British

The Poet with his literary disciples in 1912; (standing from left) Charuchandra Bandyopadhyay, Dwijendra Narayan Bagchi, Manilal Gangopadhyay and Prabhat Kumar Mukhopadhyay; (seated from left) Karunadhan Bandyopadhyay, Yatindramohan Bagchi and Satyendranath Datta.

Government not to compose any more songs that might fire patriotic fervour"'. Sumit Sarkar has also quoted in his *The Swadeshi Movement in Bengal*, 1903–08, the following official report: 'Babu Rabindranath Tagore, as friend of Aurobindo Ghosh, was the aristocratic champion of the party (Yugantar). He is an immaculate turncoat and has managed to save his skin by openly recanting his former revolutionary ideas and principles.' This is, however, nonsense. Rabindranath did not have to recant, for he never harboured any revolutionary ideas and principles—revolution, of course, here means sedition—nor encouraged others to practise them. All he did was to explain the reasons that were driving the Bengali youths to violent methods of resistance to the soul-less British administration.

The retreat from active political life yielded a rich bunch of poetry and plays, which were markedly different from Rabindranath's earlier writings. The difference was not certainly abrupt. The transition from *Naivedya* (1901) to *Kheya* (1906) to *Gitanjali* (1910) is a reflection of the Poet's spiritual progression—not a linear change but a manifestation of the motifs of surrender, acceptance and separation from the Power that moulded his poetic life. The tranquility of surrender, the joy of acceptance and the sorrow of separation are inextricably intertwined with the joy of finding the source of that Power—call it God, guiding spirit, transcendence of self, immanence of God in Man, of Brahma in Nature, or whatever. This was evident in the plays of this period, namely, *Prayaschitta, Raja, Achalayatan* and *Dakghar,* as well as *Saradotsav* which were different in character from the earlier feeble imitations of the Shakespearean model. The new plays were rooted in India's indigenous dramatic form, which baffled not only Western critics and audience but English-educated Bengali readers too.

The boat and boatman are recurring images in Rabindranath's poetry and songs. *Kheya* or the boat was not new in his poetry but the first and last poems of the book of poem, *Kheya,* were the first of the fifty-five poems written over one year and set the tune of these poems. Needless to say, all writings have an external stimulus, though the import of the writings may transcend the externalities. The first and last poems we are told by a teacher of Santiniketan, Nagendranath Aich, were written in a house called *Gairik*. At the south of the Ashram there was a canal wider then and there were tugged at the bank two boats, called *Chitra* and *Sonar Tari,* which were used by schoolboys and schoolteachers learning how to ply a boat. These boats provided the Poet with the images of *Kheya.*

The transition, over a decade, from *Naivedya* to *Kheya* to *Gitanjali* has been described by Prabhat Kumar Mukhopadhyay succinctly in his biography of Rabindranath and introduction to his complete works. He was a teacher and librarian of Santiniketan and had seen Rabindranath from close quarters from 1909 onwards with a break of two years. An employee of Santiniketan, his biography was surprisingly not a hagiography.

In fact, the first two volumes of his four-part biography came out in Rabindranath's lifetime and Rabindranath was not entirely pleased with some of the critical comments. The observant Prabhat Kumar, however, continuously revised his biography, enlarging it as he came across new materials through letters, memoirs, newspaper reports, in addition to the Tagore archives assiduously built up by Rathindranath at Santiniketan. According to him, Rabindranath became the secretary of the Adi Brahmo Samaj at the bidding of his father but he never took the job seriously. His early *Brahmasangit*—devotional songs—were more or less directed by his father's enunciation of the Brahmo religion. The Adi Brahmo Samaj slowly died as Rabindranath increasingly lost interest in institutional religion. The deity in *Naivedya*, Prabhat Kumar wrote, accepted the homage from the devotee from a distance; the poet of *Kheya* got flitting and indistinct expressions, somewhat mysterious, of the deity; the deity and devotee in *Gitanjali* (1910) were close to each other; the intimacy would gradually grow in *Gitimalya* (1914) and *Gitali* (1914).

The Poet in Calcutta, 1910.

A scene from Dakghar, *played at Santiniketan and Calcutta many times during 1917 in which the Poet played the roles of Gaffer, Watchman and Thakurda.*

Plays of a different kind

The transition from his earlier plays to the plays of this period was also not abrupt. *Prayaschitta* was written on the rambling story of *Bauthakuranir Hat*, condensed necessarily for the five-act drama (to be again shortened into a four-act *Paritran*, 1929) but the character of Pratapaditya, the tyrannical king of the novel, insensitive to the miseries and desires of the subjects, was softened and made a bit more humane in the drama. The principal difference between the novel and the drama is the introduction of the character of Dhananjay, the proponent of non-violent non-cooperation of the subjects to wear out the stubborn king. Dhananjay foreshadows M.K. Gandhi's non-violence, but not Gandhi's type of non-cooperation and is the prototype of the grandfatherly figure, Thakurdada, in many of Rabindranath's subsequent plays. Rabindranath often used to play the part of Thakurdada when these plays were staged at Santiniketan. *Saradotsav, Raja, Achalayatan* and *Dakghar* have been loosely called symbolic dramas and were never staged outside Santiniketan during the playwright's lifetime. The only exception was *Dakghar*, which was successfully staged in Calcutta and abroad.

The problem of symbols is that they mean different things to different people. For example, *Dakghar* (*The Post Office*) meant to Gandhi something beyond the playwright's imagination. *Dakghar* was staged at the Bichitra

Hall of Jorasanko on 31 December 1917 to entertain delegates to the INC session in Calcutta. Among the audience were Annie Besant, the president of INC that year, Bal Gangadhar Tilak, Sir George Woodroffe (the chief justice of Calcutta High Court), Srinivas Sastri, Gandhi, Bipin Chandra Pal, Sarojini Naidu and G.S. Arundale (a participant in the Home Rule movement). Arunprakas Bandyopadhyay, nephew of Brahmabandhav Upadhyay and a student of Santiniketan, was asked by his Gurudev to interpret the story to Gandhi during the performance. *The Post Office* (translated by Devabrata Mukhopadhyay and drastically revised by the playwright, 1913) had been successfully staged in Dublin (17 May 1913), London (10 July 1913), Berlin (June 1921 in German version) and New York (10 December 1921). At Jorasanko it was performed in the original language. Arunprakas has written about the impact of the performance. Tears welled up in Besant's eyes; Sarojini Naidu often drew up her veil to hide emotions; Arundale took up Asamukul Das (the Santiniketan student who excelled in the role of Amal, the protagonist in the play) on his shoulders and danced in joy. Malavya correctly explained the theme and significance of the play but what confounded Arunprakas was the explanation given by Gandhi. Amal represented India, his illness was India's misery caused by the British, represented by Amal's guardians and neighbourhood chiefs; the joyous curdseller represented the free dominions like Australia and Canada in the Commonwealth; and the letter Amal expected from the king would come from the British Parliament!

Rabindranath was pleased by the German production in Berlin, although this interpretation was somewhat different from his conception. *The Post Office*, translated by Andre Gide in 1924, was enacted on the French radio in June 1940, the evening before Paris fell. Rabindranath was extremely moved by the news reported to him when he was at Mungpoo, a cinchona-producing station, near Darjeeling. He was, however, spared the sad news of a Polish director, Janusz Korczak, producing the play in a Warsaw ghetto in 1942—all the people in the ghetto were later killed in a German concentration camp.

Fascinating was the response of the great German philosopher, Ludwig Wittgenstein (1889–1951) to the German translation of *The King of the Dark Chamber* (Raja, translated by Kshitis Chandra Sen) in 1921. Ray Monk, the biographer of Wittgenstein, devoted considerable space to the subject. Wittgenstein wrote to a friend that the play failed to make an impression:

> It seems to me as if all that wisdom has come out of the icebox; I should not be surprised to learn that he got it all second-hand by reading and listening (exactly as so many of us acquire our knowledge of Christian wisdom) rather than from his own genuine feeling. Perhaps I don't understand his tone; to me it does not ring like the tone of a man possessed by the truth.

Another scene from Dakghar.

A few months later Wittgenstein wrote to another friend that he was reading the play and this time with much more pleasure believing that there was indeed something grand in the play. The play became one of his favourite books, so much so that he gave or lent it to a number of friends. Some seventeen years later, in England, he returned to the play in Tagore's English translation. He wrongly believed that Tagore was the translator though that was no fault of his own. In 1914, Macmillan passed it off as Tagore's translation, knowingly or unknowingly, and in a later advertisement acknowledged the translator's name. Again Wittgenstein thought he was unable to enjoy the play because of the translation and he and a friend made their own translation of the passages they liked most.

Ray Monk explains why Wittgenstein was so haunted by the play. Its allegory of religious awakening echoed many of Wittgenstein's own thoughts. The King who lived unseen by his subjects was a perfect metaphor for Wittgenstein's attitude to unsayable religious truths. Surangama, the maid, had a faith in him, though she did not wish to see the King. Wittgenstein aspired to be a Surangama, although like Sudarshana, the Queen, he wanted to see the truth, not in the darkness, but in broad daylight.

By 1908, Brahmacharyasram or the residential school at Santiniketan had around hundred students and fifteen teachers causing the founder delighted as well as concerned at the same time. He was delighted for the expansion but concerned not only for the infrastructural poverty but also for the quality of teachers, some of whom coming with orthodox methods of teaching and ideas of education ill fitted with what Rabindranath aspired for. The school attracted police attention too because of the revolutionary turmoil in Bengal at the time. Many teachers at Santiniketan had a revolutionary background. To compound

Above: With Pratima Devi, 1926. Below: The Poet in 1910 with the newly married Rathindranath and Pratima, along with Mira (left) and Madhurilata (right). Photographed by Sukumar Ray.

the problem, a teacher in east Bengal, Hiralal Sen, dedicated a book of poems, *Hunkar* (Loud Threat), to Rabindranath without informing or taking his permission for the dedication. The teacher was arrested and produced in court and Rabindranath was summoned to Khulna, a town in east Bengal, as a witness. He had written a letter to Hiralal, knowing of the dedication and advising him social work and not to indulge in inflammatory poems.

At the mango grove, Santiniketan, 1910—the Poet's birthday celebrations, for the first time, by the inmates of the Ashram.

However, Rabindranath refused to pass any judgement on the book saying he did not know what constituted sedition. Hiralal was sentenced to imprisonment. When Hiralal was released from prison, he was invited to join Santiniketan as a teacher. But he was being shadowed by informers and had to be taken off from the school and was sent to Silaidaha to assist the supervision of the estates.

In 1910, Rabindranath married his son to a widow. This was unthinkable when Devendranath was alive (he died in 1905). Adi Brahmo Samaj did not approve of widow marriage and Devendranath was against social reforms through legislation. He intervened when a widow of his family was about to be remarried by her mother. The widow was the wife of Balendranath, a poet and essayist who assisted his uncle Rabindranath when he edited *Sadhana* and co-founded Tagore & Co. at Kushthia.

It was Balendranath who first conceived of the Brahmacharyasram at Santiniketan before Rabindranath took up the idea. After his untimely death, the widow was sent to Allahabad to her mother's place and was about to be remarried when Devendranath sent Rabindranath to stop the marriage. Rabindranath succeeded to bring her back. This was just one instance of the awesome hold of the grand patriarch over the family even when he was an old man of eighty-three.

In 1910–11, Rabindranath, amidst all his busy schedule, creative works and estates supervision, had a lonely family life. His wife and two children had died, daughters married and son had married recently; he had none at the age of fifty to look after him. There was a curious report in *The Bengalee* that he intended to remarry. He sternly asked a sub-editor of the paper to contradict the unfounded news. It is believed that Devendranath wanted him to remarry after his wife's death. If the father really wanted, it is unlikely that the son would not have complied. Rabindranath discounted all family tales regarding his remarriage proposals—Sucharu (1874–?), a daughter of Keshab Chandra Sen, and Priyambada (1871–1935), a widow and a poet of some merit, were some of the names of his allegedly prospective bride. In 1927, when *Lekhan* (Jottings) was published, Priyambada's five short poems were by mistake included in that book of short verses—an unintended compliment to a junior poet by the senior poet.

Rathindranath (1888–1961) had come back from the USA, after obtaining a bachelor's degree in agriculture and was sent to the estates to implement modern methods of agriculture. In his memoirs, *On the Edges of Time*, he writes (the name of the book derived from a poem of *The Gardener*):

> Hardly had I got home than father took me out on a tour round the estates to make me acquainted with the people and teach me the details of management. It was a novel experience for me to travel with father—just the two of us—in a house-boat. Successive bereavements and particularly the loss of Sami had left him very lonely and he naturally tried to pour all his affection on me as soon as I returned home. As we drifted along through the network of rivers so familiar to both of us, every evening we sat out on the deck and talked on all sorts of subjects. I had never talked so freely with father before this and I had to make considerable effort to break the ice. I think father must have been hugely amused to hear me

Rabindranath, with many friends and admirers, had a lonely family life.

prattle and glibly repeat copybook maxims on agronomy, genetics, evolution and such subjects as were still fresh in my mind. Most of the time he would listen patiently but when he did talk he told me about the social and economic conditions of our rural folk, the problems of their life and his own experience in dealing with them. Rarely would he talk about literature, probably thinking that my training in the sciences barred me from appreciating the arts. Father and son never came to a more intimate understanding of each other than in this winter of 1910.

Nobel Prize medal.

Translating his own poems, and the Nobel Prize

Rabindranath is one of the few great writers in the world, if not the lone one, who extensively translated his own poems, plays, songs and essays in English. But he was reluctant to do this, not only at the time he began this exercise but also throughout, to the end of his life. Two English artists and art connoisseurs can be traced as the principal motivators: A.K. Coomaraswami (1877–1947) and William Rothenstein. Coomaraswami was a Tamil Christian of Ceylon, brought up in England. He was in Santiniketan in February 1911 and asked Rothenstein, who was visiting India, to come down to Bolpur so that the latter could know the Poet better. Rothenstein regretted his inability for lack of time. Coomaraswami wanted to translate Tagore, who paraphrased for him some of his poems. Coomaraswami, in his *Art and Swadesi* (1912), devoted a chapter to Tagore's poems, quoting eleven poems, some done in collaboration with Ajit Kumar Chakrabarti (1886–1918), a teacher in Santiniketan, some with Tagore. Two of them were earlier published in *The Modern Review*.

Rothenstein was the driving force behind the foundation of the India Society in London on 15 June 1910 to promote Indian culture. He came to India to acquaint himself with the paintings and sculptures of India and could not but visit Jorasanko to see the collections of

The Poet at Hampstead, London, 1912. From left: Somendra Chandra Dev Burman, Dr D.N. Maitra, John Rothenstein, William Rothenstein and Rathindranath.

Abanindranath Tagore and his elder brother Gaganendranath Tagore (1867–1938), the two eminent artists of Bengal. He just chanced to meet their uncle Rabindranath but was not able to develop a rapport with him immediately. He knew that Tagore was a poet and he had read his short stories in *The Modern Review*. After his return to England, he requested Tagore to send his poems and stories as and when they appeared in the journals. He also pleaded a Bengali preacher, Pramathalal Sen and the famous Indian philosopher, Brajendrakumar Seal, who were in London at that time, to urge Tagore to send translations.

Tagore had earlier seen his poems translated by Roby Datta, a Calcutta University professor, who brought out his *Echoes from East and West* from Cambridge in 1909 and included eleven poems and songs by Tagore. The rhymed and literal translations did not impress Tagore, who would translate his poems in prose eschewing literal translations. Goaded by his friends abroad, he asked Ajit to translate his poems, which were sent to Rothenstein.

In a letter to Ramendrasundar Tribedi on 17 November 1913, Rabindranath wrote that he began translation of his poems for *Gitanjali: Song Offerings* with the poem: 'No more noisy, loud words from me', which featured as the eighty-ninth poem of that book of verse. Incidentally, this was the second poem in the autographed manuscript that Tagore had presented to Rothenstein on his arrival in London in 1912—the manuscript is now in the custody of Houghton Library, Harvard, as the library's collection of Rothenstein papers.

Which 'loud words' did the Poet have in his mind? Were they the biting remarks made by the Poet's literary enemies on the occasion of his fiftieth birth anniversary celebrated by the Poet's admirers in the Town Hall of Calcutta? Or the bitter attacks by the orthodox Hindus on the Poet's play *Achalayatan* (The Unmovable Institution) and the Poet's defence? Or the various lectures he delivered in January–March 1911? His lectures on religion or Indian history, however serious, drew crowds who seemed to have been more attracted by the Poet's presence than the themes of his lectures—the unruly crowd trying to enter halls by jumping windows and breaking doors. For about one year, the Poet had been feeling restless—writing letters to friends and acquaintances that he was feeling suffocated in his own surroundings, he needed to break free and derive a new lease of life by moving abroad. His acquaintance with Coomaraswami, Rothenstein and Count H. Keyserling, who visited Calcutta in 1912, might have urged him to meet liberal writers and thinkers of the West. He planned to take a long break and bought tickets to London—the embarkment date was 19 March 1912; but the journey had to be held back as he fell ill and could not reach the dock. He retired to Silaidaha and would sail on 24 May 1912 from Bombay.

The intervening two months Rabindranath spent in translating his poems. Almost one year later, on 6 May 1913, after the surprisingly rapturous response from the English poets and critics on his translated poems, he wrote to his niece Indira, that to pass time he resorted to translating his old poems—just to revive the emotions he felt when he had written those poems. This is not entirely true. The first three poems as well as the other thirteen poems in the manuscript which was used for most of the poems printed in *Song Offerings* were written in Bengali and almost immediately translated; the Bengali ones were included in *Gitimalya* in 1914. He had obviously the English public in view when he translated his just-written poems.

The India Society had planned a public dinner in honour of Tagore in London even before he reached London. That dinner would take place eventually on 10 July 1912. The Society dinner was earlier contemplated before Tagore read out his English poems in London. The city was aware of Tagore, the poet and short-story writer, before the famous 7 July 1912 gathering at Rothenstein's place.

Tagore with his son and daughter-in-law arrived in London on 16 June and handed over his manuscript of poems to Rothenstein the next day. On 19 June, W.W. Pearson (1881–1923), who had been in Calcutta since 1907 as a botany professor in the London Missionary College, invited a few English writers and distinguished Bengali people for a reception for Tagore. That was the first meeting of Tagore and Pearson, who embarrassed Tagore by welcoming him in Bengali style—bending and touching his feet.

In that reception Sukumar Ray (1887–1923), who was later the most famous Bengali writer of children's poems and stories in comic style, read out an essay on Bengali literature that included his own translations of Tagore's poems. Among the guests was Cranmore Byng, the editor of 'Wisdom of the East' series, who told Ray to translate more of Tagore's poems which he wished to publish. But Rothenstein, who was also there, had other ideas. He had already read Tagore's own translations and thought 'here was poetry of a new order which seemed to me on a level with that of the great mystics'. He had got the manuscript typed and sent out copies to Stopford Brooke (1832–1916), A.C. Bradley (1851–1935) and W.B. Yeats. The critics enthusiastically reacted and Yeats was ecstatic. Meanwhile, Rothenstein arranged a poetry session at his house on 7 July where a very diffident and nervous Tagore heard Yeats reading out a number of his translated poems. He was diffident because he was long out of touch with the English as it was spoken in England those days. The guests made no comment and took their leave. Among the guests were Yeats, Ernest Rhys, Thomas Sturge Moore (1870–1944), Robert Trevelyan (1872–1951), May Sinclair (1865–1946), Henry Nevinson (1856–1941), C.F. Andrews (1871–1940) and Evelyn Underhill (1875–1941). Tagore felt miserable at the lack of response whatsoever till the next day when he was flooded with compliments—they were silent the previous night because they were so overwhelmed that they had lost words to express their feelings.

In the India Society dinner, which was presided over by Yeats, the few more important people present among the seventy other guests were—

At the time of writing
Gitanjali, *1910.*

E.B. Havell (1861–1934), J.D. Anderson (1852–1920) and H.G. Wells (1864–1946). Of course, the India Society promoters—T.W. Rhys Davids (1843–1922), the chairman; T.W. Rolleston (1857–1920), the treasurer; and Arthur H. Fox Strangways (1859–1948), the secretary were present.

What followed the publication of *Gitanjali: Song Offerings* (November 1912) and a year later, *The Gardener* (October 1912) can be briefly described as a Tagore cult in London. Stopford Brooke, the religious poet, who had written to Rothenstein after reading the Tagore manuscript: 'I wish I were worthy of them', did not at all approve of Tagore's participation in hectic activities in London like play-readings and poetry recitals—the image of a saintly poet did not go well with those mundane events. D.H. Lawrence (1885–1930) reacted in May 1916 violently: 'this fraud of looking up to them (European civilisation vis-à-vis Eastern civilisation)—this wretched worship of Tagore attitude is disgusting.' E.M. Forster (1879–1970) was more elaborate while he reviewed *Chitra* in 1914 about this hysteria over Tagore:

> To hearken is better than the fat of rams, but seldom as popular. It requires a silent atmosphere, and, when the voice is Apollo's, an ear attentive to beauty. Rare in all places, it is almost unknown in cultured London, where there is noise without and deafness within.

Forster further clarified:

> The Londoner, and still more Londoness, prefers adoration to attention. It proves less fatiguing in the long run and induces a pleasing glow. It implies enthusiasm and enthusiasm is surely what we all need. It implies elevation and breadth.

He concluded:

> Consequently London is the city of Booms, of transient fanaticisms that raise the spirit of fever heat and pass leaving it a little weaker. There is no connection between boom and the next. The rams are driven hurriedly from altar to altar, and their blood has scarcely cooled to Emil Reich before it is poured in unexampled profusion to Mr Tagore.

Hence, he analysed:

> The reviewer, while affecting to be above such hysteria, is really involved in it, and it is difficult to listen through the noise and nonsense of the last two years and catch the authentic voice of Tagore beyond. He is a good writer. But how good?

However, Forster did not answer this question conclusively:

> To that there can be no answer until the adoration and the reaction all adoration entails have passed away, until the mess of the sacrifices has been cleared up, and Beauty can pronounce across the subsiding dust.

Forster's review of *Chitra,* it may be noted, in passing, was favourable and of *The Home and the World,* 1919, a bit condescending.

In October 1912, Tagore sailed to the USA. He received an ecstatic letter from Rothenstein who wrote on 7 November 1912 that the first review of *Gitanjali* had been published in the *Times Literary Supplement*. A book reviewed within a week of publication in a newspaper of the *TLS* standing was indeed a surprise. Whether it was a handiwork of Fox Strangways who was the music critic of the paper or because the proof-copy had been sent to the reviewer, or the reviewer might have been already familiar with the poems (presumably Stopford Brooke or A.C. Bradley) can be only speculated upon because the *TLS* reviewer is never named. But the *TLS* review set the tone of the subsequent reviews; it described *Gitanjali* as the 'Psalms of a David of our own time'.

In Chicago, 1913.

The Society printed only 750 copies of *Gitanjali*, 500 for distribution among the members and the rest for sale. The rave reviews by the *TLS* and in *Nation* by Evelyn Underhill (16 November 1912) and Rothenstein's efforts induced Macmillan to reprint it four months later. The 1913 Nobel Prize catapulted its sales and *The Manchester Despatch* reported on

19 February 1917: '*Gitanjali* has reached its thirty-seventh thousand.' By 3 February 1914, its sale had been 19,320 copies, of *The Crescent Moon*—4,200, *The Gardener*—6,080 and *Sadhana*—3,500.

By November 1912, Rothenstein sent manuscripts of poems, plays, essays, short stories to Macmillan. As advised by its dependable editor, Charles Whibley (1859–1930), it brought out a lower-priced *Gitanjali* and noting its commercial success published *The Gardener* and *The Crescent Moon*, all in 1913. Whibley was not impressed by the translated stories and plays and asked Macmillan to defer their publication. John Masefield (1878–1967) made his famous observation on the translated plays—*Chitra, Malini* and *The Post Office*: 'the plant won't transplant'. The first two were translated by Tagore himself during his stay in England. Robert Trevelyan was impressed by the classic mould of *Malini* but Macmillan did not venture to publish it then. Tagore had read out *Chitra* and *The King of the Dark Chamber* in 1913 at London and Macmillan published these as well as *The Post Office* in 1914. After the Nobel Prize in 1913, Macmillan did not stint in printing Tagore, who proved to be a gold mine to them, indiscriminately to the detriment of Tagore's interests.

The Nobel Prize in Literature in 1913 was an intriguing affair, from first to last. Sturge Moore had proposed Tagore in a strange manner:

> As a fellow of the Royal Society of Literature of the UK, I have the honour to propose the name of Rabindranath Tagore as a person qualified in my opinion to be awarded the Nobel Prize in Literature.

The proposal was strangely undated. It had to be made before 1 February 1913 according to the Swedish Academy schedule—the Academy was entrusted by the Nobel trustees for the Nobel award for Literature. By 1 February 1913, Tagore had only one publication in English—the India Society edition of *Gitanjali*, which carried a note that these were translated prose from Bengali poems. Translations are not admissible for the Nobel award—the proposal ought to have been dismissed outright. Was it due to this that Moore framed his proposal in that fashion? He did not care to mention who Rabindranath Tagore was, which part of the world he came from, in what language he wrote and why he considered Tagore worthy. A slight elaboration would have betrayed that he was proposing translations for the Prize. The telegraphic language seemed to carry an impression that Moore's certificate was enough, although he was a poet little known beyond England. From his letters subsequently written, it was clear he knew little about the Nobel Prize history. He thought Thomas Hardy had already won the Prize, unaware that the Royal Society to which he belonged had proposed Thomas Hardy that year.

It appears that the Swedish Academy needed a proposal just as a matter of technicality and it did pick up the proposal in right earnest. To a point, the Academy proceeded correctly. It entrusted a member of the Nobel Committee, Per Hallstrom (1866–1960) as a specialist to evaluate Tagore. Hallstrom had only *Gitanjali* at his disposal. In order to assess it he needed to know what the English critics thought of *Gitanjali*. He asked the Nobel Library at Stockholm for some English reviews of *Gitanjali*. The Library asked Times Book Club, which asked Macmillan, which asked Fox Strangways and who asked Tagore himself for the critical appreciations and eventually Hallstrom got hold of the reviews which appeared in the *TLS* (7 November 1912), *Fortnightly Review* (March 1913) and *The Nineteenth Century* (April 1913). He was glad that his assessment was corroborated by the English critics. The four (or five)-member Nobel Committee of the eighteen-member Swedish Academy took note of Hallstrom's assessment and decided to wait and know more of Tagore, how Tagore was viewed in his own land and recommended Emil Faguet, a French literary historian, for the award. Hallstrom also suggested, while appreciating *Gitanjali*, that there should be an assessment of the value of the originals. Customarily, the Nobel Committee forwards its recommendation by June of the concerned year which is circulated among the eighteen members of the Academy for their verdict. Surprisingly, Carl Heidenstam (1859–1940), a member of the Academy but not of the Nobel Committee, lobbied hard for Tagore. He strongly protested against the Nobel Literature Prize becoming totally Euro-centric and insisted that the Academy should break through this self-imposed barrier. He also reminded the members that Nobel intended to find and encourage new writers. Tagore admirably filled the bill and he had Hallstrom to add to his note with an appreciation of *The Gardener* which was published as late as the end of October 1913—the award was to be announced

The Poet in London, at the time of Sadhana *lectures.*

in November 1913. The Academy had the right to reject its Committee's recommendation. It did, by a 12–01 vote, by declaring Tagore the winner. But how did it get across the barrier of 'translation'? By a clever phrasing—it was not awarding Tagore for his Bengali writing but treating his English as original writings. The citation for the award was:

> Rabindranath Tagore because of his profoundly sensitive, fresh and beautiful verse, by which, with consummate skill he has made his poetic thought, expressed in his own English words, a part of the literature of the West.

The chairman of the Nobel Committee, Harold Hjarne, in his presentation address on 10 December 1913 mentioned *Gitanjali: Song Offerings, The Gardener, The Crescent Moon* (all books of poems) and *Sadhana* (a collection of eight lectures given by Tagore in the USA and UK in 1912–13, the basic theme of which was the relation of faith to thought).

Tagore was a chronic sufferer from piles. He availed himself of this long sojourn abroad and underwent operation, when he came back to England from the USA. He was all his life scared of surgery and had tried homeopathy in the States but the bleeding persisted. Fortunately his nephew, Surendranath was present in London when Rabindranath came back to London and he persuaded his uncle to go for an operation. The operation was successful but Tagore was confined to Duchess Nursing Home the whole of July of 1913 and he had to suffer all the post-operation miseries. He expressed his agony in a letter to Rothenstein: 'It is dreadful to have to watch helplessly the indignity that is being daily offered to my poor body in the name of science of healing, as if the body were no more than a mere piece of flesh and bones.' Tagore was very sensitive about his body and his friends and acquaintances seldom saw his bare body, except in times of illness.

This tour abroad helped Tagore overcome his inhibitions in writing English, which he considered a foreigner's language. But minor irritations were bound to occur. His fame as a writer in English caused surprise among his friends, not to talk of his enemies. D.L. Ray, who had criticised his poems as inscrutable, if not meaningless, and called his love poems like *Chitrangada* indecent, enlarged his old play, *Anandabiday* to incorporate his suspicion that Andrews wrote for Rabindranath's English pieces. Ray must have been provoked to read Andrews, contributing a euphorious article to *The Modern Review* of August 1912: *An Evening with Rabindranath*. Ray's comic opera staged at the Star Theatre in Calcutta on 16 November 1912 was, of course, violently stopped by Tagore's admirers and Ray had to run for his life. Tagore who was abroad could only feel pity for such kind of petty jealousy. But Valentine Chirol was a different proposition.

Chirol, the British journalist, with the infamous *Indian Unrest* to his credit ascribed *Gitanjali* to Yeats. Tagore could laugh off the suggestion that Andrews wrote for him, but Yeats could not be brushed off so casually, because the allegation had a modicum of truth. Yeats edited *Gitanjali* and *The Gardener*, Moore edited *The Crescent Moon*, Rhys edited *Sadhana: the Realisation of Life*. There was nothing unusual about it; every publisher worth the name has an editor or appoints an editor to judge, select and edit a manuscript it intends to publish. The question is: what was the extent of revisions? Yeats was ambiguous, Rothenstein was non-committal and Tagore was indignant at the suggestion that Yeats extensively revised his poems.

The original draft (Rothenstein manuscript) is there, the printed book is there, and it is easy to find the revisions. But matters got complicated when Tagore stated that he was with Yeats during revisions, suggesting that those were a collaborative exercise. The drafts with Yeats' penciled corrections were lost and there can be no vindication of either Yeats' or Tagore's stand. Of course, it was a private war conducted in correspondences but it was no less bitter. When Chirol described *Gitanjali* as the handiwork of Yeats, it was no more private. In a long letter to Moore on 17 February 1914, Tagore wrote:

> An incident will show you how the award of the Nobel Prize has roused up an antipathy and suspicion against me in certain quarters. A report has reached me from a barrister friend of mine who was present on the occasion when in a meeting of the leading Mohammedan gentlemen of Bengal Valentine Chirol told the audience that the English *Gitanjali* was practically a production of Yeats. It is very likely he did not believe it himself it being

> merely a political move on his part to minimise the significance of this Nobel Prize affair which our people naturally consider to be a matter of national rejoicing. It is not possible for him to relish the idea of Mohammedans sharing this honour with Hindus. Unfortunately for me there are signs of the feelings of antagonism in England itself which may be partly due to the natural reaction following the chorus of praise that *Gitanjali* evoked and partly, as you have said in your letter, to the bitterness of disappointment in the minds of the partisans of the candidates for the Nobel Prize.

The last sentence was a reaction to Moore's letter of 22 January 1914:

> I am often angered when references to you catch my eye in the papers now for there is an itch about them to treat you as unjustly as before they were fulsome in their praise. Your having won the Nobel Prize when Hardy had been the official candidate of the Royal Society of Literature (that is the only candidate for whom the voters were canvassed) has made you a certain number of enemies whose ill will is not solely due to the fickleness of their minds.

Moore had earlier congratulated Tagore, on the announcement of the Prize, informing Tagore that only Kipling and Hardy had won the Prize. Tagore had also written to Rothenstein about Chirol but Rothenstein said that his English friends could refute only if Chirol was on record.

Things came to a head when Robert Bridges (1844–1930), the poet laureate, wanted to revise a poem from *Gitanjali* for inclusion in his intended anthology, *The Spirit of Man* (which was published in 1916). Tagore put his foot down, refusing to be revised again. It needed tact from Yeats to persuade Tagore for this revision with the plea that Bridges was the greatest stylist of his era and it would be graceful if Tagore concurred with the old poet.

Tagore had met Bridges when he came to one of his *Sadhana* lectures at Oxford. He also went up to the poet laureate's residence to pay his homage. Ultimately, he agreed to Bridges' revision of poem no. 67 of *Gitanjali*: 'Thou art the sky and thou art the nest as well.'

Tagore was chary about more revisions by his English friends because the Swedish Academy had awarded his 'English words'. When Chirol talked about Tagore's English, an angry Tagore wrote to Rothenstein (as also to Moore): 'It is annoyingly insulting for me to be constantly suspected of being capable of enjoying a reputation by fraud.'

During the five-month-long imbroglio around *The Spirit of Man*, which involved Yeats, Rothenstein and Macmillan, Tagore had written to Rothenstein on 4 April 1915:

> And if it be true that Yeats' touches have made it possible for *Gitanjali* to occupy the place it does, then that must be confessed. At least by my subsequent unadulterated writings my true level should be found out and the faintest speck of lie should be wiped out from the fame I enjoy now. It does not matter what the people think of me but it does matter all the world to me to be true to myself.

When Tagore sent the manuscripts of *Fruit-Gathering* and *Lover's Gift* to Rothenstein in 1915, he made it clear that he did not want any revision and Macmillan should publish these as they were. But these two were also revised by Yeats, ignoring Tagore's direction. *Fruit-Gathering* was published in 1916 and *Lover's Gift* and *Crossing* in 1918.

When Rabindranath was abroad, Pearson and Andrews paid a visit to Santiniketan. Both of them were living in Delhi, Andrews, a professor at St. Stephens College and Pearson, a house tutor. Pearson had earlier gone back to England as he did not feel like continuing teaching at the Calcutta Missionary College. He was so impressed with the ambience of Santiniketan that he wished to join the school as a teacher and his prayer was gratefully accepted by Rabindranath abroad. Andrews was invited at the Viceregal Lodge at Simla on 26 May 1913 by Viceroy Lord Hardinge to talk about Tagore, who was hardly known in India although he had taken London by storm. In the chair, the Viceroy described Tagore as the poet laureate of Asia. The Viceroy was well aware that on 9 May 1913, E. Montagu, then a member of the British Parliament, had attended a gathering in London when Tagore read out his *Chitra*. What Montagu said in his vote of thanks was quoted in *The Times* the following day. Montagu's speech has been often

The Poet in Calcutta, 1914.

misquoted by his biographers. What he actually said was reported in the newspaper:

> He said that on his Indian tour he heard a story of a traveller, who, entering a little village near Darjeeling, saw a group of men sitting round the evening fire reciting the ancient poems of their land. When they had finished a little boy of twelve—one of those lonely young travellers who wandered all over the country— unable to read and write, recited what proved to be the most moving item of the evening—a poem he had learned from hearing it read. The author of the poem, thus ranked with the classical writings of ancient days, was Mr Tagore. If he wished to know the feelings of the people towards a teacher of beauty, love, religion and patriotism like Mr Tagore he would desire no better testimony than that of the village group; nor could he wish for any better justification for his own admiration not only of Mr Tagore's poetry, but also of his great, almost incalculable, service to the Indian people.

Both Ernest Rhys and, following him, Krishna Kripalani thought it was Montagu himself who heard the boy reciting Tagore.

All encomiums notwithstanding, the Santiniketan school was in dire straits for lack of funds. The teachers had to be housed, students had to be fed—not to talk of salaries (even measly as they were) to be paid to teachers and workers. Even the grocers of Bolpur refused to supply provisions on credit. The royalties Tagore received and gate receipts from his lectures and recitals had been sent to the school by Tagore but these could only lessen the debts. The Nobel award was a windfall for the teachers in many senses of the term, not the least of which was financial.

But the school and later the university constantly suffered from funds crunch. An experience, though of a later day, of the teachers will be indicative. The teachers lived in brick houses with thatched roofs. In the rainy season, a few teachers could not sleep at night as rain-water poured through leaks. Exasperated, they resolved to seek repairs and went up to their Gurudev, who in that early morning looked totally dishevelled and miserable. He could not find a dry spot in his room—he also spent the night sleepless. The teachers came back ashamed that they were complaining.

In 1912–13 financial year, there were in Santiniketan 189 students, 25 teachers and clerical staff and 47 menials. The tuition fees realised were only Rs 3,100. Expenses were incurred in building classrooms, hostels, teachers' quarters, guest houses. And foreign guests were on steady increase after Tagore was a Nobel winner. Not for nothing Andrews said, 'Rathi writes poetry in brick and mortar.' Rathi was the pivot—it was Surendranath Kar (1892–1970), an artist-architect of Santiniketan who designed the low-cost buildings, which won wide acclaim for what came to be known as the Santiniketan style of architecture.

Rabindranath had to find money for his school. Prior to his departure for England in 1912, he had sent in a collection of prose pieces, *Pathsanchay*, at the insistence of Ramananda Chattopadhyay (1865–1943), the editor of *Prabasi*, to Calcutta University, for its recommendation as a textbook for students of matriculation examinations. Rabindranath himself handed over a copy to Vice-Chancellor Asutosh Mookerji (1864–1924). But the University's textbook committee did not approve it. It is strange that Asutosh did not wield his power on the committee though he himself was an admirer of Rabindranath and in the following year, before the announcement of the Nobel award, he proposed to confer a D. Litt. degree on Tagore—the proposal was readily accepted by Lord Hardinge despite adverse reports by the Criminal Intelligence Department. The degree was eventually given on 26 December 1913, at a special convocation at the Governor's House in Calcutta, by Chancellor Lord Hardinge.

Reuters broadcast the news of the Nobel Prize in Literature and an evening daily of Calcutta, *Empire*, picked it up on 14 November 1913. The news predictably produced national joy in India and exultation among Bengalis. The *Indian Daily News* of Calcutta made an interesting point:

> There is one striking fact about the award of the Nobel Prize for literature to Mr Rabindranath Tagore. He is a unique example of an Indian who had nothing to do with a University, and he is not a product of Lord Macaulay and British Government education. This

> has been already dwelt on, but if he had been to the University, the odds are that he would have been steam-rollered by the curriculum of that institution into the semblance of a pedagogue.

Again, the same paper, on 19 November 1913, announced:

> But as Babu Rabindranath Tagore is now staying at Bolpur it has been settled to go there on deputation in a special train which will leave Howrah on Sunday morning (the 23rd instant) and come back to Calcutta the same evening. Anyone who loves Bengali literature can join this party on purchasing a ticket for Rs 3.4 to meet the train fare and other necessary expenses...it is to be noted that there is only accommodation for 500 people in the special train.

The notice was signed by six dignitaries among whom were Surendranath Banerjea (1848–1925), Brajendranath Seal (1864–1938), P.C. Roy (1861–1944) and Nilratan Sarkar (1861–1943). The train did leave as scheduled and returned duly, but the passengers came back crestfallen. There was no dearth of ceremonial arrangements at Bolpur and Santiniketan. Reverend Andrews in Indian attire (*dhoti* and *chador)* led the schoolboys and teachers to welcome the deputation at the station, the students sang their school song in Bengali ('She is our own, the darling of our hearts, Santiniketan' in Rabindranath's English) all along the route, while village policemen with red turbans and blue tunics stared in amazement at the unusual spectacle of 500 well-dressed gentlemen and ladies that included authors, scientists, doctors, pleaders, judges, reporters trudging the dusty village road, as the women blew conch shells standing at the well-decorated entrance of the Ashram. Everything was in order except the Poet himself. He refused to accept the honour supposed to be paid on behalf of the nation and said it although couched in poetic words.

What prompted the refusal still remains an enigma. It was on the spur of the moment that the Poet reacted in that fashion. Was it because of the presence of some in the crowd who were his sworn enemies? The enigma has not been solved—the Poet never explained, then or ever. The refusal was bound to produce adverse comments which were ably defended by the famous politician, Bipin Chandra Pal, in the monthly journal, *Hindu Review*.

Chartering a special train, a deputation of 500 Tagore admirers assembled at Santiniketan on 23 November 1913.

Almost half of the songs and poems of *Gitimalya* were written by the Poet during his restful days in Silaidaha where he had retired, unable to sail for England. A few were written abroad and another large bunch when the initial excitement caused by the Nobel award died down. Nine were written at Ramgarh, where he spent about a month to escape the heat of the plains.

Ramgarh, a quiet mountain village at 7,000 ft near Almorah, has acquired some significance not because the Poet enjoyed joyous days in the company of his family and friends among whom were Andrews and barrister-poet and musician Atulprasad Sen (1871–1934), but because of a strange letter the Poet wrote about these Ramgarh days. The letter did not speak of bright sunny days, the Himalayan peaks splendidly in clear view, or the beautiful gardens and orchards, or the simple village people coming to him for medical treatment (the local postmaster thought Dr R.N. Tagore was a medical man). His son said that Father practised

Sarojini Naidu on the Tagore Craze

I was passing one day through a hospital in Budapest—a surgical boarding it was, I think. Great many beds were lying there. People knew that I was coming and under every pillow a hand was put and a book was brought out and everybody said Tagore, Tagore and Tagore. The book was a new translation in Hungarian of one of Tagore's plays.

One year I spent the winter in Scandinavia. You know that it is from Sweden that the Nobel Prize came to Tagore. So naturally Sweden was full of Tagore, and the Swedish lady, who translated *Gitanjali* before England had heard of Tagore, was one of my hostesses...It was only when I passed on to Norway on the Norwegian mountain slopes where there were scattered farm houses ...where in those little solitary houses cattle were tending and for nearly six months there was nothing but darkness—it was there that I found farmers in families—peasants, living by provision for aeons throughout in the winter in the collected works of Rabindranath...

I happened to be in England when *Gitanjali* was published. My great friend, the great Irish poet of this generation, William Butler Yeats, was mad when he read *Gitanjali* in translation. He absolutely went mad. He thought there was the great message of hope for which the heart-sick and the soul-sick was so long waiting. When Tagore came to England in 1913, very beautiful with beard and locks and robe, the whole of cold England became warmed up in the sun of his song. We saw spectacles, sometimes comic, but very sincere, of five old ladies sitting in a row in a bus and reading *Gitanjali*. Funny spectacles were witnessed in unexpected places.

(From *Tagore Centenary Souvenir,* Tagore Memorial Publications, 1961, New Delhi)

Revision of His English

Edward John Thompson took Tagore literally when the Poet requested him to run a pencil over his English. When Thompson made liberal use of pencil, Tagore wrote him this letter from Santiniketan on 18 November 1913:

> I hope we are friends and you will not misunderstand me. I have done a wrong to you and I must ask your pardon for it. While you were minutely going over my MSS your very kindness embarrassed me and prevented me from being frank with you—which was foolish on my part and absurdly Oriental—and for which I have been feeling ashamed ever since. The *Gitanjali* poems are intimately personal to me and the pleasure I have of polishing their English versions is of a different nature from that of an author revising his works for publication. Every line of these should be as closely my own as possible though I must labour under the disadvantage of not being born to your language. In such a case I have to be guided by my instinct, allowing it to work almost unconsciously without being hindered by more than casual suggestion from outside. I think the method that Yeats followed while editing my book was the right one in selecting those poems that required least alterations and rejecting others in spite of their merits. There is a grave risk of my overlooking crudities of language—the evidence of which you will find in *The Gardener*—but still I must go on with my work unaided till I have done what is in my power to do.

homeopathy to his heart's content at Ramgarh. But the letter talked of a sense of frustration, a guilty conscience for neglecting his family, his school, his estates, an apprehension of death, a suicidal tendency. The letter is undated, written to his son, after the Poet's return from Ramgarh. The Poet had some problems with neuralgia that caused intense pain in the ear. He himself diagnosed his melancholia in Ramgarh as the side effect of the medicine the doctor prescribed to lessen the pain. He felt death was near at hand and suffered from a sense of guilt thinking that he had failed to realise his ideal and that he was causing problems in the family by being over-possessive. But he was at the same time sure that the symptoms would pass and he would recover himself. The son did not notice any melancholic trait in his father's behaviour but later thought, reading the Poet's letters to Andrews and the interpretation Andrews made of these, that the Poet was undergoing some unrest. The *Gitimalya* songs written at Ramgarh might not have reflected the unrest but the three long poems written at Ramgarh did show the turbulence of the soul. Andrews thought that the Poet had some premonitions about the impending World War—but however far-fetched the interpretation might seem, the Poet himself accepted the idea—he had dark moments; those might not be premonitions of the War, but he did feel severe mental strains. The poems concerned are no. 2 (written on 19 May 1914), no. 3 (written on 20 May 1914) and no. 4 (written on 26 May 1914) of the book of poems *Balaka*. The poems no. 2 and 4 were translated immediately and sent to Rothenstein for publication in London newspapers. Eventually the second poem's translation, 'Is it the Destroyer who comes?' was published in *Crossing* and the third poem, 'The trumpet lies in the dust' in *Fruit-Gathering*. The First World War broke to everybody's surprise on 28 July 1914 and England joined the War on 4 August 1914.

The introspective *Gitali* poems and songs were slowly yielding to a larger vision of the world as well as the society. *Balaka* (Flying Cranes), as a whole, is taken as the definitive point of departure. The launch of a new literary magazine, *Sabuj Patra* (Green Leaves) by Pramatha Choudhury (1868–1946), an eminent prose-writer and husband of the Poet's niece Indira, might have acted as a catalyst; the magazine promised to purge Bengali literature of its overbearing sentimentalism, using reason as its vehicle. Rabindranath contributed short stories every month since the inception of the journal for nine months; he added three more later. These were the stories which the writer described, as referred earlier, too formal at the cost of freshness.

Castleton Cottage in Darjeeling
where the Poet composed
Mayar Khela.

The Poet's *nomadic* mood

The long stay abroad and the award of the Nobel Prize were followed by a restiveness—Santiniketan, Silaidaha, Calcutta, Surul (land purchased there to build an adjunct to Santiniketan, for agricultural reconstruction), Bodh Gaya, Allahabad, Delhi, Darjeeling, Ramgarh, Agra, Jaipur—all the places visited in 1914 not according to a plan but as the mood seized him. He was not worried that the school would suffer by his absence; on the contrary, he deliberately made himself scarce to enable the teachers and staff stand on their own, without the overbearing guidance of the founder-financier. But he had to think of the funds for the school.

A portion of the earnings from the interest of the Prize money deposited in the bank was earmarked for the school. The management of the bank became problematic because neither Surendranath nor Rathindranath were wise on monetary matters and spent the bank money in unviable projects and Rabindranath had to plead Pramatha to take care. However, the physical motion lent itself to a sense of motion in his *Balaka* poems, which yearned for equilibrium between motion and motionlessness.

The World War itself was an unsettling affair. Rabindranath had no reason to morally support any of the warring nations out to grab colonial spoils in Africa and the Far East but he had developed a warm friendship with English writers and thinkers, who had to bear the brunt of the War. How the War disrupted the world will be evident from an apparently insignificant letter from J.D. Anderson on 3 September 1914, the Cambridge professor in Bengali, with whom Tagore was corresponding on the metric style of Bengali poetry.

> What a change has come over Cambridge—over the world, since I last wrote to you! The quiet lawns and gardens you know and love...are now covered with hospital tents...this is the result of foolish and wicked teachings of German professors, historians, philosophers—of Nietzsche and Jreischke and men like Mommsen and Rudolph Eucken...Just before the war broke out, I sent a copy of your *Gitanjali* to Mme. Gilson, a Belgian writer of great personal and literary charm...She promised me that she would show your book to Maeterlinck. Well, poor Belgian cannot think of poetry or philosophy now.

Tagore wrote a poem on 22 August, no. 5 in *Balaka*, which he translated as 'The Boatman' ('The Boatman is out crossing the wild sea at night'), and included in *Fruit-Gathering*. Andrews, always too eager to find symbols in Tagore's poetry, thought the girl whom the boatman is out to reach was Belgium, which was grasped by Germany on 3 August, compelling England to join the War. The boatman and the Poet's soul, as we have seen earlier, are too frequent an image in Tagore's poetry. But the Poet too concurred with the spin Andrews put on it!

The US was untouched by the War in the first phase and Tagore was selling briskly there. *Prabasi* quoted George Brett from Macmillan US, stating that poetry, of all the genres of literature, was the best-seller and Tagore equalled Tennyson in sales. *The Gardener* had sold 100,000 copies (*Prabasi* was reporting in July 1914); one shop in Los Angeles sold 500 copies of *The Gardener*. The journal reported next month that *Gitanjali* had sold 800,000 copies. The sales figures appear to be preposterously high and such

Left: With the German publisher, Kurt Wolff, 1921.
Facing page: At Darjeeling, 1914.

reports led Tagore to believe that he was being duped by Macmillan. As it was, Fox Strangways, who had consented to be the literary agent for Tagore, gave up the job in disgust. There were too many intermediaries—Rothenstein, Andrews, Tagore himself—instructing Macmillan and there was a total confusion. Macmillan made a mess of *The King of the Dark Chamber* partly because of this. The sales were falling in the War-devastated Europe but the condition in the States was not dismal. When Tagore demanded a revision of terms, George Brett gladly furnished the sales figures from 1912–13 to 30 April 1916 and agreed in November 1916 to pay 15% immediately and 20% from May 1917—the American royalties Tagore got till then was 10% of the sales. According to Brett's figures, Tagore's books sold 15,875 copies in May–October 1916—sales then were brisker because of the Poet's American tour. Brett informed Tagore seven months later that the European war was affecting the sales of literature books and he had to defer publication of new books from Tagore.

To feed the magazine, *Sabuj Patra,* Rabindranath had to write two novels—*Chaturanga* and *Ghare-Baire*—the two entirely different in character from each other. *Chaturanga,* purported to be a long story, turned out to be a novel, serialised in 1914, just after Rabindranath contributed seven stories consecutively to that magazine, and *Ghare-Baire* was written in 1915, one month after *Chaturanga* was concluded. Both the novels were lyrical in prose, but one dealt with a metaphysical dilemma and the other political.

As it happens almost everywhere, novels are written to meet demands from magazines. All the novels Rabindranath wrote, excepting one (*Char Adhyay*) were serialised in magazines—*Bauthakuranir Hat* in *Bharati; Rajarshi* mostly in *Balak; Prajapatir Nirbandha* in *Bharati* as *Chirakumar Sabha; Chokher Bali* and *Naukadubi* in *Bangadarshan; Gora* in *Prabasi; Yogayog* in *Bichitra; Sesher Kabita* in *Prabasi; Dui Bon* and *Malancha* in *Bichitra*. The last three and *Char Adhyay* were translated after the writer's death, the first three never. *Chokher Bali* was translated as *Eyesore* in *The Modern Review* in January–December 1914 by Surendranath Tagore but not brought out in book form by Macmillan and did not get attention from outside reviewers. J.D. Anderson did review it in *Asiatic Review* in July 1913, but he reviewed the original Bengali novel, which had made a stir in Bengal for its in-depth study of women's mind. *Naukadubi* (*The Wreck*) was translated in 1921 by J.G. Drummond, ICS, who did not know Tagore personally, but sent his manuscript for Tagore's approval. *The Wreck* sold the most among all translated novels of Tagore, but it was never seriously regarded in Bengali, first for its prolixity, and second for its contrived accident and confusion of identity. True to its tradition of handling Tagore, the publisher never mentioned it as a translation and reviewers were at a loss and thought Tagore was interpreting in his own

English, for the benefit of the West, the sacredness of Hindu marriage, without explaining the customs, values and motivations. *Char Adhyay* was translated but not approved by the novelist.

Gora in Bengali is considered to be the best novel by Tagore for its epic range. In its English incarnation, *Gora* by Pearson, in 1924, was dismissed by Western critics mostly because of the stilted English but Leonard Woolf, while reviewing *Uncle Tom's Cabin* in the *Nation* and *Athenaeum* on 9 February 1924, mentioned *Gora* for its content and the able handling of social, political and psychological problems confronting contemporary Bengal. Leonard committed the same mistake as Georg Lukacs did in 1922 calling *The Home and the World,* a Gandhi novel. *Gora's* environment was of Bengal in the 1880s and not 1920s, while *Ghare-Baire* depicted the 1905–08 of Bengal and not India of the 1920s. Bengal was undergoing vast changes, from decade to decade.

Tagore made an intriguing comment in response to Pearson's query if the novel *Gora* had any connection with Sister Nivedita (1867–1911), an Irish devotee of Swami Vivekananda. In his obituary on the Sister (he was prodded by Jagadis Chandra Bose to write it), he made no secret of the fact that the Sister's aggressive nature had put him off. He was rebuffed by the Sister at a very early stage of acquaintance when he vainly proposed to appoint her as a tutor for his children. Soon he realised that she was no British governess. Her militant worship of Mother Kali; her hatred of the Brahmo religion; her encouragement of the revolutionary youth of Bengal in the Swadesi movement could not be compensated, as far as Tagore was concerned, by her immense sacrifices for the sake of India; her contribution to Bengali literature (she edited, almost rewrote, Dineschandra Sen's magnum opus, the history of the literature of Bengal); her help to Jagadis Chandra by not only obtaining funds for the publication of his path-breaking findings in physics and botany but also in writing the first drafts of his findings; her school for girls whom she had to solicit in the face of Hindu orthodoxy. Tagore did admire her resolve to serve India although she lived in slum-like areas of Calcutta, living a penurious life and fighting the orthodox Christian missionaries. But Tagore suspected that the Sister abhorred his Santiniketan. He said so to Edward Thompson in so many words, 'She had a great hatred for me

Above: With W.W. Pearson. Facing page: Sister Nivedita, who reportedly influenced the Poet to re-write the end of the novel, Gora.

and my work, especially here (Santiniketan) and did all she could against me.' Tagore perhaps suspected that she was influential in dissuading Aurobindo Mohan, Jagadis' nephew, from visiting Santiniketan.

Tagore informed Pearson that the Sister visited him at Silaidaha for a few days and he had told her a story 'which came very near to the plot of *Gora*'. The Sister was angry at the idea of *Gora* being rejected by his disciple owing to his foreign origin. So Tagore changed the end of the plot—Sucharita accepts Gora. It does sound improbable. *Prabasi* began serialising *Gora* in August 1907 and finished it in June 1910. For nearly three years, Tagore had been writing and sending to the magazine chapters in monthly instalments. The plot and characters were growing as he proceeded, according to their own momentum. The Sister was out of India during August 1907 to July 1908 and thereafter not in touch with Tagore. She heard him telling the plot before Tagore started writing the novel. That he would abide by a request to change the end of the story—not in a way the story developed, but by an external request from a woman he hardly admired, before he began to shape the story, is truly perplexing.

Chaturanga, four years later, was as condensed as *Gora* was meandering. It was contemporaneous with *Gitali*, and the two had affinity in the sense that Rabindranath was seeking a way out from within himself in both the works. The novel was complex in form, the main character, as seen by his close friend, seeking Truth through reason and then emotion, and failing in his efforts retiring to a quietude, unsettling the life of the girl who was fascinated by the seeker of Truth. The friend, however, retained his composure through the convulsions, deeply affected but not resigned to the vicissitudes.

Chaturanga did not cause any tremor among the Bengali readers who were totally upset by *Ghare-Baire*, which, as they saw it, was a distortion of the Swadesi movement. Formwise, this novel too was a series of monologues from the three central characters, clashing in their ideals and practice. Rabindranath had to interpret himself what he wanted to convey but not to everybody's satisfaction. The central figure, a woman, who was coming out of home into the world, was somehow lost in the polemics of revolution. Tagore was relieved when the West accepted the novel translated by Surendranath in 1919, with some warmth. Although Forster deplored the Babu English, he did appreciate its merits,

Tagore never refused to pose for photographs, in spite of occasional irritation.

as did Yeats, Lady Gregory, Rothenstein, Herman Hesse and Brecht. Lukacs confused the character, who resisted the violence-preaching Swadesi leader with constructional programmes, with Gandhi, but he did notice that it was at the intellectual service of the British police. The translation of *Chaturanga* by an unidentified translator attracted no attention in 1925 when it was clubbed with some stories haphazardly strung together. By that time the West lost interest in Tagore, bewildered by Macmillan publishing him, without any notes on when Tagore had written the works that were being presented in translations.

Not only short stories and novels, Rabindranath contributed a musical drama, *Falguni,* translated by himself as *The Cycle of Spring to Sabuj Patra*. The play was staged at Santiniketan with great aplomb but when performed at Jorasanko on 29 January 1916, the songs did not click,

Songs Out of a Failed Journey

When Rabindranath visited Gaya in October 1914, a stranger introduced himself as the manager of a local zamindar and asked if the Poet wished to visit the Barabar Hill which was known for its Buddhist caves. An ardent student of Buddhism, the Poet was willing but would he be able to brave the arduous journey? No problem, assured the manager. He would arrange the palanquin for the Poet from Bela Station, two stations away from Gaya, pitch tents at the foothills of Barabar where the Poet would travel by palanquins from Bela, send caterers for refreshment—the Poet was just to go by train to Bela—the rest would be taken care of by the manager.

The Poet was accompanied by Charuchandra Bandyopadhyay (1877–1938), a novelist and Tagore follower; Asit Kumar Haldar (1890–1914), an artist and the Poet's relation; a servant; and two other gentlemen. The team arrived along with the manager at Bela Station but there were no palanquins in sight. The others took an elephant-ride to Barabar, fortified with some fruits brought by the manager. The Poet waited and waited at the Bela Station waiting room but no palanquin arrived. The manager went out in search of the missing palanquin and never came back. One of the persons who stayed back with the Poet managed to get two palanquins in a nearby village.

The advance party arrived at Barabar but found an endless stretch of arid land burning in the midday sun. There were no tents, not to speak of caterers. The palanquins were late to come and so the advance party utilised the time by visiting the caves. No sign of the Poet's palanquin. They were hungry and made use of the fruits—the oldest member, Charu, snatching a pear and banana and saving them for the Poet. At last the Poet's palanquin arrived. The Poet rested under the lone tree at the foothills. Learning that his companions had already visited the caves, he said he was too exhausted and lost interest in the caves. He took the banana but not the pear which he said he was too old to chew. The troupe went into the village in search of whatever foodstuff was available and the Poet pleaded Charu not to forget the servant if anything could be found. Something was found but the companions were reluctant to offer the tasteless, rancid, stale food to the Poet. The party came back repeating the tiresome ride to Bela Station. It was evening. They waited for the train back to Gaya. The Poet walked up and down the platform. The companions could not gather courage to go near the Poet—unwashed, unfed, exhausted and pale-looking. Charu, after some time, joined the Poet, who noticing Charu at his back, said, 'There is a necessity to brave suffering in this life', and went on talking. Charu regretted that he did not record the Poet's sayings, which were better than what he used to hear the Poet at the Ashram's morning and evening prayers. The train was yet to come. Charu brought a chair from the waiting room and placed it on the platform. Passengers on other trains peeped from their windows to watch the remarkable figure seated on the platform. Was he a zamindar, a king or a sadhu? Charu thought, he was all the three combined. The fruitless journey, however, produced four remarkable songs which are a treasure in the Tagore songs repertoire. One would hardly believe that these were caused by the irritation and disappointment of a failed journey. The Poet translated three of the four songs.

'To move is to meet you every moment' (*Fruit-Gathering*, no. 13). It was written when the Poet was waiting for the manager who went out to fetch a palanquin.

'I will meet one day the Life within me' (*Fruit-Gathering*, no. 21). This was written during the return trip on the palanquin from the Barabar Hill.

'Comrade of the road/Here are my traveller's greetings to thee' (*Crossing*, no. 78). This was written while returning to Gaya.

and the response was not as expected. Thompson saw the performance and wrote:

> I was one of the audience at the unforgettable first night when it was staged at the Jorasanko house by the Santiniketan boys, and the scenery and the small boys' appearance—as Spirits of the South Wind, and the Bamboo, and other distinguished personages—and their singing were too ravishing for words. It was a complete musical and scenic success. The songs have lived. Greatest of all was the Poet's acting as Baul, the Blind Bard.

The play was staged for the benefit of the famine-distressed people of Bankura, a district in Bengal. The objective was achieved—it was a full house. However, newspaper reviews were not that exciting. A disappointed Thompson wrote again:

> I saw him next day, when he was to return with me to Bankura. But his nervous energy was drained. When the mood held him, he had daemonic vigour; but it ebbed suddenly and completely. Press notices had begun, and he was discouraged by the play's mixed reception; two days later, he was on the edge of collapse. He cancelled his arrangements and fled from Calcutta to the wild ducks and reed beds of Shelida, where he rested.

Santiniketan became a tourist attraction after the Poet became an international celebrity. Lord Hardinge, by conferring the University degree, had somehow made Tagore acceptable to the ever-suspecting police, who were harassed with violent activities of the Bengali revolutionary youths. Lord Carmichael, Governor of Bengal, 1912–17, paid a visit on 20 March 1915. Hereafter, all the governors of Bengal thought it mandatory to visit Santiniketan, often upsetting the simple life there. On 3 June 1915, Tagore was honoured with knighthood. A close relation congratulated him, not forgetting to mention, 'from harassment by the CID to such a distinction, clearly shows a change in the policy of the government'. But the conclusion was drawn too soon. Tagore was highly regarded by the upper echelon of the government, causing resentment among the police officials, who would prove to be a nuisance in the near future.

How Gitanjali *was Published in German*

There are many versions of how the German edition of *Gitanjali* was published by Kurt Wolff. Wolff's own version:

> I am no longer certain (Wolff was reporting fifty years after publication) who mentioned to me that a book of poems by an Indian writer by the name of Rabindranath Tagore had just been published in London, poems with a unique flavour which nonetheless appeared to be eminently translatable. I think it possibly, or even probably, was Franz Blei, since he was always sniffing out new talent and had an excellent nose for it...It wouldn't do any harm to inquire about the book and the German translation rights, I thought. The title of the book was *Gitanjali*. A copy arrived, and with it the information that no German publishing house had made an inquiry. And then, sad to say, it fell victim to an all-too-common vice in publishing houses: the book lay around for weeks before anyone took a look at it. I, the publisher, was unfortunately unable to do so, since at the age of twenty-six I could neither speak nor read English...*Gitanjali* was sent out to readers, as so often happens, what they had to say was so contradictory that the reports cancelled each other out.
>
> 'Our German Ruckhert wrote more inspiring poetry on India,' said one. 'These are beautiful verses of great delicacy and originality, with a monotonous strain characteristic of Eastern lyric poetry,' said another. The third reader reported, 'These are not poems but elevated prose...I strongly advise rejecting it.'
>
> After brief vacillation I decided in favour of publishing—not least because everyone agreed that that there would be no translation problems, since the poems involved neither rhymes nor complicated meters. This decision then received support from a most unexpected quarter: Rabindranath Tagore was awarded the Nobel Prize for Literature in 1913, even before the German edition appeared.

Martin Kampchen has quoted this radio essay in his *Rabindranath Tagore in Germany: Four Responses to a Cultural Icon* and examining Wolff's diary and letters suggests Wolff's version may be true. But he informs that other versions had a comic side. Willy Haas, one of the editors of Wolff's publishing house, has written in 1971 in a German daily newspaper. Haas claimed that when the news of Tagore's winning the Nobel Prize reached Wolff's publishing house, he was there. Kurt Wolff said, 'Hasn't a book of poetry by this man been offered to us? Where is the manuscript? Give it to me.' Haas writes:

> People searched and searched, but nobody could find it. Finally we found out that the manuscript had been read and rejected by one of the main editors of the publishing firm. It had left one hour earlier with the last mail.
>
> Without losing a moment, Kurt Wolff rushed to his car and drove to the main post-office. He was away for over an hour, but then he returned with the manuscript under his arm. Surprisingly he did succeed in having the huge mountains of the evening post inspected, under the supervision of the director of the post-office and got back the manuscript. Presumably this was possible only because he knew the director personally.
>
> There was tension in the room as the manuscript was unpacked. A few pages were read and the editor who had turned it down was applauded. It was indeed a rather weak affair. But Kurt Wolff with his proverbial luck naturally knew the translator. He telephoned her that the manuscript was accepted, but it had to be revised, and he probably immediately settled the question of royalty with her.

Wolff died eight years earlier, Kampchen writes, implying that Wolff could not contradict the story given out by Haas.

Lost in the world of books.

Against materialism and nationalism

Tagore's nomadic mood (as written to Rothenstein) or the migratory instinct (as written to Thompson) was only whetted by a tour of Kashmir which inspired his famous no. 36 of *Balaka,* translated by the Poet as 'When like a flaming scimitar the hill stream has been sheathed in gloom by the evening' (*Fugitive,* III 29). The poem ends with this passage:

> I feel in my own being the rush of the sea-crossing bird, cleaving a way beyond the limits of life and death, while the migrant world cries with a myriad voices, 'Not here, but somewhere else, in the bosom of the faraway'.

Tagore had long desired to visit Japan. But Japan in 1916 was totally different from the Japan of 1905 or the Japan of Okakura. In a letter, he told Rothenstein outright that Japan's joining the Allied Power in the War and grabbing land beyond its own shores was an indication that it might be planning to grab India too. But his friends and Japanese publishers were inviting him. He had written to the Japanese scholar R.N. Kimura (1882–1925) who was financially assisted by Tagore to organise his tour in Japan:

Above: Attending a reception in Rangoon, 1916.
Below: At a tea-ceremony reception at the house of Muraiyama, the proprietor of Asahi Shimbun, Japan, 1916.

> I want to know Japan in the outward manifestation of the modern life and in the spirit of its traditional past. I also want to follow the traces of ancient India in your civilisation and have some idea of your literature if possible. I doubt not that you will be able to help me. I must ask you to protect me, while I am there, from pressure of invitations and receptions and formal meetings.

Tagore, however, had to postpone his plan because the collection of rent from the estates had fallen; students, who mostly came from East Bengal which was affected by the fall of jute export owing to the War, were getting thinner; and there were problems in his own family—his two daughters living in Jorasanko quarrelled among themselves, the elder leaving Jorasanko, never to return. Eventually, Tagore had to go on his own but he had no money.

Tagore's money problem was solved. The Keedick Agency from New York invited him on a lecture tour in the USA. He had to give forty lectures and he would be paid $250 for each lecture; besides he would be paid $2,000 for transport costs. Keedick would arrange the passage and lectures if Tagore agreed. Tagore did not. He would make his own arrangements for passage as and when it suited him. Moreover, he was not prepared to give forty lectures and make himself cheap. He had another equally good offer from James Pond of another lecture bureau, certified by George Brett of Macmillan. Tagore accepted the terms and went to the States via Japan where he spent three months.

Above: At a girls' school, Karnijaoa, Japan 1916. Below: The Poet in Japan.

Tagore sailed for Japan on 3 May 1916 and when he reached Tokyo on 5 June, after stoppages at Kobe and Osaka, a crowd estimated between twenty and fifty thousand greeted the Poet who had won the Nobel Prize for Asia. When the Poet sailed for the USA on 3 September, only a few were present at the port to see him off.

Japan did not get the Poet it expected; the Poet did not get the Japan he dreamt of. Kimura could not save him. The Poet was pestered by reporters and he lost patience. On 1 June, Tagore delivered his first lecture, 'India and Japan', to a crowd of 3,000 listeners sitting on mats. The lecture was reported by the most influential newspaper of Japan, *Tokyo Asahi Shimbun*, as 'Tagore Curses Civilisation'. On 11 June, the Poet

delivered his second lecture, 'India's Message to Japan' (which formed after revision the first chapter of *Nationalism*, as 'Nationalism in Japan'), at the Tokyo Imperial University. He did not attack Japan's aggressive policy in China or the materialistic ambitions of Japanese but he criticised the materialism of the West which was ominous for Japan.

> The political civilisation which has sprung up from the soil of Europe and is overrunning the whole world, like some prolific weed, is based upon exclusiveness...It is carnivorous and cannibalistic in its tendencies, it feeds upon the resources of other peoples and tries to swallow their whole future.

Romain Rolland considered the lecture a landmark for humanity. Even poet Noguchi (1875–1947) welcomed the message. But by and large, the Japanese could realise that the veiled attack was on them. In the third lecture, 'The Spirit of Japan', on 2 July 1916 at Tokyo's Keio University, he deplored the Japanese excitement to imitate the West, even in dresses, school buildings and home furnishings. This lecture formed the second part of 'Nationalism in Japan' in *Nationalism*. Tagore could have left Japan earlier but Pond wanted him to delay the departure. He spent a few delightful days with graduate women students, who were on a mountain summer camp, reciting his poems and talking about religion with them. He also spent some days with the widow and daughter of Okakura. He liked Japanese painting and dance but not the music. The short verses he used to write while asked for autographs in Japan were later, along with others, collected in *Stray Birds* in November 1916.

Above: On way to the US, 1916. Left: At Illinois, Urbana, 1916, with members of the Cosmopolitan Club of the Illinois University. Facing page: In Japan, 1916.

Earlier, Tagore had spent about five months in America, from October 1912 to March 1913. The Seymours, Arthur and Mayce, of Urbana formed a band of devotees, later known as the Tagore Circle. The professor had introduced him to the professors of the University of Illinois. The Unitarians of Urbana had asked him to read four papers. Harriet Monroe, the editor of *Poetry* which published six poems of Tagore had invited him to come to Chicago and introduced him to a rich widow—Harriet Moody—and thus the friendship of Moody (1857–1932) and Tagore ran like a golden thread through all subsequent American visits of Tagore.

The four-month stay in America in 1916–17 was a hectic one for Tagore who had to travel across the continent delivering lectures to earn money for his school. All the lectures drew full houses, mostly women, a point his American critics later never forgot to mention. The sheer spectacle of his presence, 'the poet who looked like a poet', reported widely in newspapers made Tagore's face and clothes familiar to all Americans. Pond's overdrive to publicise Tagore had its negative side also. The bare fact that *Chitra* was produced in Berlin conveyed the wrong notion that Germans involved in the War were trying to earn the loyalty of Indians. Headlines screamed all over the continent that a group of Indians was trying to kill Tagore. Lala Hardayal, the famous revolutionary (1884–1939) had founded in 1913 a Pacific Coast Hindusthani Association, which was known as the Gadar Party following the name of its Urdu mouthpiece *Gadar*. Ramchandra Bharadwaj, the leader of the party in 1916, sent two angry letters to American papers denouncing Tagore's anti-nationalist preaching, which at a time when India was fighting for freedom, was playing into the hands of the imperialists. What happened on 5 October 1916 in front of the San Francisco hotel where Tagore was staying at was a scuffle between two members of the Gadar Party with a Sikh professor and his two companions who came to invite Tagore. Ramchandra denied that his Party had planned to kill the Poet. But the American police made a mountain out of the molehill and shadowed Tagore wherever Tagore went in San Francisco. Tagore could do nothing about it except issuing a newspaper notice that the news of Indians trying to kill him was a badly conceived rumour.

Facing page: With Paul and Mira Richard among others at a Buddhist temple, Nara, Japan 1916.

Tagore delivered his lecture, 'The Cult of Nationalism', twenty times through the length and breadth of the States and although America was yet to join the War, the message did irritate Americans. When he reached the east coast, the criticism rose in crescendo. Whether or not

Left: At Bichitra Hall, Jorasanko, on his fifty-sixth birthday. Right: At Strasbourg, 1921.

Tagore could sense the hostility, he cried a halt to his lectures though they were always attended to the brim, no dissent ever raised, and though this meant a great monetary loss for him.

Physically he was tired, more so mentally. He had already written to Harriet Monroe on 4 October 1916, 'I am like a show lion in a circus now.' He was also fed up with reporters misreporting at will. He had to tell a reporter at Detroit on 9 November 1916, 'I often wonder why some newspapers send men to see me at all when they would save time and trouble by simply putting a reporter down to a typewriter and letting him dream out what I might say. I say it is an un-American efficiency to go through a lot of trouble for an interview in which the only true thing is my name and the name of my hotel.'

Not for nothing, hence, the *Rocky Mountain News* had reported on 17 October 1916 that Tagore, when asked which American marvel had impressed him most, had ironically replied, 'The American newspaper reporters.'

Tagore also did not realise the absurdity of running down the American greed while he was himself earning money by giving lectures. He had to bear with the *Tribune* columnist of Minneapolis describing him on

15 November 1916, as 'the best businessman' scolding Americans at $700 per scold while pleading with them at $700 per scold. However, taken as a whole, Tagore's second American visit was a grand success, not only monetarily but also because the Tagore 'craze' during his first visit had turned out to be a Tagore 'cult'. There were more gushing praises than scathing criticism.

Tagore left San Francisco for India on 17 January 1917. He had seen Woodrow Wilson, the Democratic candidate, winning California and being re-elected as the President of the US in November 1916. Pearson, who had accompanied Tagore as his secretary during the Japan and US tour, wrote to Andrews, who also was with Tagore but had gone back after the three-month stay in Japan, of Wilson's victory in California. He explained the unexpected victory as the outcome of Tagore's lectures on the cult of nationalism—for six weeks Tagore talked against militant nationalism in every big city of California and Wilson kept the US out of War.

Pearson might have overestimated his Gurudev but *New York City Sun* did report on 19 November that Tagore was glad that the President was re-elected because he considered him an idealist; the Poet had read and enjoyed several of his speeches and books. He had no occasion to meet Wilson as he would President Hoover in his next tour but on 9 February sent a telegram to Brett that he intended to dedicate *Nationalism* to Wilson, if permitted. The US, however, entered the War on 6 April. Wilson replied through his adviser to Brett:

> Will you not express to Sir R. Tagore my warm appreciation of the motives which prompted him to make this request and my regret that it seems unwise for me to comply with it, not because of any lack of sympathy on my part for the principles which he so eloquently supports in his book, but because just now I have to take all sorts of international considerations into my thought and must err at all on the side of tact and prudence.

Actually Britain's special liaison agent in the US advised Wilson against granting this permission as Tagore had 'tangled up in some way with the Indian revolutionaries' in the US who were conspiring with Germany to overthrow British rule in India. The police bureaucracy of India did everything to spite Tagore. *Nationalism* was dedicated on September 1917 to Andrews. *Personality,* a collection of some lectures delivered in

In Germany, 1921.

the US, was also dedicated to Andrews; it was published in May 1917. Pearson had *Balaka* dedicated to him earlier in 1916.

Tagore came back to a disturbed Bengal. The British had no intention to relinquish its stranglehold on the colony and by June 1917, ninety-nine persons in Bengal were imprisoned and 705 interned without trial. Tagore's lecture translated by Surendranath as 'The Small and the Great' was given in this context. His interventions on behalf of his countrymen have been referred earlier. His ties with the INC had been snapped since 1908 for multiple reasons. However, he was dragged into politics again in 1917.

Annie Besant was interned in Madras for her Home Rule movement and the internment led Rabindranath to address an invited audience at Rammohun Library and to the general public at Alfred Theatre. The address was meant for the government but more for his countrymen who were divided amongst themselves for social and religious hangovers. The INC session, held at Wellington Square, began with Rabindranath reciting 'India's Prayer': 'Thou hast given us to live' (*Poems*, no. 61). The first day's session ended with a choral song, rendered into English later by the Poet into no. 59 of *Poems*: 'Thy call has sped over all countries of the world.' The INC session 1917 had a record number of delegates—nearly 5,000.

Bal Gangadhar Tilak raised funds for the Home Rule movement and sent Rs 50,000 to Tagore with a request to plead for India in the US. Tagore was tempted to accept the offer but sent back the money—the funds were raised for a political movement but Tagore could not make political speeches. Tilak later assured Tagore that he was not expected to make political speeches but spread the Indian ideals in the US. However, Tagore made preparations for going to Australia on his own and also intended to visit the US again, but he had to abruptly call an end to such plans. The Indian Police was overactive. Tagore was implicated in the San Francisco Conspiracy case, US, thanks to police machinations in India.

When the World War broke, the Indian revolutionaries sought help from the enemy of the enemy—Germany—who was too eager to help with arms and money. One Dr Chandrakanta Chakrabarty was sent to the US with plenty of money. Dr Chakrabarty was shadowed by the US police as well as British intelligence. Ramchandra, the Gadar leader and Dr Chakrabarty were arrested along with their companions from various places in the US. There was no coordination among the revolutionaries and Ramchandra was shot at and killed inside the court during the prosecution by one of the so-called revolutionaries. The judgement was delivered on 23 April 1918—imprisonment for all for various terms, the least for Dr Chakrabarty who was suspected to be a double agent, usurping German funds in his own interest. This was known as the Indo-German Conspiracy or San Francisco Conspiracy case. During prosecution, Dr Chakrabarty claimed that Tagore had come to the US to serve their cause. The claim got wide press coverage and Pearson protested against the wild allegations. Learning all these, Andrews met W.R. Gourlay, private secretary to Bengal's governor, who showed Andrews all the Japanese and the US paper cuttings implicating Tagore. Tagore wrote a long letter and a telegram to the US President asking protection against such calumny. The President did not respond. American officials made some gestures to investigate and ignored the paper reports, but did not have the courtesy to inform Tagore that they considered the reports a bad joke. Tagore cancelled his passage to Australia and the US.

More bad news awaited Tagore. Both Andrews and Pearson were being shadowed all the time in Japan and the US during Tagore's tour. Andrews had come back from Japan. But Pearson did not from the US, staying back in Japan and later in China where he was arrested for writing an anti-British tract, *For India,* in September 1917, which got immediately proscribed in India. He was deported to Britain where he suffered internment. Tagore pleaded for Pearson in a letter to the new viceroy, Lord Chelmsford, but with no success. Pearson was freed after the War.

Tagore's disenchantment with the British rulers grew when the news of the Jallianwala Bagh massacre, perpetrated on 13 April 1919, belatedly reached him. Punjab, under Lieutenant Governor Michael O'Dwyer, was oppressed beyond endurance. The Defence of India Act, 1915, lapsed with the end of the World War and was replaced by Anarchical and Revolutionary Crimes Act, known commonly as Rowlatt Act, more stringent than its predecessor. Gandhi had launched his Satyagraha; the country observed *hartal*; peaceful agitators were fired upon in Delhi; Gandhi was forbidden to enter Delhi and Punjab. On 13 April about 10,000 people, mostly villagers, assembled at a garden in Amritsar called Jallianwala Bagh without knowing that there was a ban on any such congregation of people. General E.H. Dyer ordered fire, after closing the only exit from the garden. Officially 379 people died, unofficially more than a thousand. As all these reports trickled out in the press, Tagore sent Andrews to Gandhi, volunteering to enter Punjab with Gandhi. Gandhi did not respond. Tagore asked Bengal's leader Chittaranjan Das (1870–1925) to call a protest meeting. Chittaranjan suggested Tagore as the lone speaker. In disgust Tagore wrote his famous letter to Chelmsford renouncing his Knighthood.

The letter was dated 31 May 1919. Chelmsford did not know how to handle this renunciation and sought advice from the Secretary of State, Montagu, suggesting that he would write to Tagore to the effect that he was unable to relieve him of the title and so did not propose to make any recommendation to His Majesty. Both King George V and Montagu concurred with the suggestion. Tagore was informed accordingly. The British press in India was furious at the slight of the King; the vernacular press less than congratulatory. Even the Congress session, held later that year, did not think the renunciation of Knighthood important enough for a discussion or resolution. Gandhi some years later called the Poet in his article 'The Poet and the Charkha' in *Young India*, 5 November 1925, as Sir Rabindranath. Ramananda Chattopadhyay, the editor of *The Modern Review* objected. A Bengali scholar from Bombay wrote to the editor that Macmillan was still using the title in books by Tagore. The editor replied that the recent books did not carry the title. To stop this controversy, Tagore sent an open letter to *The Modern Review* stating that he valued his Knighthood and so renounced it when political leaders were unable to launch an adequate protest. He concluded the longish letter saying: '...I do not like any addition to my name—Babu or Srijut, Sir or Doctor, or Mr, and the least of all, Esquire.'

Gurudev with the Mahatma.

Raising funds for a dream

Visva-Bharati, the dream project of the Poet, formally commenced on 3 July 1919, although its founding stone was laid on 23 December 1918. Its motto was derived from a *sloka* from the Yajurveda: *Yatra Visva Bhabatyekriram*. The educational mission of Visva-Bharati has been explained by the Poet on many occasions. Simply stated, as the Poet said in a lecture broadcast by Radio New York, on 10 November 1930:

> I am an artist and not a man of science, and therefore my institution necessarily has assumed the aspect of a work of art and not that of a pedagogical laboratory...I represent in my institution an ideal of brotherhood where men of different countries and different languages can come together...

But Santiniketan could not hold him long at any time. He travelled over the north-east of the country for over a month, October–November 1919, and invited by Gujarat Sahitya Parishad, he went to the western part of the country in March 1920.

On 2 April, he delivered his important lecture, 'Construction versus Creation', at Ahmedabad's three-day Gujarati Literary Conference. He visited Sabarmati, Bhavnagar, Limdi and then went back to Bombay. The Native States liberally presented him with gifts and donations.

Gandhi was ecstatic that Tagore praised *khadi*. He wrote in *Nabajivan* on 25 April 1920, later translated in *Harijan*:

> When her (Sarala's) maternal uncle saw her in this (*khadi*) dress, he also remarked, 'If you don't feel embarrassed yourself, there is nothing wrong with the dress. You can go anywhere in it'. There was a big party on the 11th at Mrs Petit's in honour of the Poet and she had to decide whether she could attend it in *khadi*. She then remembered the Poet's remark and honoured that party by attending it in this same *khadi* dress. She received no less respect than she used to in her costly silk saris...Thus the uncle and niece, who have acquired a reputation in the country for their artistic sense, did not reject from that point of view at any rate. On the contrary, they introduced *khadi* as a dress for women in gatherings of rich people.

In view of the bitter prolonged debate between Gandhi and Tagore later, on the issue of *charkha* and *khadi*, Gandhi's expectations were far from fulfilled. Sarala would have to bear the brunt of her uncle's anger over the *khadi* fetish. It is not known if the uncle knew that his niece Sarala (1872–1945) was having an affair with Gandhi at that time. Gandhi's infatuation with Sarala has come to light only recently.

As it was, her relation with the uncle was never easy—she clashed with him during the Swadesi movement of 1904–05; she was angry that her uncle showed his preference for other magazines when she was editing *Bharati* in 1902–05; she also condemned her uncle performing *Varshamangal* when the country was in the thick of the Non-Cooperation movement in 1922; she openly quarrelled with him on editorial ethics in 1926.

Unlike his tour in south India, the one to west India was beneficial for Santiniketan. Tagore had travelled to the southern part in January–February 1919, on an invitation from the state of Mysore. He visited the hill station of Ooty from where he went to Palghat, the business centre of the Nilgiri Hills, Salem, the industrial centre of Madras, Trichinapoly, Srirangam, Kumbhakonam, Tanjore, Madura, Madnapalli and Bangalore.

In most places, he delivered lectures on education. The reception everywhere was regal but donations were meagre. On the contrary, west India paid rich dividends in terms of one-time and annual grants. The credit should go to Gandhi who insisted, when he learnt that the Poet needed rest and was planning to go abroad again, that the country was going through troubled times and needed Tagore and Andrews to face the problems. He suggested that the Poet could recoup his health at Matheran, a hill station, and Ambalal would be happy to host him. During his trip in west India, Ambalal was the host at many centres.

Ambalal Sarabhai (1890–1967), one of the leading industrialists among Indians at the time, and his wife Saraladevi were lifelong devotees of Tagore. Sarabhai lived in his famous palace, Retreat, in Shahibag gardens, which were created by Shahjahan, the Moghul prince and the governor of Gujarat. The gardens in the twentieth century became the residential areas for Gujarat Cotton mill-owners. Tagore stayed several times at Retreat like many celebrities of the time.

The Sarabhais became family friends of Tagore and all the children of Ambalal went to England for further studies with references from Tagore. Ambalal's children were talented: Mridula (1911–78), a leading social worker; Bharati (1912–?), a writer; Leena (1915–?) a painter; Geeta (1921–?), a musician; Gora (1923–?) and Goutam, designers (co-founders of the National School of Drama at Ahmedabad); and Vikram (1919–71), the architect of India's Space Programme.

They all spent at least some time in Santiniketan. Ambalal and Sarala sought references from Tagore when they went abroad holidaying. Ambalal introduced many industrialists to Tagore.

On the night before her death, Sarala was reading out Tagore's *The Parrot's Training* to her nurse and died in her sleep. She was keen to take advice from Tagore on the education of her children. Mrinalini (born 1918), who married Vikram, was a leading dancer and choreographer in India had decided that she wanted to be a dancer when she was in Santiniketan in 1938. Tagore gave her a leading role in *Chandalika*. She writes in her memoirs:

> Here was an artist asking me to choreograph dances! It was as though something deep within me was liberated and given the

Women students at Santiniketan.

> authority to be my real self! It was a moment of such intense joy, that the radiance, not of his words, but of his acceptance of my individuality, still remains within my heart...For me, the enchantment came alive each time Gurudev said, 'Here is the music. This is the story. Dance it as you wish'. I felt so elated, so free to express myself. Finding new forms from traditional techniques was my need and it was Gurudev who first understood and encouraged this creative urge.

Though the south, north-east or west of India received Tagore warmly, the Poet was keen to spread his educational ideals that had led to the foundation of Visva-Bharati beyond the Indian shores. An invitation from Australian universities had come long ago and was renewed again. Tagore was ready for the trip but abandoned the idea when he learnt that the universities were facing attacks from a section of racist Australians for inviting him. Hence, he started on his journey from Bombay on 4 May 1920 for a fourteen-month trip to Europe and America—fourteen unpleasant months, except the months spent in Europe.

In London, Tagore met his old acquaintances but the meetings took on a new hue. In 1912–13, he was an unknown poet whom London had brought into limelight; there was a patronising indulgence given to Tagore. Now, Tagore was more famous than any one of them and he spoke to them not as a diffident man intruding into a foreign language, but as a man with firm political, artistic and educational ideas. Rothenstein differed, rather strangely, with Tagore on the issue of the necessity of official patronage for the advancement of Visva-Bharati. Tagore would have none of it. He met Montagu, an old friend, but could not convince the secretary of state. It was more important to Tagore that the British condemned the Jallianwala Bagh monstrosity outright than investigating and punishing the guilty. Montagu agreed but pleaded that he had to work within his limitations.

Apart from his meetings with old friends, Tagore was glad to make acquaintance with the Russian painter Nicholas Roerich (1874–1947) and the Austrian art critic Stella Kramrish (1895–1993). The latter was grateful at Tagore's invitation to visit India, which she was able to do after nine months. She stayed at Santiniketan, taught German and made the artists of the school aware of the European trends in painting. In France, the Karpeles sisters, both admirers of Oriental art, visited Tagore almost every day when he was in Paris. The elder sister Andre (1885–1956) later became a familiar figure at Santiniketan.

Henry Bergson (1859–1941), the famous French philosopher came to meet Tagore in Paris. Unfortunately, Bergson was vexed when Tagore–Bergson talks titled as 'The Arch from the East to West' was published in *The Modern Review* without his knowledge. The same thing would happen when Tagore–Einstein talks were published, to Einstein's annoyance, in *The New York Times* in 1930.

Tagore's contact with the French billionaire Albert Kahn (1860–1940) and the French poet Comtesse de Noailles (1876–1933) would help him to mount his first exhibition of paintings, in 1930, in Europe.

This third trip to America during October 1920 and March 1921 yielded drastically less than what Tagore hoped for, partly because Pond failed as an organiser and partly because America had changed in these four years, peopled by whom Gertrude Stein (1874–1946), the expatriate American socialite and writer, called 'the lost generation'. There were only four public addresses and several receptions but little publicity in newspapers.

Tagore's letters to Andrews, which were edited by Andrews and published from Madras as *Letters from Abroad* (1924) and enlarged as *Letters to a Friend* (1928), bear testimony to his frustrations and discontent with himself. The only redeeming feature was the company of Harriet Moody. Pond partly succeeded in the latter part of the tour to organise some lectures in Texas which Tagore had not visited earlier.

The 'five million dollar' dream which Tagore jokingly told to a friend was pricked into thin air but Tagore had the good fortune of meeting Helen Keller (1880–1968) at her home. Keller presented him her book, *The World I Live In*, inscribing a line from *The Gardener*, 'Yes Master, I Forget,/I ever Forget, that the/Gates are shut everywhere in the house/ where I dwell alone!'

Tagore had been widely translated in major languages of Europe and continuously requested by translators for permission. He was hardly in a position to know the people who asked permission. The celebrated Spanish couple, Juan Ramon Jimenez (1881–1954) and Zenobia Camprubi (1887–1956) who came to know each other while translating Tagore and got married, were the most important as well as celebrated translators among all translators in any language.

Jimenez, the Nobel winner in 1956, is considered to be one of the most, if not the most important Spanish poet and one-third of his total works was translations from Tagore, who, according to Spanish critics, influenced him most. Jimenez knew little English but his friend, later wife, Zenobia knew English and translated Tagore from his English works. Jimenez contributed subtle touches extensively but the works used to be published under Zenobia's name, even though Jimenez by that time was an established name in Spain.

The couple invited Tagore to Spain and the latter accepted it. After many changes and cancellations by Tagore, they were expecting him on 27 April 1921 and got busy in rehearsing *The Sacrifice*. But without any explanation Tagore cancelled the visit. All the elaborate arrangements in Madrid came to naught. Tagore hardly knew that he had unknowingly hurt his best translators and devotees.

The continental receptions to Tagore, when he returned from America to Europe, were exceptionally enthusiastic—in Paris, Strasbourg, Geneva,

With Sylvain Levy at Josephine Garden, Strasbourg, 1921.

Lusanne, Lucerne, Basel, Zurich, Hamburg, Copenhagen, Stockholm, Berlin, Munich—but none to beat Darmstadt where Count Keyserling organised a Tagore week.

Among the elite in Europe, communication was no problem but Tagore overwhelmed ordinary people with his appearance—'more Christ-like than Christ'. Among the elite were Romain Rolland, Sylvain Levi, Vincenc Lesny, Moriz Winternitz and Sten Konow. Levi (1853–1935), the French Orientalist, was the first visiting professor in Santiniketan in 1921–22, followed by the three Czech Orientalists—Winternitz (1863–1937) in 1923–24, Konow (1867–1948) in 1924–25 and Lesny (1882–1953) in 1928–29. Lesny would be publishing in Czech, *RabindranathThakur,* in 1937.

In Stockholm, Tagore delivered his Nobel award acceptance speech on 26 May 1921. Earlier, the Nobel award winners had no problem in attending the Prize award ceremony, which is presented every year on 10 December—Alfred Nobel's death anniversary—as they were all from Europe. Tagore lived in a far distant continent and sea-voyage was time-consuming, flights by air were experimental. In fact, when the Swedish hosts arranged Tagore's return to Berlin by hydroplanes, Sven Hedin (1865–1952), the famous explorer and writer, intervened and arranged train bookings; he thought air journey was too risky.

The European response overwhelmed Tagore. When *Svenska Tageblatt*, a newspaper of Stockholm requested Tagore for an autographed letter for publication and offered money for Visva-Bharati, Tagore politely refused the money but sent a letter expressing his astonishment at the European demonstrations in his honour. In the letter he related one incident.

> The other day when I rested alone in my room in the hotel at Hamburg there entered two shy German girls with a bunch of roses as their offering for me. One of them who spoke broken English said to me, 'I love India.' I asked her, 'Why do you love India?' She answered, 'because you love God.' The praise was too great for me to accept with any degree of complacence...the nations love their own countries and that has only given rise to mutual hatred and suspicion. The world is waiting for a country that loves her God and not herself, and only that land will have the claims to be loved by men of all countries.

Rabindranath came back to his country which convulsed with the Non-Cooperation movement. Even Santiniketan, which he had declared out of bounds for politics, was not untouched by the movement. His trusted teachers, Nepalchandra Ray (1867–1944), Bidhusekhar Sastri (1878–1957), Andrews, even his eldest brother Dwijendranath (1840–1926) were enticed by Gandhi's spirit of Non-Cooperation.

Subhas Chandra Bose (1897–?), refusing the coveted ICS job, was coming back to Calcutta by the same ship Rabindranath took. Subhas sought advice from Rabindranath, who told him to take up constructive work to serve the country. Subhas was the students union secretary of

Presidency College, Calcutta in 1916, when Prof. E.F. Oaten, the chemistry professor of the college, was beaten for his abusive words to students. Subhas was not among the group who assaulted Oaten but accepted responsibility and was expelled from the college. Rabindranath defended the students in two long articles, one in Bengali and the other in English, in two leading magazines. He did not support student indiscipline but condemned the English professors' colonial attitude that caused students' grievances.

Rabindranath might not have known Subhas in 1916 but the latter was well aware of the defence. Subhas was undecided about what to do, but reaching Calcutta he joined the Non-Cooperation movement under the guidance of Chittaranjan who gave up his fabulous profession as a barrister and joined Gandhi. Rabindranath felt like an exile in his own motherland. He started writing children's poems once more to get away from the stifled clime—the poems were compiled into *Sisu Bholanath* (1922).

The Poet at Surul, which would eventually be the seat of Sriniketan.

One of the important occasions abroad was Tagore's meeting with Leonard Elmhirst (1893–1974), an Englishman who had earlier travelled all over India and was willing to serve Indian agriculture, and was studying agricultural science at Cornell University in the US. Learning this, Tagore asked him to see him at New York and invited him to join Santiniketan. But Rabindranath, at home, had no surplus funds to start an agricultural university. Elmhirst secured funds from Mrs Dorothy Straight, whom Elmhirst knew and later married. Funnily, Mrs Straight had already met Tagore and was not at all impressed by what appeared to her, 'as the wooliness of the Poet's ideas and the phony business of his dress and play-acting'. But Elmhirst's gushing letters persuaded her to contribute funds to Santiniketan and later she became a whole-hearted promoter of Sriniketan of which Elmhirst was the principal architect. Elmhirst came to Santiniketan in November 1921. Forty years later, he told an interviewer

on the occasion of Tagore's birth centenary, his first experiences:

> But at the end of six months Tagore said, 'Elmhirst will you formulate your findings because I want you to come with me to Calcutta and talk to the students in the University there about what you have found? Can you sum up, what are the three main troubles?' And I said well the odd thing is that they all begin with M: Monkeys, malaria and mistrust...Before we went to bed (at Surul), the students came to me and said, 'But, Sir, there is no sweeper.' The sweeper is a man who traditionally in India looks after the lavatories. I said, 'There will be a sweeper in the morning.' In the morning after they had visited the latrines and had gone to have their bath and their breakfast, I went myself to empty those buckets. And two of the boys, who had been trained under the Poet saw me doing this, ran up to me and said, 'But, Sir, you are our teacher, you mustn't do this, we will do it.' Now for four of the boys who were Brahmins, this was really something they felt they couldn't do. And it was three months before they were able to break their own traditional restrictions and do it. But while this was going on, Tagore was himself digging a trench in his own garden and emptying his own bucket into that trench.

In Santiniketan school, Rabindranath had introduced co-education as early as 1908, and with some hiccups, the system was well entrenched. Girls had no problems in participating in musical or dramatic performances. Rabindranath had taken girls along with boys to Calcutta for various public performances, although within the precincts of Jorasanko. Nobody criticised; at least, not publicly. However, when *Saradotsav* was mounted at Alfred Theatre on 16 September 1922 and at Madan Theatre on 18 September, Rabindranath defied letters from two Brahmo leaders who did not favour girls and boys participating in *Varshamangal* presented

Left: Students at work in the Sriniketan farm.
Facing page: Leonard Elmhirst, the architect of the village reconstruction programme at Surul.

earlier at the Rammohun Library Hall (16 August), Madan Theatre (17 August) and Alfred Theatre (19 August). One of the letters came from Krishnakumar Mitra (1852–1936), editor of *Sanjibani*, a militant Swadesi leader exiled during that movement, and a Brahmo leader. The other letter-writer was also a Brahmo. The letters were surprising because the Brahmos promoted female education and defied the *purdah* of women. As expected, the performance of *Saradotsav* drew praises from all newspapers, except *Sanjibani*. Such Brahmo orthodoxy had featured in his novel *Gora* in the character of Haranbabu, professedly emancipated but essentially conservative.

In 1922, Rabindranath had written another play—*Muktadhara*—and immediately translated it—*The Waterfall*. It had a message against machines—machines which were used against humanity. When he read out the play to select gatherings, some people thought it portrayed Gandhi in the character of Dhananjay and propagated Gandhi's non-violence and anti-machine ideas. Rabindranath was annoyed with such interpretations. *Muktadhara* essentially celebrated the call of the road to people confined within their homes. It had nothing to do with Gandhi's Non-Cooperation. Strangely, the play was never staged by Rabindranath and the play never clicked when performed by various troupes after his death—probably the play was internally, both thematically and structurally, flawed.

In 1922, Rabindranath ended the contract with Chintamani Ghosh (1854–1928) for the publication of his books and entrusted the

Visva-Bharati Trust with the copyright of all his Bengali books. In the beginning, his friends, relations or he himself were publishers of his books. However, from 1884 onwards, several publishers came forward for printing and selling his books till the Indian Publishing House, a Calcutta subsidiary of the Indian Press of Allahabad, was given the right to publishing Rabindranath. Chintamani, a professionally competent publisher, used to publish Hindi and English books. When Charuchandra Bandyopadhyay, later a novelist and professor, joined his firm, he established Indian Publishing House in Calcutta and Charuchandra was able to secure Rabindranath's confidence and earn for his firm the right to publish Rabindranath in 1908. Rabindranath was happy with the conscientious publisher who never thought of commerce with regard to Rabindranath's books. In 1914, when Rabindranath visited Allahabad he wanted to meet his publisher, Chintamani. At the meeting, Rabindranath made an astounding request—could Chintamani print and publish *Gitali* in one week? Initially reluctant to accept such a challenge, printing processes being what they were then in India, Chintamani delivered the goods by inducing his printing staff to work seventeen hours a day. Rabindranath was taken aback to get copies within a week and wanted to give something to his publisher. The publisher wanted Rabindranath to sing the song, '*amar matha nata kore dao he tomar*', a song from *Gitanjali* which he had heard in so many tunes that his only wish was to listen to the correct tune. The grateful Poet sang the song, needless to say; but whether correctly or not, it is hard to say as the composer often forgot his own tunes!

In September 1922, Rabindranath went on a two-month tour—Poona, Mysore, Madras, Coimbatore and Ceylon. There were great receptions; crowds thronged railway platforms when they knew that the Poet was travelling; he delivered lectures in packed halls. Gretchen Green, recommended by Dorothy Straight and funded by Harriet Moody to come to Santiniketan and help village women learn elementary hygiene, landing in Bombay, met Rabindranath at Poona. At some places villagers, at other places businessmen, presented him with garlands of currency notes. Rabindranath wrote to Indira that he was travelling with a begging bowl, not in his hand but in his voice—delivering lectures, singing songs, reciting poems. On his way back, he visited Trivandrum, Quilon, Ernakulam, Alwaye, Madras, Bombay, Ahmedabad and Benares. In February 1923, he once more undertook a journey and travelled to Benares, Lucknow, Bombay, Ahmedabad, Karachi, Porbandar, and returned to Bombay. Donations collected were handsome.

The Poet with his students in Santiniketan.

Financing a Dream

Kalidas Nag (1891–1966), the historian and a Tagore follower, wrote this letter to Romain Rolland on 28 November 1923:

> Our Poet has taken to the programme with all the passion and resources at his disposal. Santiniketan is his last great dream, his last great fight to destroy the barriers between man and man and to lay the foundation of international peace and amity.
>
> But to realise this dream we must have money and also an efficient army of collaborators both inside and outside India...With the exception of Macmillan's royalty which goes to meet his personal expenses, Tagore has given everything that he has earned personally: (the ancestral property goes to the son) his whole Bengali works, their sale-returns, the Nobel Prize, and so on. But the establishment of Santiniketan, the expansion of educational, artistic and economic enterprises, demands fresh supply of funds, mere interest on the consolidated capital is not sufficient, invitation of distinguished guests from Europe like Prof Sylvain Levi of Paris, Dr Winternitz of German University of Prague and other teachers had strained the finances to its utmost: the deficit budget was met miraculously by the staging of some of our Poet's dramas in Calcutta. But that was a makeshift...The country unfortunately is now preoccupied with politics and Tagore has no political programme! Still, after a month's tour through western India and Gujarat he has managed to raise Rs 80,000 (£1,600). That gives us a hope that the country may gradually awaken to the needs and requirements of the new-born university...

At Peking, 1924, with Kalidas Nag, Elmhirst, Kshitimohan Sen, Gretchen Green, Nandalal Bose, among others.

The message of the East

Tagore's next venture abroad was facilitated by Jugaldas Birla, belonging to the famous business family of the Birlas, who advised by Madanmohan Malavya, contributed Rs 10,000 for Tagore's journey to China. The large amount allowed the Poet to take along with him Kshitimohan Sen, Nandalal Basu (1883–1966), an artist, Kalidas Nag (1891–1966), a historian and Elmhirst as secretary of the Poet. Malavya was impressed by Rabindranath's sympathy for Hindu Mahasabha, in view of Swami Sraddhananda's (1857–1926) re-conversion of Muslims to Hindus and expected that the Poet would lecture on Hinduism. However, in China, Tagore did not talk on Hinduism but on the Eastern civilisation.

Tagore left Calcutta on 21 March 1924, reached Shanghai on 12 April and left on 30 May 1924. Chronologically, Tagore addressed about a hundred teachers and students at Shanghai on 13 April; an assembly of a few thousand students at Hangchow on 15 April; around 1,200 listeners at the Commercial Press conference room at Shanghai on 17 April; about a thousand students at Nanking on 20 April; a few thousand students at Provincial County Hall, Tsinan (Shantung) and 200 listeners at Shantung Christian University on 22 April; an assembly of Anglo-American Association and then a group of boys and girls at

Pei Hei, Peking, on 25 April; an assembly of more than a thousand at the National Normal University, Peking, on 26 April; at a Buddhist temple and then scholars at the Navy Club, Peking, on 27 April; an assembly of more than 10,000 at Altar of Agriculture, Peking, on 28 April; students of Tsing Hua College, Peking, on 1 May; teachers on 6 May at Peking House and elsewhere in Peking on 8 May; delivered his first public talk at the True Light Theatre on 9 May, 10 May and 12 May; further addressed students in Peking on 18 May; members of the International Institute, Peking, on 19 May; at the Confucian Hall of Self-Examination, Peking, on 20 May; school students at Hangkao and at Wuchang ground on 25 May; and finally gave a farewell speech at Shanghai on 29 May.

These talks were all extempore. *Talks in China* was published chronologically in 1924 but the volume was withdrawn, perhaps because of the shoddy production, and then brought out again in 1925 according to the category of people who were addressed. The talks had been made out from Elmhirst's notes and newspaper reports. The talks were dignified in spite of the hostility shown by students. In fact, Tagore knew that China was going through troubled times and when in 1923 the president of the Universities Lectures invited him, he sent Elmhirst to China to reconnoitre. Elmhirst could not gauge the depth of the discontent. Elmhirst himself wrote in his diary that at Shanghai on 17 April, almost at the beginning of the lecture tour, students protested with flags against Tagore's message. They thought that the Poet was pacifist, all-spiritual, anti-communist and against industrialisation. It is doubtful if they at all listened to the Poet's message or understood his English. The climate, preceding the tour, was charged with acrimonious debates among the contending intellectuals. Four Marxists—Kuo Mojo, Mao Tun, Chu Chiu and Chan Tu-hsin—wrote strong newspaper articles against Tagore's anti-nationalist and anti-materialist stand.

Tagore was aware of these criticisms but he was assured by his supporters and admirers that they needed Tagore to bring some sanity in China which was driven not only by Marxists and non-Marxists, but by liberals and conservatives, by followers of Confucius and Lao Tse and modernists. Chen Tu-hsin, the general secretary of the Communist Party which was founded in China in 1921, had asked 'Why do we welcome Tagore?' He wrote:

At a monastery in China, 1924.

> Having added to the chaotic thought of Lao Tse and Chaung-zu, the chaotic thought of Buddhism, we have suffered enough, and are more than grateful to the Indians for their gifts. Now there is no need to add Tagore to all this.

On 10 May, at the True Light Theatre lecture, pamphlets were distributed at the conference stating why the protesters were objecting to Tagore's message. They thought Tagore was feudal in outlook (because he was eulogising China's past which looked down upon women and pampered rich feudal lords); he was against industrialisation whereas China needed rapid industrialisation; he preached spiritualism to the common people who were extensively exploited by foreign powers and warlords; he was adding his theory of Brahma to the Chinese minds when they were already burdened with the theory of Ying and Yang, Tao, Confucius and Christianity.

Tagore wanted to know the content of the pamphlets. The Chinese hosts were reluctant to tell him. Tagore learnt it from some Japanese friends and cancelled his successive three public talks. The communists were incensed to watch Tagore's itinerary—meetings with the Manchu Emperor, Chinese warlords, American ambassador, Anglo-American association, Japanese Buddhists, and so on.

Tagore with the former Chinese Emperor.

However, it was not all criticism. The Crescent Moon Society formed at Peking Normal University celebrated the Poet's birthday in a grand way, calling him Chu Chen-Tan (meaning bamboo, representing ancient India, thunder and morning which added up to mean Rabindra). One of the greatest actors of China, Mei Lang-Fang, treasured a hand-fan gifted by Tagore with a four-line inscription in Bengali, although he was peeved when the Poet, invited to his production of a play, walked out in the middle of the play—that was the ultimate insult to a director. It was not entirely the fault of Tagore—he was tired with preliminary songs and the play started at 11 in the night. Lang-Fang had earlier staged *Chitra* and sought Tagore's advice regarding the lights used. Tagore had told him, for a Puranic tale, the décor did look colourless. Lang-Fang used the lights as suggested by Tagore in his subsequent productions.

Returning to Calcutta, Tagore reported his tour in a lecture at the University Institute on 22 July 1924. He said that there was resistance in China but not much. Kalidas Nag, however, confessed to Elmhirst that he apprehended even physical assault on 25 May at the Wuchang ground lecture when students were shouting: 'Go back, you slave of colonial rulers.'

Tagore retained interest in China, in spite of his not so happy Chinese adventure. One of his Italian guest professors, Giuseppe Tucci, taught Chinese in Santiniketan along with the Chinese professor, Lim Ngo Chiang in 1925–26. Tan Yun-Shan, an enterprising Chinese youth who studied in Santiniketan in 1928–31, formed a Sino-Indian Cultural Society at Nanking, which wanted Visva-Bharati to be its centre in India. He raised funds in China and Cheena-Bhavan was built in Santiniketan in 1937. Tan was a class-friend of Mao-Tse-Tung. In 1934, Tagore had told him not to imitate the USSR, instead develop their own communism. Tan was, however, not a follower of the Chinese Communist Party, but of Chiang Kai-Shek's Kuomintang. When Tai Chi-Tao, a very senior Chinese official, came to Santiniketan with a large number of delegates in 1940, he said to Tagore in an interview that took place on 12 December 1940:

> Your visit in 1924 not only brought to us the message of India but also inspired us to know ourselves and saved us from the strangling hold and fatal glamour of the materialistic West. Our cultural renaissance, in fact, dates from that event...When the present troubles are over I shall myself come over here and on behalf of my country, my people and my Government escort you to China and all possible arrangements can be and will be made for your comfort and convenience.

Tagore had said, 'Thank you, I look forward to that day.'

Año II. Buenos Aires, del 10 al 16 de Noviembre de 1924. Núm. 96.

Radio Cultura

Revista Semanal de Radiotelefonía, Literatura y Arte

RABINDRANATH TAGORE

Rabindranath Tagore está con nosotros.

Esta noticia encierra para muchos la deleitante alegría que emana de las fiestas silenciosas del espíritu. Difícilmente habrá abrigado jamás el territorio de la República Argentina un hombre tan grande, un corazón tan perfecto, una imaginación tan clara, una inteligencia tan luminosa capaz de bañar en suave luz los misterios más insondables.

¡Rabindranath Tagore!... Yo no sé qué labios puedan pronunciar este nombre sin temblorosa reverencia; no sé quién, al pensar en él, no sienta deslumbrado el espíritu y conmovido el corazón; no sé quién haya ejercido en el mundo una influencia más decisiva sobre los corazones...

Rabindranath Tagore está con nosotros. Estoy por afirmar que ha llegado aquí atraído por el inmenso amor que le profesamos; por esa milagrosa fuerza de atracción que tiene todo lo grande, desinteresado y puro. Es su llegada un triunfo misterioso de nuestra voluntad ardiente, la que le ha puesto en camino de estas tierras feraces, donde alientan tantos corazones entusiastas, que se sienten atraídos por la perfecta y suave armonía de sus canciones, breves y sencillas, que penetran en los cerebros como una luz y animan las almas en un deseo vehemente de ser buenas.

De juro los que más anian al santo maestro no podrán verle, ni conversar con él, ni oir su palabra, ni besar sus manos sagradas que saben acariciar suavemente a los niños y tenderse humildes a Dios para implorar la felicidad del mundo; pero hemos de sentir todos la beneficiosa influencia de su espíritu luminoso que tan asombrosa fuerza de irradiación tiene.

Por Rabindranath Tagore hemos aprendido a amar la India y hemos envidiado, con santa envidia, a los afortunados niños que en las Moradas de Paz se educan, dirigidos santamente por él, y que por él han aprendido la ciencia incomparable de dirigir los ojos al cielo, y de mirar con mirada serena, hacia el alma propia, fortalecida por la meditación...

¡Maestro! Muchas cosas tienes que enseñarnos a nosotros, turbulentos occidentales que arrastramos una vida desalentada por la consecución de los más groseros ideales.

Sea tu visita para nosotros aliento purificador que nos ayude a penetrar el hondo sentido de la vida y nos haga más nobles y más buenos.

¡Maestro! Que tu permanencia entre nosotros sea grata, como tu visita a nuestro suelo es grata a mi corazón.

Rafael Ruiz López.

DÍMELO

¡No me escondas tú el secretó de tu corazón! ¡Dímelo a mí, que yo soy tu amigo, sólo a mí!... Dímelo tan dulce como te sonríes, que no te oirán más oídos, sino mi corazón.

La noche es profunda; está la casa silenciosa; el sueño amortaja los nidos de los pájaros... ¡Anda, dime tú, en un llorar vacilante, en un tímido sonreír, en una dulce vergüenza, en un dolor dulce, el secreto de tu corazón!

Rabindranath Tagore.

Rabindranath Tagore's stay in Argentina featured in Radio Cultura, *1924.*
Inset: Spanish version of a Tagore song.

An Argentine adventure

From near Peking, Elmhirst wrote to Ranu Adhikari (1906–2000), who was a fervid Tagore-worshipper, on 17 May 1924:

> He has delivered over twenty speeches and addresses and given countless interviews...he no longer talks of leaving this existence at an early date, but of going to Italy and Russia and Heaven knows where.

He was prophetic. On his way back, in Japan, he received an invitation allegedly from the Peru Government to attend the centenary celebration of the country's Independence on 9 December 1924. Tagore accepted it. Romain Rolland learnt it from a letter from Kalidas Nag and warned Tagore that he should not be trapped by the dictator ruler of Peru, who was trying to legitimise his dictatorship. He also wrote a letter to this effect to an editor of an Argentine newspaper. He intended to personally brief Tagore in France when Tagore would be on way to Peru, but Tagore could not make his scheduled meeting with Rolland as he got in France an earlier ticket than expected. At Buenos Aires, Elmhirst found to his dismay that the Peruvian consul knew nothing about the invitation to Tagore. However, funds and tickets were made available by the Peru Government. Meanwhile, Rolland's letter to Buenos Aires as well as another one from a Peruvian exile in Argentina were published causing a Peru—Argentina political crisis. Providentially, Tagore was attacked with virulent influenza and doctors advised total rest for him—a long journey whether by train or boat to Lima was totally unacceptable to them. Elmhirst wanted to pay back the money given by the Peru Government which was, however, gracefully refused by the Peruvian consul. Tagore stayed for two months in Argentina, as a guest of Victoria Ocampo (1890–1979).

At Villa Miralrio, San Isidro, Argentina, 1924.

Ocampo was at that time estranged from her husband and had developed an intimate friendship with her husband's cousin. Being a Catholic for whom divorce was not possible, she was going through a troubled marital relationship. She was fond of the French novelist Proust's works, but was feeling stifled, when she chanced upon Andre Gide's French translation of *Gitanjali*. She sought solace from Tagore, who, she learnt, would be going to Lima via Buenos Aires. She was excited that she might get an opportunity to meet the Poet himself and wrote an article in *La Nacion* on Tagore.

She did meet the Poet at Plaza Hotel but she was totally tongue-tied, overwhelmed by the Poet's presence. She volunteered to act as a hostess and arranged the Poet's stay at a newly-built house of a friend at San Isidro. The house was called Miralrio, meaning river-view, next to their own house, Villa Ocampo, where her parents refused to accommodate the Poet.

Tagore stayed in Villa Miralrio from 11 November 1924 to 3 January 1925 with a brief stay at Chapmadal at Ocampo's friend's house. Chapmadal was some 400 miles away from Buenos Aires, near the Atlantic Ocean.

Tagore wrote twenty-two poems in this period, of them only two at Chapmadal. However, he had been writing poems all through his sea-voyage to Argentina—altogether twenty-three poems, before he reached Buenos Aires. This was unusual. He once told Ajit Chakrabarty that Saraswati used to bid farewell to him when he donned Western dresses—he could not write in his mother-tongue in foreign attire.

He was perhaps tired of giving lectures in China and Japan and gave vent to his innermost feelings, getting this long respite. He said so in one of the letters. There is no reason to believe that he was possessed by the Muse in the form of Ocampo—he was already seized. But there were poems inspired by Ocampo—there were definite marks of her presence in those poems. These poems were special and ambiguous—a reason why Tagore asked Elmhirst on 20 November not to send those poems to India which might upset his near ones. In fact, Rathindranath and Pratima, who were in Paris at that time, were wondering what held back Tagore in Argentina. They were not aware that money became a problem at the latter stage of his stay at Argentina.

The Poet with Victoria Ocampo, Paris, 1930.

Ocampo went through various stages in her relation with the Poet. When she first saw him, she was awed in his presence. He was her father's age and she indeed felt like a daughter. She needed some time to overcome her shyness and awkwardness. She did not stay at Miralrio, in deference to her relatives' and friends' sensibilities. By nature she was not at all a timid girl. In her own words, 'Little by little he partially tamed the young animal, by turns wild and docile, who did not sleep, dog-like on the floor outside his door, simply because it was not done.' Since she was keeping herself aloof, the Poet used to send her letters, which any other woman could have interpreted wrongly. On 14 November, he wrote to her, explaining his understatement in thanking her for the hospitality:

> My market price has risen high and my personal value has been obscured. This value I seek to realise with an aching desire which constantly pursues me. This can be had only from a woman's love and I have been hoping for a long time that I deserve it.

A page from the manuscript of Purabi.

The Tagore–Ocampo correspondence is marked by this ambiguity—love has so many connotations, depending on the context. Naturally, it is tempting to read the letters and poems written on these days any way one likes. Ocampo–Tagore's relation also upset Elmhirst, who himself had felt attracted to Ocampo and that complicated matters. Ocampo had written much about Tagore when she was herself an international celebrity, editor of the *Sur* magazine and founder of Sur publications, sought after by intellectuals like Count Keyserling and Jose Ortega Y. Gasset (1883–1955) who were named by Ocampo's biographer, Doris Meyer, as her suitors. But even a frank and bold woman like Ocampo never explained the nature of 'love' she felt for Tagore. When *Purabi* was dedicated to her, she was perplexed what the dedication was for. She did not know Bengali and the text of the volume remained unknown to her. Once she asked a Bengali interviewer what the word *Purabi* meant. It might mean the east, she was told and she wondered if the west should not have been more appropriate. *Purabi* might also mean an evening tune, and she felt that the latter connotation was relevant. Very attentive to the Poet's comforts, the resourceful Ocampo made the captain of the ship, by which he was to come to Europe, pull off the doors of the cabin to place a sofa for the Poet during the journey. It was reached to Santiniketan and the Poet used it to his last days. But Ocampo was irritated to read the Poet's views of modern Argentina, which he formed in the course of his talks with intellectuals of Argentina. The Poet said that Argentina had become too Westernised, forgetting its own heritage. Ocampo agreed that communication might have been a problem due to scant knowledge of English of the Spanish-speaking Argentines but she thought Tagore was too enchanted with W.H. Hudson's (1841–1922) portrayal of the arcadian Argentina to understand modern Argentina.

In his diary, Elmhirst termed his experiences in Argentina as the 'Argentine Adventure'. He could have termed his experiences in Italy in 1925 and in 1926 as the Italian Misadventure. However, he did not, because he did not accompany Tagore in the Poet's tour of Italy in 1926—as a point of fact, he was not allowed. But that is another story. On his way back from Buenos Aires, the Poet arrived in Geneva on 19 January 1925 and left Brindisi on 4 February 1925. The principal personality involved in the Poet's tour in Italy was Carlow Formichi (1871–1943), a professor of Sanskrit in Rome University, who was made out as the villain by Nirmalkumari Mahalanobis (1900–81) in her memoir, *Kabir Sange Europe* (With Tagore in Europe). Formichi was invited as a guest

With Ocampo to whom he had dedicated Purabi.

lecturer in Santiniketan in 1925–26 and he impressed Visva-Bharati as a learned professor with great love for India and Tagore's institution. Mussolini (1883–1945), thanks to Formichi's persistent efforts, donated a large library of Italian books to Visva-Bharati. During his 1920–21 tour in Europe, Tagore was promised similar gifts of French and German books to Visva-Bharati. Additionally, Mussolini sent Giuseppe Tucci (1894–1987), a famous Indologist, paid by the Italian Government, for a professorship at Visva-Bharati. However, what happened to Tagore in Italy in 1925 and then in 1926 has been vitiated by conflicting reports, sometime by the same persons and it is not easy even now what Tagore or Visva-Bharati later thought of Formichi and Tucci or for that matter, Mussolini.

The Role Reversed

One evening my guest expressed the wish to hear some modern European music. I arranged for the Castro Quartet to come out to San Isidro.

On that day Tagore felt depressed, having presumably received disturbing news from India. He did not come down from his room on the first floor. He just left his door ajar. The musicians sat down to play, with their music-stands before them, in the middle of the empty hall on the ground floor. I had to limit myself to pointing in the direction of the room upstairs where Tagore was sitting.

I could not help smiling to myself, remembering an incident I had read in Tagore's Reminiscences...It is true that my friends did not play on a landing before a closed door. Debussy, Ravel and Borodin could reach the Poet through a half-open door. I always wanted to tease him a little about this, telling him that without wishing it the young Indian student had had his revenge. But I did not dare.

(From *Tagore on the Banks of the River Plate*
by Victoria Ocampo)

With Prasanta and Nirmalkumari (Rani) Mahalanobis, as travel companions in Europe, 1926.

Regal reception in Europe

In 1925, Tagore's stay in Italy was short, only for two weeks. He could only visit Genoa and Milan and had to cancel his visit to Turin. The Duke of Milan, G. Scotti, chairman of the reception committee at Milan, a playwright and writer, struck a warm friendship with the Poet. In a crowded hall, Tagore gave a talk—'The Voice of Humanity'. Formichi wrote in his book on India in 1927 that he was embarrassed while interpreting Tagore's talks in Italian to the audience and 'the scene changed completely. The enthusiastic approval which had surrounded the Poet in the beginning was replaced by harsh criticism, angry debates and the stirring up of suspicion and hate.' Formichi was writing after his bitter experience in 1926, and therefore, may not be wholly relied upon. But in 1925 itself, Sudhindra Bose, a professor in the US, wrote an article in *Forward*, reporting criticisms hurled on Tagore which made him leave early. However, *The Modern Review* contradicted Sudhindra Bose by publishing an article written by Sudhirkumar Lahiri who was in Italy, denying any such criticism of Tagore. The debate was pointless as Tagore himself said after the 1926 visit, 'reports of fascist atrocities reached me from time to time and I had serious misgivings about coming back to Italy'.

Elmhirst also told Rolland on 19 January that Tagore was upset at the manifestations of fascism. Rolland's diary on India has been translated by

Right and facing page: The Poet received by officials at Naples, 1926.

Abantikumar Sanyal in Bengali. Either Rolland or Sanyal is wrong about the date of this entry in the diary. Elmhirst and Tagore arrived in Genoa on 19 January 1925. According to Rolland's diary, on that date, Elmhirst met Rolland after Tagore left for India. However, Elmhirst confirmed in his introduction to an interview of Tagore with the Duke of Milan, subsequently published in the *Visva-Bharati Quarterly,* that Tagore was upset by the manipulation of press interviews and misreporting of his speeches, and the Duke of Milan, Scotti, saw to it that doctors advised Tagore not to continue the tour.

The question is why Tagore accepted the Italian Government's invitation in 1926. Tagore rationalised with the explanation: he was entranced by the scenic beauty of Italy; he was eager to meet the great minds of Europe; and he had to redeem his pledge to his friends whom he promised a visit sooner than later. But Rathindranath and Prasanta Mahalanobis did not approve of Tagore's visit, knowing the nature of fascist Italy; they, however, did not have the courage to say it to Tagore. When they found that Tagore had made up his mind, they decided to travel with him and guard him against misinterpretations of his interviews.

Nirmalkumari (Rani) narrated a breath-holding suspense story describing how Formichi manoeuvred and prevented Prasanta and Rani from joining Tagore on the boat and how they succeeded in eluding the

watchful eyes of Formichi but a bit too late. Formichi had already started his game at Rome, arranging a meeting where Tagore and Mussolini would be present. Formichi tried to prevent Rathindranath and his wife too to accompany Tagore on the boat, but Rathindranath insisted that they must look after the health of Tagore. The boat carrying Tagore and family reached Naples where Elmhirst from London and Karpeles from Paris came to receive the Poet. They came to join him on this Italian tour. Mussolini had invited Tagore and conveyed an idea that he could take as many members he liked to accompany him. A special train was waiting at Naples and as soon as Tagore embarked on the train, it moved. Elmhirst ran to board the train but Formichi pushed him out on the plea that there was no room for others. In disgust, Elmhirst returned to London. Karpeles stayed back with Rathindranath and his wife at Naples till Prasanta and Rani reached.

Tagore stayed in Italy from 30 May to 22 June 1926—in Rome from 30 May to 15 June, in Florence on 16 and 17 June, in Turin from 18 June to 22 June. Tagore met Mussolini on 31 May and 13 June, met a reporter from *Tribune* on 1 June and another reporter from *La Voce Republican* on 3 June, attended a reception thrown by the Governor of Rome on 7 June, addressed an assembly including Mussolini at *Unione Intellectuale Italian* on 8 June, attended a grand reception at Colosseum on 10 June, met King Victor Emmanuel on 11 June and Benedetto Croce on 15 June. The most sensational was the meeting with Croce. Tagore was told by his friends that he must not leave Rome without meeting Croce but Tagore did not know where and how to meet him. Formichi assured him that he would try. Croce (1866–1952) was not a fascist and Formichi made no attempt to arrange the meeting. A student of Croce, Captain Rapicovoli told Tagore that if Tagore requested Mussolini himself for a meeting with Croce, he would try. The anti-fascist captain belonged to the royal family. Mussolini asked Formichi if Croce was in Rome and the latter said he did not know but would enquire. On June 15, the Captain brought Croce from Naples at the dead of night. Croce, who was in fact interned in Naples, had a closed-door meeting with Tagore. When Formichi came to know of this meeting, he could do nothing but gnash his teeth.

Later that year, the Tagore–Croce interview, as reported by Prasanta, was published in the *Visva-Bharati Quarterly*. The interview was short and inconsequential but Rani wrote in her memoir that Tagore told them the morning after the interview that Croce had expressed surprise to read newspapers reporting Tagore's fulsome praise of Mussolini.Croce said that writers and artists had been censored and there was no freedom of mind under fascism.

Rani and Prasanta had a strange, and till today unexplained, experience according to Rani's memoir. Apprehending that Tagore would be and in fact had been misreported by the fascist propaganda machine, Prasanta and Rathindranath used to send detailed weekly reports from Italy. On their return to India, they were surprised to note that none of the reports were published in the *Visva-Bharati Quarterly*. Not only that, they found no trace of the reports in the Visva-Bharati office. In 1941, Rathindranath found the reports in the Visva-Bharati godown and sent those to Prasanta, who again lost them and refound them in 1969. When Tagore sadly remarked in *Prabasi* in 1940 that none of his assistants thought that Tagore's European tour in 1926, which featured his meetings with so many European thinkers, deserved to be recorded, Rani got down to reconstruct the tour through her numerous letters she had written during the tour to acquaintances in Calcutta. Surprisingly, the bunch of letters she collected was getting lost time and again. When in 1940 she got back the bunch, she was at a loss to find that her letters from Italy were missing!

Meanwhile, another sensational drama was being enacted at Villeneuve in Switzerland, where Rolland lived and arranged Tagore's stay for recuperation of health. Tagore stayed there during 22 June and 4 July 1926. Rolland was gathering information, as was his method of knowing a man he considered important. He wrote books on Vivekananda, Ramkrishna, Gandhi, without ever visiting India. Tagore hoped Rolland would be writing on him. Rolland never did. Rolland–Tagore correspondence was, of course, published by Visva-Bharati in 1945.

Rolland was disheartened to see Tagore, who was thinner and paler than what he had seen of him in Paris three years ago. However, Tagore was pleased to see that Rolland had arranged accommodation in the very room at Hotel Byrone where Victor Hugo stayed. Over the first few days, they talked about music and art. Prasanta hinted about Formichi conspiracy but could not elaborate in the presence of the Poet. After some days, Rolland was stunned to hear Tagore praising Mussolini who according to the Poet had restored Italy's economy and discipline in life, who had to enforce some kind of regimentation when the country was sinking into anarchy. Rolland listened silently, feeling that Tagore loved to talk and needed to unburden himself. Another stumbling block for a dialogue was that both of them needed an interpreter, Tagore knew no French, Rolland little English. Rolland's sister was the interpreter.

Rolland invited Tagore to his house, Villa Olga, and talked about the other side of Italy, where students, teachers and liberal thinkers were murdered by the fascists. Rolland thought Tagore was shocked, his face shrunk in agony. Tagore however, changed the subject and rambled on India and Gandhi. In the evening, Prasanta came alone and told Rolland how Tagore was cheated by Mussolini. He read out his own notes. Prasanta told Rolland that he had no idea who invited Tagore in Italy and when he asked Tucci, who was teaching in Santiniketan, he

Facing page: The Poet in Switzerland, 1926, with Madeleine Rolland, Prasanta, Rolland, Pratima and Rani, among others.

was rebuffed. He told how Tagore was cut off from his companions in Italy. In his talks with Mussolini, Tagore did point out that Mussolini was being criticised by the outside world and Mussolini pleaded that he knew but that was the price he was paying for he loved his country. Tagore met many people, but all screened by Formichi. None of his old acquaintances met him and those who met had changed overnight—all praises for fascism. Even Croce allegedly talked about spirituality and Scotti told him his lips were sealed.

Needless to say, Rolland–Tagore talks were not confined to fascism only but Rolland was seeking ways of exorcising the enchantment of fascism out of Tagore. Prasanta had already apprised Tagore of all the evil deeds Mussolini perpetrated as detailed by Rolland. Rolland knew that mere debates or discussions would not be enough and that Tagore was too sensitive to bear a brute attack. He invited Georges Duhamel, a novelist and essayist, from Paris, to take an interview of Tagore on fascism. But Tagore thought he would be more comfortable if Duhamel framed his questions and he would react in his own way. Rolland and Duhamel were hoping that Tagore would shake off his ambivalence after listening to the fascist atrocities. They were disappointed. Duhamel was so shocked when Tagore read out an essay that he felt like going out in the middle of Tagore's reading. Rolland knew better and restrained Duhamel from a rude response. However, Duhamel refused to accept the essay for the paper in which he intended to publish Tagore's views. Tagore consented to revise the essay in view of Duhamel's points—the essay was too full of praises for Mussolini—to be a balanced view; his 'buts' were feeble and lost in the lyrical outbursts of adoration of Italy, Duhamel said. They felt that Tagore was hesitant to criticise Mussolini after enjoying his hospitality which was given on a grand scale (1,000 school children and around 30,000 people rising from their seats as the Poet arrived at the Colosseum, for example). Tagore commented on things he had seen and held that he had not seen any sign of oppression. In fact, Rolland thought how Tagore could even be made responsible for what the Italian press had said.

Above: Villa Olga, Rolland's house.
Facing page: With Rolland, 1926.

In a desperate attempt to make Tagore see the truth Rolland requested two Italian exiles—Salvemini and Salvadori—to meet Tagore in Vienna. They wrote to Tagore how they were tortured by fascists. The famous socialist, Matteoti, was murdered in 1924. The lawyer, who fought for the murdered leader, Modigliani, met Tagore in Vienna, accompanied by Angelica Balabanoff, a famous writer, once a co-worker with Mussolini, now a severe critic. Tagore was now willing to make amends for his hasty appraisal of fascism. His open letter to Andrews was published on 5 August 1926 in *The Manchester Guardian*. His interview with the wife of Salvadori was published by the same paper on 7 August, a reply from Formichi on 25 August and the Poet's rejoinder to Formichi on 20 September. Rolland was not happy with the Poet's initial letter but consoled himself with 'something, better than nothing'. He quoted relevant passages from Tagore's letter to Andrews and gave wide publicity of Tagore's criticism of fascism in several languages in several papers.

The controversial tour and Tagore's condemnation of fascism had the natural consequence. The sponsorship of Tucci's post at Santiniketan was withdrawn and Tucci left Santiniketan but not India. Manilal Patel, a teacher at Santiniketan, told Rolland (noted in his diary 20 October 1929) that Tagore was face to face with Tucci at a hill station and Tucci did not greet the Poet. Patel later asked Tucci for a recommendation for a trip to Europe; Tucci said, 'Give up the job at Santiniketan and then come to me.'

The Modern Review made a nasty crack on Tagore's turnaround in Italy. It was then a votary of Mussolini and asked why Tagore had accepted the invitation in the first place and if he had accepted, what sort of courtesy was it that he should denounce the host now? Possibly Tagore was not abreast with current world politics—that could be pardoned for a poet but what about his 'knowledgeable' assistants—asked the temporary editor, Asok Chattopadhyay, the son of Ramananda who was also on tour in Europe at the time. Tagore wrote a long bitter letter debunking the language of Asok and asked if this was the return to his three-decade-long service to *Prabasi* and *The Modern Review*. A taciturn Ramananda wrote back that factual misstatements, if any, would be corrected. *Prabasi* did correct the misstatements—it said that it had learnt later that Rathi and Prasanta did oppose the Poet's acceptance of Mussolini's invitation.

That was not the end of the story. It was argued that fascism did not bare its fangs in 1926 and so Rabindranath could be forgiven for the tour. But Tagore met a tearful Formichi in America in 1930 and asked him if he could possibly visit Italy again. No problem, said Formichi, just write a letter to Mussolini. Tagore wrote a letter to Mussolini, thanking him for his magnanimous gifts, lavish generosity shown to him and hoped that the misunderstanding was forgotten. He forwarded the letter to his son to examine if it would be all right to send the letter to Mussolini. It was believed till the other day that his son withheld the father's inopportune letter, but now the evidence has surfaced that the son did send the letter.

Formichi, whom the Mahalanobises thought to be a fascist agent and a two-faced villain, was asked by the editors of *The Golden Book of Tagore* for his contribution in 1931 and Formichi obliged. And the other villain, Tucci, was conferred the highest honour of Visva-Bharati, the title of Desikottam, although after the death of Tagore. Tucci was, of

Left: With Pratima and Rathindranath, in Rome, 1926.
Facing page: In Switzerland, 1926.

course, a true scholar, a great Indologist and a talented linguist. He had picked up Bengali in his short stay at Santiniketan and translated *Lipika* in Italian.

Tagore's grand continental tour was resumed after his days with Rolland—Zurich, Lucerne, Vienna, Paris, London, Totnes in Devonshire (where Elmhirst, inspired by Sriniketan, founded Dartington Hall),

Right: With German intellectuals, 1926.
Facing page: The bust by Jacob Epstein.

Oslo, Stockholm, Copenhagen, Hamburg, Berlin, Munich, Nuremburg, Stuttgart, Dusseldorf, Dresden, Prague, Vienna, Budapest, Belgrade, Sophia, Bucharest and Athens; and then again, from Athens to Alexandria, Cairo and back to India in December 1926.

Rathindranath summed up the receptions in continental Europe with a statement, 'At every railway station huge crowds would gather to have *darshan* or just touch the hem of his robe—a sight which hardly fitted in with our conception of the rationalistic and unemotional people of the West.' The ovation had its comic side. The King of Bulgaria ordered a special train to reach the Poet at the Bulgarian frontier, where the Danube River touched Rumania on the opposite shore. The Bulgars transferred the Poet and his companions on to a battleship cruiser, decorated with flags and buntings, and gave a warm farewell with gun salutes and a brass band playing the Bulgar national songs at its loudest. The guests were surprised to find one solitary figure on a desolate pier on the other side of the bank gesticulating and tearing his hair—the more that man gnashed his teeth, the more amused were the Bulgars escorting the Poet. That gesticulating man was the station master of the tiny railway terminus of Rumania. The Bulgars had seen to it that the Rumanian Government did not get any definite information of the Poet's arrival so that it could not arrange any ceremonial welcome to the Poet!

In London, Jacob Epstein (1880–1959), an American sculptor of Russo-Polish descent, sculpted a bust of Tagore. The bust was criticised as it looked as if the bust rested on the beard. Epstein made the bust but in his autobiography, *Let There be Sculpture*, made rude remarks on Tagore. He was exasperated at the seemingly condescending sitter, posing as a holy man. 'On one occasion two American women came to visit him, and I remember how they left him, retiring backwards, with their hands raised in worship.' On the fringe of the bust, the sculptor inscribed a quotation from *Gitanjali*: 'I am he that sitteth among the poorest, the loneliest, and the lost.' The quotation was entirely wrong—the correct version being: 'My heart can never find its way to where thou keepest company with the companionless, among the poorest, the lowliest, and the lost.' In his autobiography, Epstein remarked that the criticism might have been correct; the bust did seem to rest on the beard, a pretension of holiness.

Rolland had hailed Tagore's speech in Japan in 1916, 'The message of India to Japan', as a landmark in the history of mankind and asked Tagore in 1919 to sign the 'Declaration of Independence of the Spirit', an appeal to stand out against universal oppression and servitude of the intellect, which Tagore signed along with around a thousand leading international intellectuals. Rolland eagerly waited to meet the Poet and saw him for the first time in April 1922 in Paris and said the memory of the meetings with Tagore would remain among the most precious in his memory. But he was increasingly feeling unhappy with Tagore's globe-trotting. The continental tour of 1926 annoyed him most as the personalities whom Tagore was meeting were all reactionary rulers of the world. His insatiable wanderlust provoked Rolland to comment on him most unkindly—Tagore loved to show himself off.

The little girl Ranu, now Lady Ranu Mukherjee, with the Poet.

A many-splendoured mind

Tagore was apologetic about his nomadic mood and missionary zeal but he could not help it. Long ago in 1902 he said it in a poem (translated by him and included in *The Gardener*: 'I am restless, I am athirst for faraway things'). He confessed on the eve of his first overseas tour in 1912 in a letter to Kadambini Debi, who used to seek his advice on spiritual and social matters, that because he was born as a Bengali in the Tagore family, he did not wish simply to carry that sole identity; he came to the world as a world citizen and he intended to bid farewell as a world citizen.

This same truth he tried to impress upon the little girl Ranu, time and again ever since she was twelve. Ranu Adhikary was the daughter of a philosophy professor of Benares. Her precocious letters intrigued Rabindranath who increasingly indulged her. Ranu never studied at Santiniketan—her sister and cousin did—but she used to come to the Ashram during her school vacation. The vivacious, sometimes audacious, girl won the hearts of everybody she met; but as she grew up without losing none of her vivacity, it was telling on her parents; more so, when she attracted rave reviews by acting as Aparna in Rabindranath's immensely successful production of *Bisarjan* in Calcutta in 1923. Her parents, scared by her suitors, wanted to marry her off but the girl pitched high—she wanted none else but Rabindranath himself. The Poet, aged sixty-three (and the girl eighteen) did not know how to get out of the ticklish situation. He could not hurt her, who was easy to be hurt; he suggested several suitable bridegrooms, some of whom were from his extended Tagore family, but all were dismissed by the girl as idiots. The Poet was relieved to learn on his return from Argentina via Italy in 1925 that Ranu had consented to an arranged marriage. Rabindranath met the boy, the son of Sir R.N. Mukherjee, who rose from the ranks to the captaincy of Indian industry, and approved of the match, even though socially the Adhikarys and Mukherjees were poles apart.

It has been suggested that Ranu inspired Rabindranath to visualise Nandini, the central character in *Raktakarabi*. True or not, Ranu was with the family of Rabindranath during April–June 1923 at Shillong, where the playwright made his first two drafts of the play (as many as ten drafts have been found). The play was about the dehumanising force of mammon versus love, machine versus individuality, organisation versus personality. Tagore immediately translated the play into *Red Oleanders* and published it in the *Visva-Bharati Quarterly* even before the Bengali play was printed in book form. Unfortunately, *Red Oleanders* evoked little response in the West which was perplexed by obtuse symbolism. And the play was never staged by the playwright—ostensibly because he could not find an actress who could do justice to the joyous, spirited, daring Nandini. The play has been differently interpreted—anti-capitalist, anti-power, even anti-West—the last interpretation made by the playwright himself, against the adverse reviews published in *The Manchester Guardian*.

Muktadhara and *Raktakarabi* could not be staged by Rabindranath but *Natir Puja* (translated by the Poet as *The Dancing Girl's Worship*) was staged in Calcutta on 21, 29, 31 January 1927 to ecstatic reviews. To protect the girls acting and dancing on a public stage—at Jorasanko, of course—the playwright added for himself a character to the play, which was eight months ago performed at Santiniketan, and appeared on the stage. *Sanjibani*, as we have noted earlier, was against female participation on public stage. It questioned what was the use of Santiniketan, if the institute had to raise money by selling the honour of its students? The all-girls cast, the superb final dance by Gauri, daughter of Nandalal Basu, minimal but effective décor carried away the Calcutta audience. The film, *Natir Puja*, produced by The New Theatres in 1932, was, however, a

Facing page: As Upali, a Buddhist monk, in Natir Puja, *Calcutta, 1927.*

catastrophe. Released in Chitra Cinema Hall, it could not run even a week, the filmgoers broke the furniture of the hall and demanded refund. They could not be entirely faulted; the 10,000 ft-long film was nothing but a picturisation of the dance-drama staged at Jorasanko. The New Theatres claimed that the film was directed by Rabindranath; if it was, the media was beyond the grasp of the many-splendoured genius. The static camera and moving girls were no entertainment for bioscope buffs.

Tagore had another go at film-making in 1930; this time, not as a director, but as a script-writer. Himangshu Ray (1892–1940), a student of Santiniketan, had executed a successful film, *The Light of Asia* (1925), directed by Niranjan Pal, the son of Bipin Chandra Pal. Himangshu sold the idea of making a film—on Christ with a script by Tagore—to UFA, the prestigious film producer of Germany. He took Tagore to Oberammergau, a Bavarian town in Germany, which used to present the passion play on Christ at ten-year intervals. Tagore saw the passion play on 23 July 1930 during his last continental tour of Europe and overnight wrote out *The Child* in English. Unfortunately, UFA was affected by the Great Depression of 1929 and the progressive producers of UFA were driven out by the Nazis. Tagore was not a professional filmscript writer; he expected that the script could be built upon the very long poem which was a sequence of images after images.

Critics, at home, never left Tagore alone and Tagore countered them in a dignified way, sometimes choosing to ignore them, sometimes meeting them with a banter but privately, sometimes losing his cool but even then checking himself from public acrimony. But in 1927, he did an unexpected thing. Getting a copy of *Rabindranath Tagore, Poet and Dramatist* by Edward Thompson, which was published in 1926 from Oxford University Press, while he was relaxing in Ahmedabad after a visit to Bharatpur near Agra and Awagarh (the Maharaja of Awagarh donated money and a palace he built for his own stay at Santiniketan to Visva-Bharati), he decided to hit back. He was angered by the patronising tone of Thompson which he ascribed to his English origin. He wrote a critique of the book under a pseudonym, Banibinod Bandyopadhyay, in *Prabasi*. In 1921, Thompson had published *Rabindranath Tagore: His Life and Work*. Even at that time Tagore did not quite approve of the book but since he knew that Thompson was getting his facts and interpretations from Prasanta Mahalanobis, he did not chide Thompson. In fact, Tagore himself encouraged Thompson while the biographer was working on him, telling him that he had Tagore's permission to quote from his works and to translate. Nonetheless, he told Prasanta, knowing that the remarks would be relayed to the biographer, that Thompson did not understand the influence of the Upanishads and the Vaishnava lyrics on his life and work and overestimated the influence of the English romantic poets. The second treatise by Thompson was much later enlarged and revised but the Poet did not live to see it.

Fortunately, his relations with Thompson were not snapped. Thompson had a major work in his plans—one of them being the *Oxford Book of Bengali Verse*, an anthology of Bengali poetry from the Middle Ages to the modern period—Tagore was supposed to edit the Bengali version and Thompson to translate it in English. The plan was made in 1921 and abandoned because of the sluggishness of Prasanta who was to help Tagore in scanning Bengali poetry for selection. Thompson revived the plan in 1929 but it did not come through, again partly for two sluggards—Prasanta and Sudhindranath Datta (1901–60) who were to select the moderns—and partly for the confusion of Oxford advisers and editors. Extremely annoyed with his two associates, Rabindranath brought out, with the help of his Visva-Bharati teachers, *Bangla Kavyaparichay* (A Bengali Poetry Reader) in 1938. But this anthology was withdrawn, as young and not so young modern poets of Bengal cried hoarse on omissions and commissions. A revised edition within weeks was promised—but the revised reader never came out.

Visva-Bharati, in 1927, was not in a good shape. Distinguished scholars continued to come as visiting professors but they too were embroiled

The Poet on his trip to Greater India.

in petty politics of the University campus, never slow to slander each other, privately to Tagore. Money problems were persistent because the University was adding many disciplines to its existing tenuous self. A generously funded magazine *Bichitra* came out in 1927 and for sheer money, the Poet contributed a novel, *Yogayog* (The Connections), in nineteen big instalments from September 1927. Another novel from August 1928, *Sesher Kabita* (The Last Poem) was contributed to *Prabasi* in eight instalments. *Yogayog* was planned on a grand scale encompassing three generations but the writer could not 'drag' it beyond one generation. Readers were expecting another epic novel like *Gora* but were surprised to find the end of the tensions between sensitive feudalism and vulgar mercantilism with the pregnancy of the heroine. Saratchandra Chattopadhyay (1876–1938), the best-selling novelist of his time, ridiculed the denouement of the novel with an observation that the seemingly insurmountable problem of incompatibility was resolved by a lady doctor!

Saratchandra had no less admiration for the Poet, even if he drew the sword with him on the issue of Non-Cooperation movement. Once he chided a reader who held that Saratchandra was a greater writer than Rabindranath with the remark that he wrote for the people like that reader but Rabindranath wrote for writers like him. But he was grievously hurt when Rabindranath refused to bail him out morally after *Pather Dabi* (The Claim of the Road) was proscribed in August 1927. Rabindranath wrote to him that he should not expect mercy at the hands of the government if he had written a seditious novel.

Compared with *Yogayog, Sesher Kabita* was a pretty novel, too pretty for some critics for its sparkling language. The theme was love and when the novel was concluded at Bangalore, his host Brajendranath Seal, a leading philosopher of his time, exclaimed how the Poet could handle a mere love story at that age. More surprise was in store for the philosopher. *Mahua* (a plant for intoxicants), a bunch of love poems written in August–December 1928, was published in 1929.

The Bengal Cooperative Organisations Society celebrated 2 July 1927 as the International Cooperators' Day at Albert Hall in Calcutta and requested Tagore to preside over the celebrations. The Poet propounded the principles of cooperation in his famous lecture of 1904—'Swadesi Samaj'—but in the agitational heat of the time, the Poet's appeal had few takers. Seven years later, the Poet delivered the presidential address at the silver jubilee celebrations of the Hindusthan Cooperative Insurance Society at the Town Hall, Calcutta. Way back in 1906, the Poet was one of the signatories to an appeal in support of the scheme of the National Cooperative Insurance Society; three years later, he lent the ground floor of Bichitra Hall in Jorasanko for use of the just formed Hindusthan Cooperative Insurance Society. He wrote out the first Bengali prospectus and joined as a signatory to the Memorandum of Association. His nephew, Surendranath, was the founder of the Society.

Facing page
Above: In the Malay Peninsula, 1927.
Below: In Siam with Indian residents, 1927.

About a decade ago, Tagore had visited Japan and later China to search for the relics of India but speeches and interviews left him little time. In 1927, he set out on a trip to what he called Greater India—Singapore, Malay, Java, Bali and Siam. The Dutch archaeologists had requested the Poet to see the historical relics of India; the Javanese asked him to see

their cultural heritage. This trip was sponsored by two Marwari business tycoons—G.D. Birla and N.D. Bajoria. Sunitikumar Chattopadhyay (1890–1977), the linguist and grammarian, Surendranath Kar, the artist and architect, Dhirendrakrishna Debbarman, another artist-teacher of Santiniketan, and Arnold Bake (1899–1963), the Dutch musician who was staying at that time at Santiniketan, comprised Tagore's team. Unlike the 1926 European tour, this tour has been vividly recorded by Sunitikumar.

The Chinese tour had gone awry partly because Tagore's English could not be adequately interpreted by his Chinese interpreters. The Greater India tour was facilitated by Sunitikumar who could interpret the Poet's speeches in Hindi. Additionally, the Tamil-Christian professor of Visva-Bharati, Aryam Williams, was already there to interpret the Poet in Tamil. The triumphal tour met a discordant note when the *Malaya Tribune*, championing English interests, attacked Tagore's politics by distorting his essay in *Shanghai Times* and projecting him as anti-English. However, the distortion was quickly corrected by another Malay newspaper. The tour earned large contributions for Visva-Bharati.

But the Greater India tour had its flip side. On return from China in 1924, Rabindranath's tour companion, Kalidas Nag founded the Greater India Society and Rabindranath was its first president. As the Society expanded, Kalidas found to his dismay that Rathindranath and Prasanta had succeeded in making the Poet believe that Kalidas intended to make the Greater India Society a rival to Visva-Bharati.

Kalidas informed Rolland that he had to take great pains to convince Tagore that it was a monstrous lie but there was a chasm between Ramananda (Kalidas married his daughter) and Tagore after the Mussolini affair. It was Tagore who introduced Kalidas to Rolland when Kalidas went for studies at Sorbonne, France and Rolland had been since then 'Master' of Kalidas. Rolland had planned to celebrate the seventieth birthday of Tagore with *The Golden Book of Tagore* to be edited by Ramananda.

Kalidas was uneasy with the proposal and informed Rolland that the relation of Tagore and Ramananda was too formal after the reaction of *Prabasi* and *The Modern Review* to Tagore's visit to fascist Italy. But Rolland insisted that he could not depend upon the so-called friends of Tagore in India who wanted to bring out the volume from France. The book must appear from India, otherwise people there would be confirmed in their wrong idea that Tagore was alienated from his own people in India and had become West-centric. Kalidas, Rolland said, must approach all the writers whom Rolland knew, with an appeal which would be signed by Rolland, Einstein (who had agreed) and Jagadis Bose. But Rolland did not know all the English and American friends of Tagore and so he depended upon Kalidas to make the final list with the assistance of Rathi. Anyway, it was decided that the book must be edited by an intellectual and at the same time edited by someone competent. Eventually, the appeal was signed additionally by Gandhi and Costes Palamas, the greatest living poet of Greece, and edited by Ramananda and it turned out to be a fabulous production. Rolland desired the contributors not to make just appropriate noises which were usually made for such commemorative volumes but to gift the Poet their best—poets with poems, essayists with essays, painters with their new paintings, and so on.

The book was presented to the Poet at the Town Hall of Calcutta on 27 December 1931 by Ramananda on behalf of the Golden Book of Tagore Committee. H.G. Wells and Shaw, vexed by too many reminders, refused to contribute. Tagore was against all such ceremonies because of that kind of avoidable embarrassment.

The year 1928 saw two more ceremonies added to the Santiniketan calendar—*Vriksharopan* in Santiniketan and *Halakarshan* in Sriniketan.

Facing page: On the steps of Borobudur Stupa, 1927.

At the age of sixty-one, photographed by Bula Mahalanobis.

Varshamangal was introduced in 1921, *Basantotsav* in 1923 and *Saradotsav* way back in 1908. The *Paushmela* was not an occasion for songs or dances —it was truly a rural fair of crafts and display of fireworks. Rabindranath and following him Rathindranath planted trees and turned the arid land of Bolpur into a green landscape—plants were gathered from within the country and abroad. The ceremonies are explained by the names given to them—celebration of rains, spring, autumn, plantations and ploughing. Occasionally, Santiniketan students and teachers staged these musical

Rabindranath as a Film Director

The New Theatres, a film studio established in 1931, acquired in the 1930s the reputation of a premier film studio in India. Located on the southern fringe of Calcutta, the studio had a thatched hut, called Golghar—the round room. Golghar was treated as a sacred place, visited by pilgrims like film personalities (Frank Capra, Jean Renoir, V.I. Pudovkin and others), writers (Saratchandra Chatterjee, Kazi Nazrul Islam and others) and national political leaders (Jawaharlal Nehru, Sarvepalli Radhakrishnan, Subhas Chandra Bose and others).

The Golghar was erected when Rabindranath Tagore was approached by the ace cameraman and director, Nitin Bose of The New Theatres for permission to film *Natir Puja*. The Poet refused to give his consent as he thought Bengali films were bad art. Many of his stories and novels were earlier filmed and these films were nothing to rave about. However, the Poet gave his permission on condition that he would himself direct the film. The proprietor of the studio, Birendra Nath Sircar, was ecstatic when he learnt the term of the Poet's consent. It was a double gain for him—the permission to film *Natir Puja* and the acquisition of Tagore as the director. He planted trees and put pots of flowers, erected a thatched hut, covered the adjacent grounds with shrubs and the Poet was pleased to see the spot, calling it a second Santiniketan. This was the Golghar.

The D-Day arrived. The Poet came with a group of Santiniketan pupils who would play out the dance-drama. Sircar, however, was taken aback when the shooting commenced under the direction of the Poet. The camera was kept static and the Santiniketan pupils acted, danced and sung before the static camera. Even then, he consoled himself that the genius that the Poet was, some magic touch would redeem the stagey production. At the end of the first day's shooting, the rush print was shown to the Poet, who gravely watched the print and told the crew to shoot the film themselves. The 10,551 ft-long film was released at the Chitra Cinema Hall on 22 March. The film was advertised as 'Directed by Rabindranath Tagore'.

Lila Majumdar (1908–2007), the famous writer, had seen the filmed play. Actually, the film was taken on a staged production at Jorasanko. In her memoir, she wrote that the Calcutta film-goers were so vexed with the film that they broke chairs, electric lamps of the hall and demanded refund of the ticket money. The film was withdrawn within a week.

The Golghar is no more, yielding itself to a Kali Temple!

The Sparkling Green Drink

Rabindranath was an early riser. As W.B. Yeats wrote in his introduction to *Gitanjali*, "'Every morning at three—I know, for I have seen it"—one said to me, "he sits immovable in contemplation, and for two hours does not awake from his reverie upon the nature of God."' The Indian gentleman from whom Yeats derived this bit of information might have exaggerated a bit but teachers of Santiniketan and visitors to the Ashram who were lodged in close proximity to the Poet's residence testified to the fact that the Poet used to rise early and meditate.

There are many who have recorded their experiences of sharing the Poet's breakfast. The Poet was a small eater and insisted on sharing food with whoever was present at his breakfast table. And a number of writers have mentioned the tumbler of sparkling green *sherbet* the Poet used to drink at breakfast. Since the experiences were common, we shall see what a pupil wrote about it.

Pramathanath Bisi (1901–85), a pupil of Santiniketan and a teacher later, found it convenient to come for his lessons at the Poet's breakfast time. Expectedly, the Poet offered him some items of the breakfast which the pupil, with feigned reluctance, used to partake. But the pupil was curious to know what the green drink was and why the Poet never offered it to him. One day, noticing furtive glances from the pupil at the *sherbet*, the Poet asked for another tumbler of green drink and offered it to the pupil, who eagerly took a large sip and did not know how to tackle the huge remnant in the tumbler. It was killingly bitter and the pupil realised it was pure *neem* juice. He gulped it down pretending that he liked it and made it a point not to come at the Poet's breakfast table for his lessons.

compositions in Calcutta for fundraising, not necessarily for Santiniketan but also for the relief of people stricken with famine or floods in other parts of Bengal. *Basantotsav* and *Paushmela* have since become tourist attractions of Santiniketan while *Vriksharopan* is now an all-India affair, officially adopted by government agencies.

Tagore visited the US three times by 1929 but not Canada. He was invited by the National Council of Education, Canada. Earlier, Tagore had refused invitations from Canada which was known for its racism. In 1916, he refused an invitation from Toronto and Montreal, publicly stating that he did not want to set foot on a country which refused Indians. Evidently, the *Kamagata Maru* incident rankled in his mind. That ship hired by a Sikh businessman of Singapore and with 351 Sikhs and 21 Punjabi Muslims on board had reached Vancouver but they were not allowed to disembark; the ship came back to Calcutta and passengers were ordered to go to Punjab by a special train. The passengers refused to obey the order and were fired upon—officially eighteen Sikhs were killed. By 1929, Tagore was more internationally oriented and accepted the Council's invitation to spread the message of Visva-Bharati.

The eleven-day stay in Canada was spent in speeches and interviews but an unthinkable incident made Tagore bitter about Americans once more. He never talked about it in the US but Dr Boyd G. Tucker, a professor sent by the Methodist Christian Mission in the US to teach at Santiniketan, and who was accompanying Tagore on the Canadian tour, angrily told the American journalists about what happened. Tagore's passport was misplaced and when he went to the Los Angeles immigration office on 18 April 1929 along with Dr Tucker and Andrews, the Nobel Laureate was asked if he knew how to read and write, if he had the money to return to his country, and so forth. The immigration officer was not impressed by the Poet's countenance which had so far swept Europeans and Americans off their feet.

The Poet redeemed his promise to lecture at Los Angeles the next day and cancelled his remaining American schedule. On his way back to Japan, he said to a Japanese interviewer that he had no rancour against the immigration officer who treated him as he would any Oriental coloured man and he expected no better.

With L.P. Jack, Principal, Manchester College, Oxford, during the Hibbert Lectures, 1930.

In the West for the last time

Oxford University invited Tagore to deliver the Hibbert Lectures in 1928. This was the first time the University invited an Asian for the lectures initiated in 1878 on an endowment from one Robert Hibbert (1770–1849) who wanted discourses on religion. Tagore had embarked on a ship on 12 May 1928 but returned from Colombo, too ill to make the voyage. The Hibbert lectures—'The Religion of Man' were delivered in May 1930. On this trip, Tagore took along with him a box of drawings and paintings for probable exhibitions in Europe and America. Tagore had no formal training in painting. During his Argentine stay:

> he played with erasures, following them from verse to verse with his pen, making lines that suddenly jumped into life out of this play: prehistoric monsters, birds, faces appeared. The cancelled mistakes in Tagore's poems gave birth to a world of forms that grinned, frowned or laughed at us in a mysterious and fascinating way.

This was how Ocampo described her first experience with Tagore's drawings, in her contribution to the Tagore centenary volume by Sahitya Akademi. Tagore developed this frenzied drawing and learning when Elmhirst sent him a special pen in 1925. Tagore himself explained his painting, in reply to Elmhirst's gift, as something that came from an excess of 'dream energy'. The problem was, in his obsession to draw and paint, he used whatever paper was handy to him—hardly a material ideal for preservation.

Tagore and his family reached Marseilles on 26 March 1930 but the Hibbert Lectures were scheduled in May. Enjoying the hospitality of M. Kahn, the rich banker who founded scholarships all over the world and was deeply interested in cultural activities and who had offered his resorts to Tagore earlier, the Poet spent a few days at Cape Martin near Monte Carlo and then proceeded to Paris. Andree Karpeles was already an established painter in Paris and knew all the important artists and authors there but organising an exhibition at short notice was beyond her power. Fortunately, Ocampo was in Europe in connection with her prospective magazine and publishing house. She was contacted; she immediately came down to Paris and installed the Poet in a suite of rooms in a hotel called Mozart Gardens. Karpeles was astounded to see the drawings and paintings. Ocampo was not too sure about their merit but when Paul Valery said they had to be exhibited, Ocampo, the newcomer to Paris, did what Karpeles or M. Kahn could not do—she organised the Tagore painting exhibition at Galarie Pigalle on 2 May, with the necessary publicity and press reviews prior and after the exhibition. The influence, power and energy that Ocampo displayed amazed even the billionaire banker M. Kahn.

Ocampo saw to it that the paintings were given a display to draw out their best. The rooms—one big and two small—were lit by invisible lights, grey velvet on the walls and the paintings could be seen from a distance, if one wished to. A staircase led to the cellar transformed to a steamer-deck, housing a bar. The paintings (125 of them) were well-selected, well-hung and well-isolated. People were coming before the scheduled opening at 3 p.m. and the crowd intensified more and more as Tagore appeared, clad in white, like a huge statue, seen from the stairs, overlooking the crowd of dwarfs, as Karpeles had remarked. The painter was surrounded quickly by Comtesse de Noailles in a long black skirt. She had written the introduction to the catalogue. The crowd stayed for a long time, seeing the pictures again and again. Some said that these paintings could not be a single man's work but the work of a whole people; some called it psychic painting; landscapes were compared with and preferred to Victor Hugo's landscapes; some compared him

With Comtesse Anna de Noailles and Victoria Ocampo, among others, at the opening of the Poet's painting exhibitions, Galarie Pigalle, Paris, 1930.

with Paul Gaugin. The exhibition time was till 6.30 p.m. but the crowd was so big and the rooms became so hot with the presence of so many visitors that Tagore retired to a little side-room. The exhibition was a grand success and Victoria Ocampo took all the credit to the great grief of Karpeles who could do nothing but admire. Her husband had been supplying special inks to Tagore before and after the exhibition and Karpeles was stunned to see her Gurudev pouring out paintings after paintings.

The Paris exhibition was followed by similar ones held at Birmingham (2 June), London (4 June), Berlin (16 July), Dresden (19 July), Copenhagen (9 August), Geneva (August–September), Moscow (17 September), Boston (30 October), New York (20 November). The paintings and drawings were reviewed, analysed, compared with this school of painting and that and such interpretations continue to be made even to this day. An interesting remark was made by the Painter when Karpeles asked before the first exhibition what he thought would be the reviewers' response. The viewers would be impressed if they were told that those were drawn 3,000 years ago, he said with a smile.

The Hibbert Lectures drew crowds, as never before, said Michael Sadler on behalf of the Oxford University and added, 'We shall never forget in Oxford the gift you have given us and the inspiration you have brought to us.'

Dr Sadler (1861–1943) knew Tagore when he came to India in 1917 as the chairman of the Calcutta University Commission to report on University education and suggest reforms. He was a friend of Rothenstein who introduced him to Tagore by a letter. Tagore entertained him with a musical evening at Jorasanko. Instead of asking Tagore to come over to Calcutta for his comments on Calcutta University, as the Sadler Commission asked others, Sadler went to Santiniketan to gather Tagore's views. The Commission's report was published in 1919, an important milestone in the history of Calcutta University.

In between the Hibbert Lectures, Tagore was asked by the Society of Friends to address their members, who were commonly called Quakers. This was the first time the Quakers asked somebody other than their members to preside over

their annual conference—the Society was formed by George Fox (1624–91), a religious leader. The British members objected to what Tagore called the repression conducted by the British Government on India—they were countered by others as well as Tagore.

After England, Tagore then went on to visit Germany once more and then Denmark and Switzerland. The regal receptions continued and leading thinkers continued to come and meet him. After staying in Geneva for about a month, Tagore made a fifteen-day visit to the Soviet Russia. He was warned against the Russian trip by his friends on ground of bad hotels, bad transport, and of course, bad ideology. Tagore refused to listen to his advisers and wanted to see for himself the transformation of men, if any, after the Bolshevik Revolution. He was invited by the Soviet Academy of Sciences in 1925 and the invitation continued to be renewed.

Above: Coming to the opening of the exhibition of his paintings, Moscow, 1930.
Below: At Frankfurt, 1930.
Facing page: The Poet with his paintings.

In Russia, Tagore did not leave an account of the visit to his companions but wrote it himself in detail—*Russiar Chithi* (Letters from Russia), which serially appeared in *Prabasi* during December 1930 and April 1931. The letters were contradictory. He praised the Soviet encouragement of mass education, cooperative agriculture and health system and he condemned the coercive method employed by the authorities to spread literacy, improve agriculture and uplift the economy of the country. It appears that Tagore was bitten in Italy and felt shy in Russia. He called the visit a pilgrimage, so overwhelmed was he to learn the transformation of a country in about a decade, but he remembered that he had to revoke his praises in Italy and hastily added that he was against all types of regimentation. In fact, his German and American friends were upset by his eulogy of the system which he expressed in his interviews and he was dubbed as the most effective propagandist of Soviet Russia. The last letter of *Russiar Chithi* was a condemnation of dictatorship in Russia. He himself translated the last letter, 'The Soviet System', which was published in *The Modern Review* in September 1931. Funnily, the Government of India overlooked the serialisation of the Bengali letters and even Tagore's English 'The Soviet System' but when Sasadhar Sinha began translating the letters in English, in 1934, taking up the last letter first, the editor of *The Modern Review* was ordered not to publish the letters any more. When the anomaly was pointed out in the British Parliament, the reason given was that *Prabasi* being a vernacular journal was not as important as the English monthly which had an international readership. The reason for the ban was not because of Tagore's pro-Soviet stance but for his condemnation of the English rule in India. *Russiar Chithi* continues to be quoted by Leftists and anti-Leftists, picking up extracts according to their convenience.

Tagore concluded his 1930 tour by a fifth visit to the US—during 9 October and 13 December. There was no lack of efforts on the part of Tagore's American friends—the press very attentive to what Tagore said or did; he talked on the radio; his public appearances were crowded; an interview was shown in movie newsreels; and President

Left: In Europe, 1930. Facing page: At the Pioneers' Commune.

Herbert Hoover met him on 29 November. But Tagore's mistrust of reporters who sometimes misquoted him to his annoyance, his previous criticisms of American greed and commercialism and his praises of the Soviet system rankled in a section of Americans. He fell grievously ill and some of his engagements were cancelled. When he resumed his lectures, an interviewer bitterly commented, 'For a man so old as he

Left: The Poet, lip-read by Helen Keller, in New York, 1930. Right: With Einstein, New York, 1930. Facing page: At Teheran, where his birthday was observed on 7 May 1932.

is and so ill, he has been making too many farewell appearances like an attention-loving prima donna who cannot tear herself away from the limelight.'

The interviewer unconsciously echoed Rolland, who was not at all ecstatic about Tagore's paintings. He came down to Geneva where Tagore stayed before his Russian visit and was irritated to hear Tagore talking about the 500 paintings and drawings he had already completed (he would create about 2,500 eventually) and the appreciations he received in Europe. Rolland was pained that Tagore gloated over his newly adopted art while his country convulsed with the Civil Disobedience movement and thousands were imprisoned.

It is true in 1930 and 1931, India was at a boiling point—Gandhi had launched Civil Disobedience on 12 March 1930; marched from Sabarmati to Dandi on 6 April to make salt, defying official ban; the Chattagram armoury was raided on 18 April; Hindu–Muslim riots had broken out once more. But Rolland forgot that Tagore was not a political leader and he had no faith in Gandhi's political movements. Ocampo took offence when Rolland was alleged to have said that Tagore was mixing with society people during his European tour. In her contribution to the Tagore centenary volume she challenged Rolland to prove his complaint. She was with Tagore in Paris and she knew whom Tagore met. She named Andre Gide (1869–1951), Paul Valery (1871–1945), Jean Cassou (1897– ?)

and George Henri Riviera (a museum curator who organised Tagore's exhibition in Paris). Were they society people? Was Anna Noailles (1876–1933) just a countess?

In America, Tagore met Robert Frost (1874–1963), Will Durant (1885–1981), Helen Keller, Albert Einstein (both for the second time) and Sinclair Lewis (1885–1951) who won the literature Nobel in 1931. Will Durant presented Tagore with a copy of his just published book, *The Case for India*, which was not banned in India, but the Indian booksellers ordering copies of the book never got their copies. Tagore reviewed the book in *The Modern Review* of March 1931 and apprehended that the book would be banned in India. He expressed gratitude to the writer who saw the miserable condition of India with his own eyes, and unlike most tourists:

> ...he has explored the history of our misfortune. Will Durant has treated us with the respect due to human beings, acknowledging our right to serious consideration ...I am specially thankful to him for the service he has rendered to the English nation by largely quoting from its own members condemning the British policy where it has cruelly betrayed its responsibility to India...

In his presentation copy of his book to Tagore, Durant inscribed the words, 'You alone are sufficient reason why India should be free.'

Back in India, on 26 September 1931, he addressed more than a 100,000-strong assembly at the foot of the Ochterloney Monument in Calcutta,

Above: At a mammoth gathering in front of Ochterloney Monument, Calcutta, 1931; photographed by Kanchan Mukhopadhyay. Facing page: At the tomb of Hafiz, Shiraj, 1932.

warning the British rulers that however mighty they were they could not last if they continued to lose trust in them from their subjects. The occasion was the killing of two prisoners, Santosh Mitra and Tarakeswar Datta, by jail guards at Hijli Jail in Midnapore, Bengal, where hundreds of Bengali youths were languishing in inhuman condition. Tagore was overwhelmed by greetings from brave Bengali young men, imprisoned in Buxa Jail on the Bhutan border, on the occasion of his seventieth birthday. He wrote back a fifteen-line poem greeting the youths who were defying death to seek freedom for their countrymen.

Tagore made his last foreign tour (Ceylon was not considered foreign then) in 1932 when Reza Shah Pahlavi, the King of Iran, invited him. He dared a long aeroplane journey by the Royal Dutch Airlines, which took immense care for the safety of their august flier—the aeroplanes then were primitive. This was the second flight for Tagore, who had made a short hop on 16 April 1921 from London to Paris.

The plane, after landing at Jodhpur and Karachi reached Jask aerodrome the next day and after a night halt arrived at Bushire on 14 April—a three-day journey from Calcutta. Tagore went from Bushire to Shiraj by road on 17 April, Ispahan on 23 April, Tehran on 29 April. He stayed at Tehran for two weeks. From there he went to Baghdad by rail on 16 May where he stayed as the guest of King Faisal. From Baghdad he again took the flight back to Calcutta on 3 June.

Tagore wrote the tour experience in 'Parasya-bhraman' in *Bichitra* from August 1932 to April 1933 in consideration of around Rs 1,000 which filled his ever-emptying coffer, even if in small measure. Tagore was grateful to the King of Iran that he could personally pay homage at the tombs of Hafiz and Sa'adi. Tagore was familiar with Hafiz from his father's reciting of Hafiz poetry in Persian. He was by this time accustomed to royal receptions, which awed his companions, but what impressed him most was the practice of Islam without any communal hatred. He would have to painfully compare the openness of the Middle East Islam with the orthodox and aggressive Islam in India.

The Poet at the Calcutta Congress, 1917, reading 'India's Prayer', as painted by Gaganendranath Tagore. Collection: Rathindranath Tagore.

In the thick of national problems

In 1933, Rabindranath received a letter from Subhas Chandra Bose, who was in jail, requesting the Poet for an introductory letter to distinguished people in Europe where he would be going for medical treatment. The Poet obliged but Subhas tore off the letter as he thought it was too impersonal and formal. The letter was 'My friend Subhas Chandra Bose is going for his treatment. I earnestly hope my friends will be kind to him and help him.'

Rabindranath had reasons to be cold and formal. In 1928, he did not view Subhas kindly, when the latter fought for the Hindu community against the Sadharan Brahmo Samaj which ran the City College of Calcutta. In January 1928, the boarders of Rammohun Roy hostel worshipped the idol of Saraswati, defying the hostel superintendent's order that idolatry was not allowed in a Brahmo institution. Seven students were fined and several rumoured to be soon expelled and rusticated. Students claimed that the hostel building was built and run at the expense of Calcutta University which was not a Brahmo institution. All the students of the College boycotted classes demanding the revocation of fines imposed. When the College authorities did not relent, guardians of students began to take away their wards with transfer certificates. The income of the College drastically fell as tuition fees were the major source of revenue. Matters took a worse turn when a Hindu benefactress who lent Rs 100,000 to City College to construct a new building was annoyed with the Brahmos and demanded the principal and interest pay-back immediately.

At this critical time, Rabindranath bailed City College out of this pecuniary crisis with a loan of Rs 125,000 from the Visva-Bharati fund. But the exodus of Hindu students continued and teachers and employees of the College had to agree to substantial pay-cuts for the survival of the College. The Hindu students were led by Subhas who believed that the Hindu community should not bow down to the Brahmo orthodoxy and must be granted the freedom to observe their Hindu rites. Rabindranath wrote an angry essay on this confrontation in *Prabasi* and translated it for *The Modern Review*, which also, being edited by a Brahmo, Ramananda, took a strong stand against the Hindu students. Rabindranath made an oblique reference to Subhas when he said in his essay, 'Would it amount to a cultivation of the spirit of Swaraj which is to give legitimate freedom of self-expression to the mutual differences in the communities that come under it?'

In 1928, Subhas was the leader of one faction of the Bengal Provincial Congress Committee. He had been a disciple of Chittaranjan Das, contrary to the expectations of Rabindranath. Chittaranjan, once a favourite visitor to the Jorasanko Tagore family and very close to Rabindranath, was drifting away from the Tagore associates. He launched a monthly magazine which preached that Bengali literature should grow on the soil of Bengal and not on Western shores. The magazine, *Narayan*, ran for nine years from 1914 to 1923 and when it folded up, Subhas regretted the closure from Mandalay Jail in a letter to his elder brother Sarat Chandra Basu (1889–1950). Sarat was a member of the Swarajya Party, the breakaway group from Congress under Chittaranjan's leadership. Subhas wrote that *Narayan* needed to exist as an antidote to *Sabuj Patra*, which was the mouthpiece of so-called progressive writers. In this *Narayan–Sabuj Patra* confrontation, there was a literary debate on indigenous realism against Bengali writers' opening up to Western literature and thoughts.

Rabindranath defended the *Sabuj Patra* group against the *Narayan* group, and held that *Narayan* writers had a distorted view of realism. Politically, Chittaranjan strongly denounced Rabindranath's internationalism, embraced Gandhi's Non-Cooperation movement and gave up his legendary career as a barrister. Chittaranjan was not only a Bengali political leader but he was recognised as an all-India leader whom Gandhi had managed to convert to his political strategies, to the great surprise of contemporary political observers. The untimely death of Chittaranjan weakened the political leadership of Bengal.

With George Bernard Shaw, London, 1931.

In December 1928, Subhas attracted wide attention by organising mass participation in the Congress annual session in Calcutta. In 1930, he was elected the mayor of Calcutta. Rabindranath requested Subhas that N. Takagaki, a leading Japanese expert in judo, be appointed by Calcutta Corporation. Takagaki had been invited to Santiniketan to teach boys and specially girls judo in self-defence and he taught students there for two years. But Santiniketan was unable to bear his expenses. Rabindranath thought that martial art was essential for the weak-bodied Bengali youths. Strangely, Subhas did not even respond to Rabindranath's request.

In August 1934, Subhas again wrote to Rabindranath from Vienna with another request. He had just finished writing his book, *The Indian Struggle*, and wanted a foreword to be written either by Bernard Shaw or H.G. Wells. Would the Poet please ask Shaw or Wells? What he added to his request angered the Poet. Subhas wrote that he was not asking the Poet, as he might not agree to write a foreword to a political treatise; nor was he asking Romain Rolland as he was an admirer of Gandhi and for that matter even Rabindranath himself was an admirer of Gandhi in spite of all his criticisms. Rabindranath wrote back that he knew Shaw too well and dared not ask him to write it. He added further that Gandhi, in spite of his politics, had a moral force which had given a new life-force to the country.

Early that year, Gandhi's followers were taken aback when Gandhi ascribed the severe earthquake that killed and damaged vast parts of Bihar to divine chastisement for the sin of untouchability. Tagore issued a public statement that it was unfortunate that Gandhi should believe a natural disaster to be an expression of divine anger, more so because Gandhi was too readily accepted by a large section of Indians. Tagore understood that Gandhi used the occurrence of earthquake to instill fear into people who practise untouchability. This type of expediency, Tagore said, would never work. He had strongly condemned Gandhi's Khilafat strategy in 1921. Though he appreciated that the end, being Hindu–Muslim unity, might have been noble, the means was entirely wrong, the Caliphate being an outdated and reactionary regime. Similarly, Tagore ridiculed the promise that Gandhi would bring Swaraj in one year if every countryman spun yarns on the *charkha*. He was not taken in by Gandhi's explanation that the masses needed motivation with such promises.

Gandhi and Tagore were poles apart in their social and political beliefs, not just in their daily mode of living, but Gandhi continued to reverentially listen to Gurudev, whom he had called 'The Great Sentinel' in *Young Indi*a of 13 October 1921 and Tagore continued to call him Mahatma in spite of his dubious politics. The chasm continued to widen as Tagore was seized with his idea of Visva-Bharati and humanism that cut across national frontiers. Subhas knew all this but also believed that he would not get Tagore on his side in his fight with Gandhi.

Tagore might not have accepted earthquake as a divine dispensation, but he was all support to Gandhi's sustained protest and agitation against untouchability. A ticklish situation arose when Tucker, a Tagore associate, argued against Gandhi who was demanding entry for the untouchables into the Guruvayyur Temple in Travancore. Tucker said the untouchables should not care about temples run by upper-caste Hindus but build their own temples. In this Gandhi–Tucker controversy, Tagore did not quite approve of Tucker's stand. If millions could be united on their own, there should not have been any problem but the cruel fact was, millions of illiterates were burdened with century-old faiths and superstitions and when they wanted entry into temples, they should be encouraged. The Santiniketan prayer hall was open to all faiths but not every priest or trustee of numerous temples could be expected to be so open-hearted.

On 15 February 1933, Tagore participated in a large gathering at Sriniketan demanding abolition of untouchability and supporting Ranga Ayer's Bill introduced in the central legislative council. For the untouchables, Tagore sent a translation of a poem on sweepers by Satyendranath Datta (1882–1922), a poet and an ardent admirer of Tagore, to Gandhi's periodical *Harijan*.

Facing page: At Udayan, Santiniketan, 1936.

In that February 1933, Rabindranath wrote a play, *Chandalika*, adapting a story from Nepalese Buddhist literature. A long time ago, Satishchandra Ray (1882–1904), a talented young graduate who had joined the

GBS and Tagore

When *The Golden Book of Tagore* was planned, writers and painters all over the world were contacted for their contributions. George Bernard Shaw (1856–1950), exasperated by continuous requests, blurted out to W. Rothenstein (quoted in *Since Fifty* by W.R.):

> To the devil with these Nitwitiketant idiots! I spend half the year telling them to put my name to anything they like that will please Tagore, and the other half telling you to tell them so.

Rothenstein also wrote about Tagore's meeting with Shaw and his wife at a dinner given by Rothenstein in 1912. Rothenstein was not present at the dinner. He wrote, 'My wife told me that Shaw was outrageous, while his wife was all admiration...' 'Old Blue-beard,' said Shaw to mine while he was leaving, 'how many wives has he got, I wonder!'

It might appear that Shaw had a poor opinion of Tagore. More so because in 1919, Shaw named a poet in one of his playlets, Stupendranath Begorr. But Shaw was unpredictable. Rathindranath wrote in *On the Edges of Time* about two meetings in 1912 thus:

> One evening we were all invited to a dinner given by Miss May Sinclair. It was a fairly large gathering of well-known writers. Father was seated next to Bernard Shaw. Conversation flowed around the table with sparkling brilliance, but to the surprise of everybody Shaw hardly opened his mouth. Father had to do all the talking. We were told Shaw had never kept so silent anywhere before. Our next meeting with him was at the Queen's Hall where we went to hear the violinist Heifetz. At the end of the concert, as we were making our exit through the jostling crowd, somebody suddenly caught hold of Father and turning him round quietly announced, 'Do you remember me? I am Bernard Shaw.'

After these two meetings, Shaw developed a friendship with Tagore. The Shaws invited Tagore to a lunch on 24 May 1913 but Tagore could not go because of his scheduled visit to Oxford. Shaw's wife met Tagore several times, attended his lectures and the performance of *The Post Office*. Shaw regretted that he could not attend the send-off dinner to Tagore who left England for India on 4 September 1913.

He wrote to Mrs Grace Rhys, who and her husband Ernest Rhys gave that farewell dinner, on 22 August from outside London:

> I am afraid there is no chance of my being in London on the 26th. It is most unfortunate that Mr Tagore should take his departure at a moment when there is nobody in London to bid him farewell. He has made an extraordinary number of deeply interested friends during his visit; and I am one of them.

There was a rumour spread by leading newspapers in India that Shaw would be visiting Santiniketan in 1927 winter. Tagore wrote a letter on 1 July 1927 to Shaw that he was being assailed from all sides with the question if the news was true. He concluded the letter with the memory of his days with Shaw in 1913:

> Please tell Mrs Shaw how I still remember the occasion when years ago we had our conversation at your house in London and how I shall appreciate the opportunity if it does come again to have it revived in another environment.

Shaw sent back a telegram on 31 July, 'Alas a poetic fiction invented by someone who knew our regard for you.'

The two met again in London in 1931 at a luncheon which *The Spectator* gave for Tagore in Hyde Park Hotel. They had a long talk. Unfortunately the talk was not recorded, neither was the meeting when Tagore visited Shaw's house on 29 May 1913.

There was another chance of the two meeting again in India. Shaw was on a cruise round the world and reached Bombay in 1933. Tagore invited Shaw by a telegram. Shaw regretted that his age and health came in the way of his landing. 'My only regret is that I shall be unable to visit you. My consolation is that the present situation in India will not bear being talked about. I understand it only too well.'

Jokingly he wrote that he had stepped ashore in Bombay for a few hours and wandered about the streets and such temples as were open to European untouchables. India was full of news about Gandhi's untouchability movement at that time.

When Tagore died, Shaw suggested that a portrait of Tagore should be displayed in the National Portrait Gallery in London. Sir Kenneth Clark, director of the gallery, agreed to hang the portraits of Tagore painted by Sir W. Rothenstein and Sir Muirhead Bone.

With Sarojini Naidu (on his right) who arranged a Tagore week in Bombay, 1933.

Santiniketan school, wrote a poem on the same theme—'Chandali'. His Gurudev, pleased with the poem, noticed a dramatic element in it and asked him to make a play out of the poem. He tried but could not master the art of drama. Thirty years later, Gurudev gave the dramatic form. He recited the play at the Madan Theatre on 12, 13 and 15 September with Santiniketan students. *Chandalika* was transformed into a dance-drama in 1938, at the request from his daughter-in-law, Pratima, and was staged at Chhaya Cinema Hall on 18, 19 and 20 March 1938. Rabindranath was present for the performance on 19 March, ignoring all requests from his relatives who were scared that the ailing Poet would again fall ill. Subhas Chandra Bose, the then Congress President, sat with the Poet among the audience. Another revised version of the dance-drama was presented by Santiniketan students on 9 and 10 February 1939 at Sree Cinema Hall.

Rabindranath had earlier written another prose drama, *Kaler Yatra* in 1932 and dedicated the play to the novelist Sarat Chandra Chattopadhyay.

It was an enlarged form of *Rathayatra,* published in *Prabasi* in 1923, in which the Poet acknowledged his debt to Pramathanath Bisi (1901–85), a Santiniketan student, then a teacher there, who had written a play on a similar subject. Pramatha was inspired by an incident at a village near Santiniketan.

The villagers were stuck during a Ratha festival when they failed to drag the chariot due to uneven ground and heaviness of the vehicle. A group of Santhal men and women were passing by. Pramatha had asked the villagers if the Santhals (belonging to the depressed classes) could lend a hand. The distressed villagers chose to ignore class prejudices. The Santhals joyfully lent their might and the chariot moved. Gurudev edited and revised Pramatha's play and asked him to forward it to *Prabasi* under Pramatha's name. The play after the Poet's revision was transformed beyond recognition and the disciple was too proud to claim the authorship.

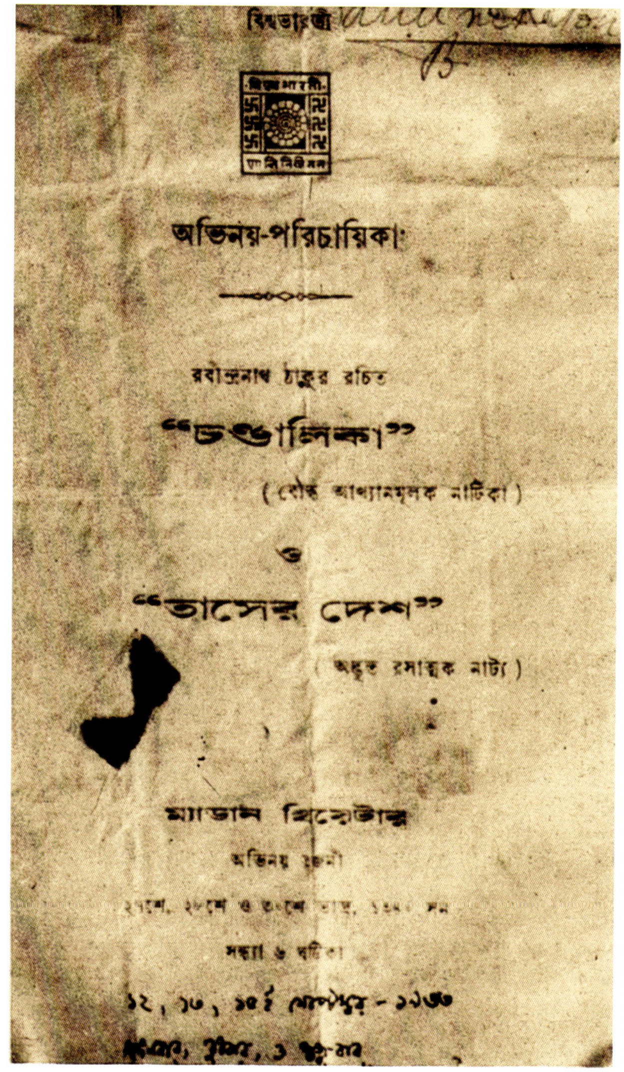
বিশ্বভারতী

অভিনয়-পরিচায়িকা

রবীন্দ্রনাথ ঠাকুর রচিত

“চণ্ডালিকা”

(বৌদ্ধ আখ্যানমূলক নাটিকা)

ও

“তাসের দেশ”

(অদ্ভুত রসাত্মক নাট্য)

ম্যাডান থিয়েটার

অভিনয় রজনী

সন্ধ্যা ৬ ঘটিকা

Announcement of the staging of Chandalika *and* Tasher Desh *at the Madan Theatre in 1933.*

In 1933, another play, *Tasher Desh* was written by the Poet and almost immediately staged at the Madan Theatre, where *Chandalika* was recited by the Poet. The play was based on the theme of a slender story, 'Ekti Ashade Galpa', written and published by the Poet in 1892. The two-act play was enlarged into a four-act play in 1938 and dedicated to Subhas Chandra Bose. These revisions and enlargements of plays were due to many factors—artistic, practical (to suit available actors) or just the Poet's fancy. The reason of revising *Tasher Desh* was, according to the inmates of Santiniketan, a bit amusing. Tagore noticed a boy getting too close to a girl during the enactment of the play at Santiniketan. He changed the sequence and dialogues to prevent this undesired proximity. He enlarged it to drive the point home to the actors! Maybe the story was true. But the Poet, on his own admission, added more songs to the play when he found the audience at Bombay, where it was staged in November 1933, unable to respond to Bengali dialogues, and on the following night, he was happy to note the audience enjoying the dance and songs, which were added overnight, and at the same time grasping the import of the drama.

Sarojini Naidu and Tagore

The Spectator in its 15 February 1913 edition wrote:

> Our two volumes of Indian poetry represent, the one on occidental culture working in an Oriental atmosphere, the other the pure inspiration of the East.

The first one was the *Bird of Time* by Sarojini Naidu (1879–1949) and the other was *Gitanjali* by Tagore. Edmund Gosse wrote an appreciative introduction to Sarojini's volume. She was made a fellow of the Royal Society of Literature in 1914, the honour denied to Tagore in 1912, due to Gosse's malice.

Sarojini, though born of Bengali parents, did not learn Bengali as she was brought up in Hyderabad and English was her first language. When she presented Tagore her *Broken Wing* in 1917, Tagore wrote to her in August 1917:

> Shall I make a confession to you? Once again while reading your poems in your last book I became only too conscious of my own broken wing in my flight in the alien sky of English diction. You make me jealous of your lyrical ease and grace in every movement of your thought among foreign words that are so friendly to you.

Sarojini, however, opted for an active political life and she was the first Indian woman to be president of the INC. She was well known for her oratory and her hearty laughter even in grim situations.

Tagore wrote this letter on 3 December 1933:

> You are great. Once I thought that you were frivolous as I am. I still hope I was not wrong but there is another side of your

> character, and I repeat once again that you are great. You have helped me as no one else could have done but what is still more important to me is that I have come close to you and known you. You have amazing gifts which would have made me envious but I have loved you and that has saved me. I am afraid my language sounds absurdly sentimental, but I do not care. I expose myself to your delightful laughter...

The gratitude was for the Tagore week in Bombay organised by Sarojini in the last week of November 1933. Tagore was accompanied by a team of forty-five students of Santiniketan who presented *Sapmochan* and *Tasher Desh,* led by Dinendranath Tagore. Tagore's pictures were exhibited with the assistance of Nandalal Bose and Surendranath Kar. Tagore delivered two public lectures. At the back of all these was Sarojini, who left her own home and stayed with Tagore at the palatial mansion of Sir Dorabji Tata to fend off visitors who were eager to see the Poet. Rani Chanda, who was with the Poet, remembers how the tight schedule made the Poet tired—he had to receive the mayor of Bombay, the vice-chancellor, the chief justice, the president of Bombay Provincial Congress and others sometime or other. A cigarette company arranged a visit of the Poet to its factory. When Sarojini learnt this, she exclaimed, 'What nonsense! The Poet will not go.' The company officials were perplexed—the managers from all over India had assembled at Bombay to welcome their distinguished guest. But a firm Sarojini sent Anil Kumar Chanda, the poet's secretary and Rani as substitutes, who were embarrassed to get a royal welcome by the factory owners.

The Tagore week fetched Visva-Bharati Rs 65,000.

Dance-drama, Chitrangada, *Calcutta, 1936, at New Empire, Calcutta.*

The last flourishes

In 1934, the Poet took his troupe to Ceylon. By this time, Tagore's dance-drama repertoire was rich: *Nabin* (a music drama written in 1931 to celebrate spring), *Sapmochan* (1931), *Chandalika* (1933), *Tasher Desh* (1933), *Sravangatha* (a music drama composed in 1934 to celebrate the rains). For Ceylon, he chose *Sapmochan*. *Raja* (The King of the Dark Chamber) was shortened into *Arupratan* (1919), which was converted to the dance-drama, *Sapmochan*, with a new story added to it. This dance-drama was singular in the sense that none of the songs used were written for this drama—nineteen songs in the first version, ten songs added in the second version and ten more songs added in the final revised form—all culled from previous compositions. It was staged in many places: Jorasanko, Lucknow, Santiniketan, Bombay (where it earned more than Rs 14,000), Madras (where the reception was cold) and Colombo.

During the sea voyage from Calcutta to Colombo, the Poet drafted a short story, which after many revisions, turned into a novel—*Char Adhyay* (Four Chapters)—in 1934. It is not clear why this political novel was written but it was a clear shocker to the Bengali revolutionaries, who were shown in their moral degeneracy which caused their downfall. Surprisingly enough, its author thought the novel was anti-British and worried that

Dance-drama, Tasher Desh, *Calcutta, 1938.*

it would be proscribed in the country. He asked Amiya Chakravarti (1901–86), who was once his literary secretary and at that time staying at Oxford, to quickly translate it and release the novel abroad. But Amiya's translation did not satisfy him and the translating job got protracted. Ultimately, he released the Bengali novel, and faced from his own people a barrage of criticisms. The released novel had an introductory section in which the Poet said that it was Brahmabandhab Upadhyay himself who had repented to the Poet that he had a moral downfall. The assertion was challenged, more so because Brahmabandhab refused to cooperate with the police and died in prison in 1907. The preface was withdrawn in the next edition which came out quickly because the novel had a brisk sale, for whatever reasons. The author again had to issue an explanation and asked readers to treat the novel as a love story—the Swadesi agitation merely forming the background. The author hoped that the lyrical prose in which the story was presented would redeem the novel but the controversy about its political purpose continues to this day. The English translation, by Amiya Chakrabarti, was released in an American magazine but made no splash in the West. This was the author's last novel.

Two other novels, both slender in volume, came out earlier. The magazine *Bichitra* was the vehicle for serialisation of both the novels, as it paid more than other magazines. *Dui Bon* (Two Sisters) was published in December 1932–February 1933 and *Malancha* (The Orchard) in

September–December 1933. Both the novels explored marital relations at the advent of a new woman. *Malancha* had the ignored wife explode at the climactic point, a rare moment in Rabindranath's novels.

Ever on the lookout for earning a handful of cash, the Poet accepted an offer in 1932 from Calcutta University to hold the honorary post of Ramtanu Lahiri Professorship. The understanding was that he would be delivering a few lectures at his convenience in two years and would be paid Rs 5,000. Only two lectures were delivered—in February 1934 and 16 July 1934. Earlier also he had accepted special university readership of Calcutta University in 1923; at that time he had given three lectures. All these, needless to say, pertained to literary criticism. Additionally, in 1934, he gave three Kamala lectures, which were instituted in memory of the deceased daughter of Asutosh Mookerji. He was also the first recipient of the Jagattarini gold medal which was instituted in memory of Asutosh's mother.

Asutosh was helpful to Rabindranath whenever he could but Rabindranath was a bit cold in his relation to the ex-vice-chancellor. In 1937, when Syamaprasad Mookerji (1901–53), Asutosh's son, was vice-chancellor of Calcutta University, the Poet agreed to deliver the convocation address. He did it, not at the Senate Hall, the usual venue of the convocation, but at the Presidency College lawn, to accommodate more than 5,000 guests. And this was the first time that the Calcutta University convocation address was delivered in Bengali. Perhaps the college lawn kindled his memory. To the surprise of everyone, he said, he was once an external student of Presidency College, but just for one day. He could not bear being ragged by classmates and bade goodbye to college education. In the convocation address, Tagore stressed the importance of teaching, both at the lowest and the highest level, in one's mother-tongue. His sustained promotion of mother-tongue as the medium of instruction bore fruit, but after his death. He, however, was happy to see the acceptance of mother-tongue as the medium of instruction up to Matriculation in Calcutta University, which was belatedly implemented, following the Sadler Commission recommendation, in 1940.

From 1932, Rabindranath must have felt that his stock of poetry was diminishing. The titles given to the collection of verses published henceforward seem to suggest that fear: *Parisesh* (Remnants) 1932, *Punascha* (Postscript) 1932, *Sesh Saptak* (The Last Melodies) 1935. Prose

At the housewarming ceremony of Udichi, Santiniketan, 1938.

poems, written sporadically since *Lipika* (Short Writings) 1922, found their final form in *Punascha* which was dedicated in memory of his grandson, Nitindra, son of Mira. Nitindra was studying printing and publishing in Germany. His parents were estranged; father Nagendra living in London and mother Mira at Santiniketan. Nitindra (1922–32) died of tuberculosis, medicines for which disease were yet to be discovered. Nagendra instituted a Nitu memorial bed in the Pearson Hospital at Santiniketan. Pearson, who acted as the Poet's secretary in Tagore's overseas tour in 1920–21, after being interned in England for writing a book, referred earlier, had resumed work at Santiniketan. He had donated the royalties from another of his books, *Santiniketan: The Bolpur School of Rabindranath Tagore*, 1917, to add facilities in the primitive hospital at the Ashram. Over the years, his admirers raised funds to improve the hospital which was named Pearson Hospital. Pearson died in a train accident in Italy in 1923.

Rabindranath reverted to metrical poems, saying in jest that he had to prove that he had not lost control of meters. He published more volumes of verse—*Vithika* (Boulevard) 1935, *Khapchhara* (Disjointed) 1937, *Chadar Chhabi* (Pictures in Rhymes) 1937, *Prantik* (On the Margin) 1938, *Senjuti*

(Evening Lamp) 1938, *Prahasini* (The Smiling One) 1939, *Akashpradip* (Beacon Lamp) 1939, *Nabajatak* (New-Born) 1940, *Sanai* (Wooden Flute) 1940, *Rogsayyay* (On Sick-Bed) 1940, *Arogya* (Recovery) 1941, *Janmadine* (On Birthday) 1941. In between he had produced two other volumes of prose poems, *Patraput* (Pot Made of Leaves) 1936 and *Syamali* (The Girl Syamali) 1936. His last poems were collected in *Sesh Lekha* (Last Writings) and *Chhada* (Doggerel) and published in 1941, after the Poet's death.

The 1930s were, however, the troubled times for Bengal. Police repressions were rampant to teach revolutionaries a lesson. The Bengal Congress suffered from factional fights and the only leader, Subhas, was abroad for medical treatment. Political stability worsened when the depressed classes in Bengal as well as of the whole country demanded a separate electorate to which the British Parliament gave consent. In protest, Gandhi undertook a fast unto death in the Yeravada Jail at Poona in September 1932. B.R. Ambedkar (1891–1956), the leader of

Gandhi and Tagore at Santiniketan, February 1940.

the depressed classes, relented after national pressure but wrested from Gandhi more seats for the depressed classes, of course within the Hindu electorate. Tagore had rushed to Poona to persuade Gandhi to give up the fast but before he reached, Gandhi agreed to what was called the Poona Pact under which Ambedkar gave up the demand for separate electorate but obtained more seats. Tagore did not realise the implication of the Pact which hurt Bengal most where the caste Hindus were sidelined under the Pact. Back in Calcutta, when he was explained the situation, he wrote to Gandhi to reconsider the Pact. However, both Gandhi and later the Secretary of State for India replied to Tagore that political parties had to resolve themselves how to solve the problem.

Tagore could do nothing but address a meeting at the Town Hall on 15 July 1936 against the communal award and the reforms proposed in the 1935 reforms bill which came into effect in 1937. Tagore was continuously frustrated by Gandhi's political strategies, particularly his fasts, which he called the moral tyranny of Gandhi. The blatantly unfair way Gandhi dislodged Subhas from the presidentship of the Congress in 1939 pained Tagore the most. Bengal politics was also in a dire mess—not all Bengali leaders were fond of Subhas. Earlier, on 21 January 1939, Rabindranath had addressed Subhas, in the mango-grove of Santiniketan, as the leader of the nation. Rabindranath himself convened a meeting at Jorasanko in 1939 asking all the Bengali journalists not to quarrel among themselves and accept Subhas as Bengal's leader. The anti-Subhas coterie raised a proviso—if there was disagreement on any point, the Poet must mediate. The Poet was irritated and called it a day. He then onwards wanted to increasingly keep himself aloof from political discussions.

On 10 September 1937, the Poet was seated in his chair in the evening at Santiniketan when he was stricken with a virulent infection behind one of his ears, medically termed erysipelas, and lost consciousness for forty-eight hours. There was no telephone connection in Santiniketan. It took time for medical doctors from Calcutta, led by Nilratan Sircar (1861–1943), to arrive. They sat by the Poet for several days. Recovering from the comatose condition, on the fifth day, Rabindranath, propped up on pillows, painted a landscape—a dark wood with faint yellow light breaking through the darkness. On 25 September he wrote the first poem of *Prantik*.

Facing page: The Poet at Santiniketan in 1938.

The Poet claimed that he did not feel uneasy when he lost consciousness, nor did he feel any distress when he regained consciousness. But he developed prostate and kidney problems which would trouble him for the last four years of life. The stately figure got bent, broad shoulders stooped. Rani Chanda (1912–97), wife of Anilkumar Chanda (1906–76), his secretary during the last years, herself a painter and writer, writes in her notes on the Poet's conversations:

> 01 January 1938
>
> He ambled up in the afternoon to the garden in the west of Konark (one of the tiny buildings the Poet had lived in). He talked for a long time, sitting in the garden. On return, the cobbled path at one spot sloped downwards with constant rainwater falling from the roof. He stepped on the spot, stumbled and somehow recovered himself. He walks so rapidly with stooping shoulders, one fears that he would fall down any moment. I remonstrated and told him he should walk with a supporting help. Affectionately, he placed his hand on my shoulders and said, 'You want me to walk with a support? Where should I find Him (or Her?) on whom I could depend?...I am the blessed son of the green earth. I am attached more to the green soil. Buildings are not for me. I want to belong to this mud house (he was dwelling then in Syamali, a mud hut, built in 1935), one day I shall blend into the soil—that will be natural. But let me first get intimate with the house.' (Author's translation).

The nomad in him did not allow him to rest at one place however frail he was. The intense summer heat of the Birbhum District, where Santiniketan was located, was another reason why he had to flee to Kalimpong, a hill station near Darjeeling and Mungpoo near Kalimpong, five times since 1938. His unstable health could not prevent him from attending

At the foundation-stone laying ceremony, Mahajati Sadan, Calcutta, 1939; Subhas Chandra Bose on the microphone.

the inauguration of Mahajati Sadan in August 1939 at Calcutta. The building was planned by Subhas Chandra Bose to be a centre of nation-building and the proposed building was named by the Poet. Neither could he be prevented from the inauguration of an exhibition at Suri in February 1940 or an exhibition at Bankura and a maternity hospital there in March 1940 or earlier in December 1939, addressing an august assembly at Midnapore where a Vidyasagar memorial was constructed.

Neither did cease his creative activities—eleven books of verse, two dance-dramas, two books of essays and two books of short stories. A special mention needs to be made of *Visvaparichay* (Introducing the Universe), 1937. This was, of course, initiated before he blacked out. He had asked one of the science teachers at Santiniketan to write a popular book on contemporary researches in the physical sciences. The teacher submitted his first draft to the Poet who took it to Almorah, where he was going, to escape the summer in the plains. When he returned with the revision, the teacher was stunned by the simple way the intricate subject was presented by the Poet. None of the jargons, none of the details of his prolix treatise, none of his sum-ups—hard to understand by lay readers—were there but all the important aspects of neo-physics were presented in lucid Bengali. The science teacher hardly knew that Gurudev was well versed in contemporary researches in physics. Gurudev said in jest that modern science was of utmost urgency in the land of Mayavad.

With Jawaharlal Nehru, Santiniketan, 1939.

Rani writes on the Poet's talk on 10 March 1939:

> I am really surprised, I can't even imagine how Mahatmaji goes on fast, breaks his fast, takes little time to regain energy and goes to Delhi to quarrel. And then he will go here, there and who knows where. My God, it is much easier to write songs (Author's translation).

It does appear song-writing was easy for him. That year, the Poet had said that it was not possible for him to write any more songs for the rain festival, *Varshamangal*. But Sailajaranjan Majumdar (1900–92), the then principal of Sangitbhavan (the department of music), made him write as many as fifteen songs, with a rare persistence. He was not happy with the old rain songs, which were being sung too often. Sometimes he wanted a song in *Behag raga*, sometimes in baul mode —how could a rain festival be complete without a baul? And also in *Bhairabi, Iman, Mallar, Kafi, Kanara*—could these be dispensed with? The Poet was surprised to hear the demand for *Bagesri*—was it possible to render *Bagesri* in a rain song? Yes, it was, the principal pointed out that the Poet did compose a rain song in *Bagesri*. A smiling Poet met his demand. Fifteen out of the sixteen songs sung in that *Varshamangal* were new; after fifteen songs, the Poet called it a day. The disappointed (actually ecstatic, to get so many new songs) singers made do with an old one to make it sixteen—they wanted sixteen to round up the sixteen parts of the moon.

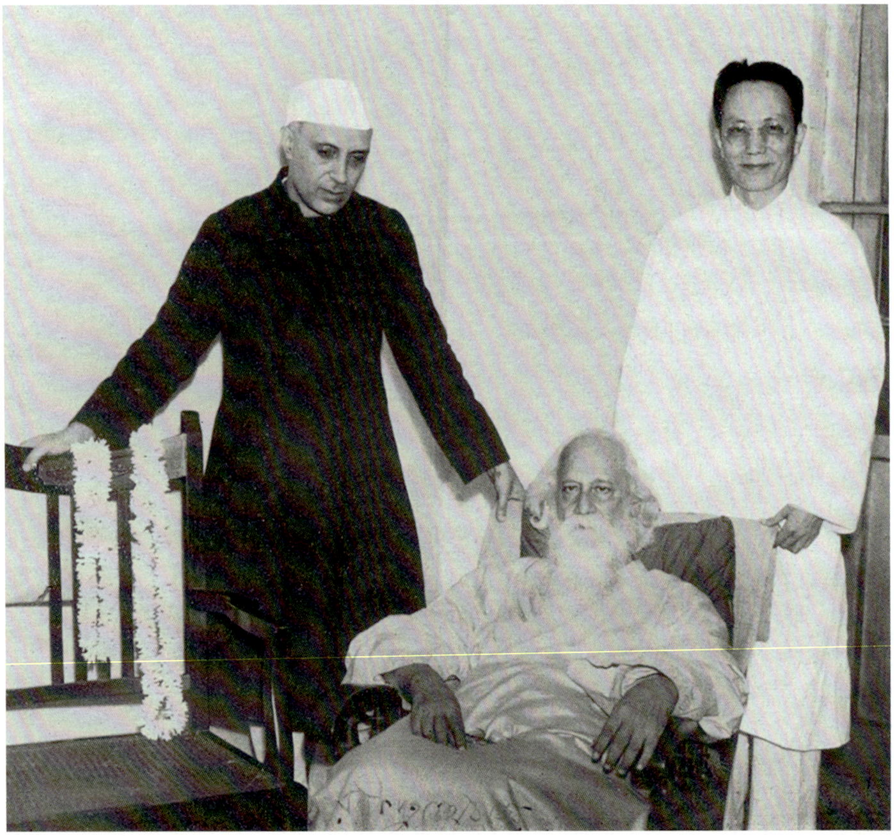

With Jawaharlal Nehru and Tan-Yun-Shan.

The two dance-dramas, were, however, enlargements of earlier compositions. *Chitrangada* was first written as a dramatic poem in 1892 and at the request of Pratima Devi, the Poet transformed it into a dance-drama in 1936. It was staged that year in Calcutta, with the Poet on the stage, reciting occasionally, and then the dance-drama was presented in Patna, Allahabad, Lahore, Delhi, Meerut getting full houses in all the cities. In Delhi, Gandhi intervened and made the Poet give up this strenuous fund-raising exercise, after sponsoring a donation of Rs 60,000 from anonymous donors. The dance-drama was, however, staged in February–March 1937 in Bombay and Ahmedabad and then in six towns of east Bengal. The troupe visited these places on its own, without the Poet, but nevertheless it drew enthusiastic and appreciative crowds in all these towns.

Syama, the second dance-drama, was a transformed poem, 'Parisodh', 1899. The dance-drama was staged at Santiniketan in October 1936 and then in Calcutta. In September 1938 it was again staged at Santiniketan and in February 1939 in Calcutta. Mrinalini performed as Vajrasen in the

Gilbert Murray to Tagore

Gilbert Murray (1866–1957), the English thinker and renowned for his works on Greek classics, wrote to Tagore on 16 August 1934, as president of the Committee on Intellectual Cooperation and asked him to sign an open letter for international intellectual cooperation. He wrote:

> You are a great poet, probably the most famous poet now living in the world and poetry is to me almost the chief pleasure and interest in life. Your life and work are inspired by a spirit of harmony, and it is in the interest of harmony between man and man that I make my appeal.

In the long letter, Murray wrote:

> ...I remember years ago a visit of yours to England, when a number of people met to give you a public welcome in some hall in London, and among other features in the entertainment, an English singer sang one of your poems. It was a gentle philosophical poem, dependent for its whole effect upon a spirit of quiet and calm. I should have liked to hear it spoken to the accompaniment of some antique stringed instrument like a harp or a cithara. But on the occasion it had been set to modern European music of a bravura style, and when the singer began, her strong soprano made me wince visibly. I looked to see how you were bearing it. No doubt you suffered, but you were the centre of all eyes and your statuesque courtesy was undisturbed.

Santiniketan performance. Her experience has been mentioned earlier, although the Poet was not impressed by her dance. She must have improved in the process, as her dance was appreciated by the press.

Tagore's famous letters to the Japanese poet, Yone Noguchi (1875–1947) and Miss Eleanor Rathbone (1872–1951) were written in this period. Noguchi was an ardent devotee of Tagore and endorsed Tagore's views on nationalism in 1916. But when he wrote a letter to Tagore in July 1938 justifying Japan's intrusion into China, Tagore wrote back two stringent letters, exposing Japan's imperialist intentions. In 1941, when Miss Rathbone from England sent an open letter to Indians, specifically Jawaharlal Nehru, advising to sink their internal dissensions to support the warring England, which had done so much for India, Tagore dictated a strong letter to Miss Rathbone, berating the so-called English mission to civilise India. He was too ill to write the letter himself, but as Jawaharlal Nehru (1888–1964) was imprisoned and gagged, the Poet firmly reacted to the gratuitous sermon. An embarrassed Rathbone consoled herself, assuming that it was not Tagore's, who was too ill, but somebody else's thought.

Dry point by the Scottish painter Sir Muirhead Bone (1876-1963).

Tagore and Bharatnatyam

Rukmini Devi Arundale (1904–86), the famous exponent of Bharatnatyam, recounts her memories of Tagore in *A Centenary Volume* on Rabindranath (Sahitya Akademi):

> The last time I ever saw and met Tagore was when Dr Arundale and I went to see him in Santiniketan a few months before passing. I was giving dance performances all over India, but I went without any accompanists thinking he was too ill to see a performance. We were treated with utmost hospitality and very gently he asked if I would give a dance recital. I told him I could not do so because of lack of accompaniments, but the request was repeated. I could not refuse and so I tried to teach one or two musicians in Santiniketan and gave two items of dance before a large audience in his home, Uttarayan. I had to sing and dance as the young musicians could not manage to learn all that was wanted in so short a time. After the dance, Tagore, who was reclining on a *chauki*, called me to him, held my hands for a long time and showered me with praise and affection. He quoted from *Malavikagnimitra* and said he understood Kalidasa's idea of the greatness of the dance only then; also that he had never before appreciated Bharata Natya which he had seen once in Madras and that his opinion of the art had now changed.

At Santiniketan, 1938;
photographed by Sombhu Saha.

The failing body

Rani Chanda was pained to see Gurudev cutting off his long curly hair. When she protested against trimming the beautiful hair, the Poet said (15 January 1938), 'I cut hair to lighten the burden on the head. Is it wise to carry unnecessary burden on the head? If you please, the build of my head is not that bad—is it?—that I will have to cover it. What do you say?'

Did he remember the exclamation, 'What a splendid head you have!' made by the headmaster of Brighton Proprietory School for Boys when Tagore, seventeen, went there for admission? The headmaster referred to the shape of the head—at first sight he knew nothing about what was inside the head.

On another day (8 April 1939), Rani heard the Poet saying that one day a German saw him in a Turkish bath and said, 'Young man, what a splendid body-frame you've got.' She saw Gurudev (12.45 a.m. at night on 10 October 1940) shaking his fingers, clinching and unclinching the fist. Gurudev told her, 'Do you think I'm practising wrestling bouts? No, my fingers are getting cramped.'

Not that Gurudev always talked of his failing body to Rani—he talked about his paintings, his music, his stories, man–woman relationship—it was Rani who wrote out the last three poems (on 27, 29, 30 July 1941), but his companions in the last few months were distressed to see the Poet trying to hide his pain which burst forth in spite of his efforts: 'My body has failed. I am living shrouded in a mist. A mist is surrounding me. I can't see properly. I can't hear either. The heart throbs. I exist. But is this existence?' (4 April 1940). Although he claimed that his brain had ceased to function and he could not find a plot, but he had to write because a newspaper had promised him a hundred rupees (saying this to Rani on 28 July 1939). He wrote *Rabibar* (The Sunday) for *Ananda Bazar Patrika*.

Gandhi, Jawaharlal, Subhas continued to come to Santiniketan or Calcutta to get Gurudev's opinion on the rapidly changing political situation of the country. In October 1937, when Tagore came to the Baranagar house, on the outskirts of Calcutta, of Prasantachandra Mahalanobis for a medical check-up, Gandhi came from Sarat Chandra Bose's house on Lansdowne Road to meet the Poet at Baranagar. On the motorcar, Gandhi fainted and was taken back to Lansdowne Road. Learning this, Tagore insisted that he must go and see him. Gandhi was staying on the topmost storey of Sarat's house. Tagore was put on a chair and the chair was carried upstairs by Jawaharlal (then forty-nine), Subhas (forty), Sarat (forty-eight) and Mahadev Desai (forty-five).

Gandhi visited Santiniketan for the last time in 1940. On 17 February he was felicitated at the mango-grove. He had earlier visited Santiniketan in 1925. Much had changed in the Ashram since then and Gandhi visited every department in Santiniketan and Sriniketan. Tagore made his last request to Gandhi to look after Santiniketan, which was his only treasure. Gandhi assured him that the treasure would not be lost. On 7 May 1941, Gandhi sent a telegram: 'Four score not enough. May you finish five'. Tagore replied: 'Thanks message. But four score is impertinence. Five score intolerable.'

At Baranagar, on the outskirts of Calcutta, 1937; photographed by Sombhu Saha.

On 26 September 1940, Rabindranath again fell unconscious at Kalimpong where he had gone, ignoring the medical advice of Nilratan Sircar and Bidhan Chandra Ray (1882–1962). There were only Pratima and Maitreyi Devi (1914–90), who was his hostess at Mungpoo. Maitreyi rushed to Darjeeling and entreated an unwilling civil surgeon to come to Kalimpong, a three-hour drive on a bad road. The British surgeon was persuaded by a crying Maitreyi on her knees to come to see the patient. He had no idea that his patient was conferred a doctorate by Oxford University barely three months ago. He asked if the patient could speak English. Diagnosing a kidney infection, he wanted a surgical operation to relieve the patient of the intense pain. But the two women resisted the

Above: Welcome to Gandhi at the mango-grove, Santiniketan, 1940. Below: With Gandhi, Santiniketan, 1940.

surgeon. Three doctors were hurriedly summoned from Calcutta and the patient was brought back to Calcutta on 29 September and then to Santiniketan on 18 November 1940.

From Rani's notes on the Poet's talks during the last days:

> 9 January 1941. (Receiving proofs of poems from the press) I sometimes feel ashamed that I've written so much. Bharatchandra Ray (1712–60), had said, 'he who talks much, talks much falsehood.' Literature is, of course, based on falsehood. How much, of what I have said, is true?
>
> 11 January. (Summoning Rani and handing over a poem on women) I've addressed it to the women of the world, you're just an excuse. Patients are like a divinity to you women. The woman who takes up nursing as a duty, takes up the nursing of the world. Women are universal, they have the power of nurturing the universe.
>
> 11 March. The body refuses to carry on. But you can see, the heart is working, the pulse is all right, the temperature is 99.6—everything is okay. But there is somewhere a Hitler working out his way.
>
> 14 March. (As Rani massages oil on his hand and wonders at the smooth skin, wrinklefree) I inherited much, otherwise how could I carry on? I've earned some. But I've spent much. Now I'll blow it out all.
>
> 17 April. Rani writes that Gurudev fondly remembers Henry Morley of London University, who used to read the text and that was enough to convey the import. How Morley was angered by an essay of an Indian student, who sang paeans on the British race and expatiated on the inferiority of Indians. Tagore, ashamed of his countrymen, wrote a counter essay on the Englishmen in India and submitted it to his teacher. He did not know how Morley would react to the criticism of British rulers and bunked from his classes till Loken Palit found him out, slapped

his back and told him how Morley praised the content, the style and the language of the student. That, Gurudev told her, was the highest praise he received in his life. And then Gurudev remembered how Bankim praised his novel, *Bauthakuranir Hat* and the poem *Sandhya Sangit* (The Evening Song).

Above: Henry Morley.
Facing page: After recovery, 1937.

23 April. Gurudev talks about Indian and Western paintings. Gurudev talks about his songs.

24 April. Gurudev talks about lyrical poetry.

27 April. Gurudev is irritated by a 'modern' Bengali poem.

15 May. Gurudev is extremely angry about somebody who suggested that India would be at a loss if the British rulers left the country.

17 May. Gurudev said women's abject dependence on men would continue till they could earn their own living.

21 May. 04.30 a.m. Gurudev wakes up. Rani washed his face, took him to the couch and opened the windows. He said, 'You've brought life to me. The morning light brings back a hope to me. I don't like at all the darkness of night. Everything seems to sink into the darkness. I wait for the dawn. The darkness fades out and a clear picture emerges.'

Afternoon. Gurudev talks about his paintings.

22 May. Gurudev talks about his short stories. He says he does not understand why his stories are called lyrical.

23 May. Gurudev makes fun with the pronunciation of, and Bengali spelling by people who live on the eastern side of the River Padma. (Rani is one of them.) Gurudev talks about the dedication of women. Mentions Vivekananda and Nivedita.

24 May. Gurudev had met a few modern writers. He said, the ultimate purpose of literature is to create joy in the mind. Modern critics know only to dissect, to ridicule. He is annoyed with an

article on his paintings in a newspaper. A painting is a painting —no matter whether it is Eastern or Western.

25, 26, 27 May. Art never imitates. It creates. Man tries to turn his dreams into reality. Modern literature deals with poverty of life. It can't solve life's problems. I tried it to do it in Silaidaha, not by art but by practical land reforms. He is annoyed by talks of proletariat art. Talks about the funny way a Polish sculptor made a bust of his. It was an amusing bust, but that was his way of seeing things.

30 May. Gurudev talks about his young students and old teachers of the Ashram.

31 May 1941. Gurudev is sad because Abanindranath was leaving Jorasanko forever. A total culture that was Jorasanko was dying. Now it will be dead; enough is enough, he said. (Paraphrased by Author.)

Rabindranath was not all his real self at this time—high fever, comatose moments. The summer heat was intense with no rainfall. The Poet had been provided with an air-conditioner by Ranu, but the machines were very primitive those days and extremely noisy. Allopathy was not working. The Indian medical treatment, Kaviraji, was tried. Doctors were sending daily bulletins to senior doctors in Calcutta, who were undecided whether surgery was the only option. Nilratan Sircar chided the juniors such as Bidhan and Lalit Kumar Bandyopadhyay who insisted on operation but Nilratan warned them because Tagore's nerve system was too sensitive to withstand surgery. They all came down to Santiniketan and after a great deal of hesitation told the Poet that he would become normal as before after an operation, which was not so great a thing. The Poet was startled. Operation? Couldn't he just drop out

like a withered leaf, as naturally? But on 25 July 1941, he was taken down to Calcutta by a special saloon attached to the train. All the inmates of the Ashram stood silently in a row, wondering if their Gurudev would ever come back.

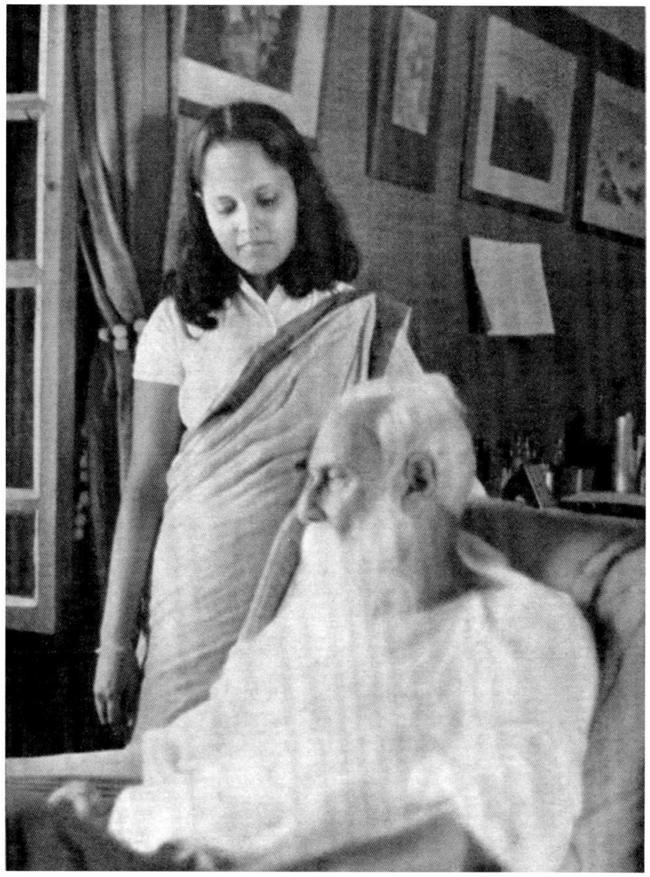

Above: Nandita Kriplani, the Poet's granddaughter, the principal nurse during the Poet's last days. Facing page: At Santiniketan, 1940.

Gurudev asked his doctors, how painful would be the operation. One of them, a distant relation, assured him that he would not at all feel pain. He had become used to intravenous injections—the surgery would be just like that. They would be operating upon him at one end and quite possibly he would be dictating a poem at the other end!

The date of operation, 30 July, was kept secret to him lest tensions created havoc with his blood pressure. It was a secret to others also, in case somebody spilled it out to Gurudev. On the day of the operation, Lalit arranged the infrastructure of the surgery and casually told the Poet, 'Let us finish off the job.' A startled look appeared on the Poet's face. He dictated his last poem to Rani and said there were few corrections to be made—he would do them later—the doctors had assured him that he would be clear-headed after the operation. The twenty-five-minute operation, supra-pubic cystostomy, was over by mid-morning and the Poet never regained full consciousness. In the evening, Lalit asked if Gurudev felt pain during the operation and Gurudev said, 'Why ask questions and be told lies?' On the third day, seeing the patient suffering from hiccups, a desperate Bidhan asked the ladies of the house, 'There are so many home remedies for hiccups, can't you do anything?' On the fifth day, Nilratan came to see the patient. He listened to the doctors, took the hands of the patient and softly massaged them. After some time, he rose and walked up to the door and cast a last glance at his long-time friend. Everybody realised, there was no hope. Bidhan dragged his tired legs out of the door. The Poet breathed his last on 7 August at 12.10 p.m.

During one of his European tours, Rabindranath received a letter dated 1 August 1920 from an unknown woman.

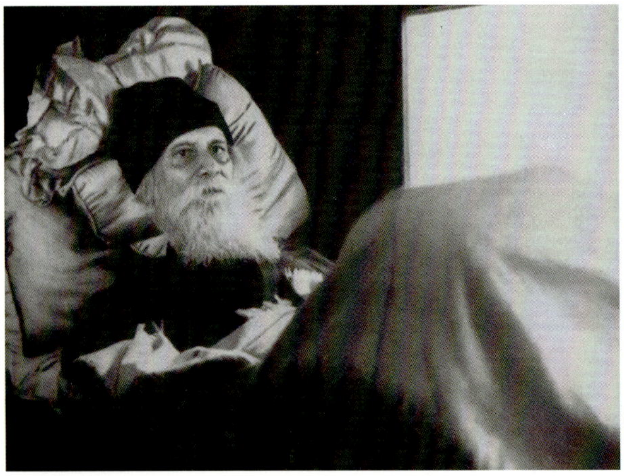

Dear Sir Rabindranath,

I have been trying to find courage to write to you ever since I heard that you were in London—but the desire to tell you something is finding its way into this letter today. The letter may never reach you, for I do not know how to address it, though I feel sure your name upon the envelope will be sufficient. It is nearly two years ago, that my dear eldest son went out to the War for the last time and the day he said goodbye to me—we were looking together across the sun-glorified sea—looking towards France, with breaking hearts—when he, my poet son, said those wonderful words of yours—beginning at, 'When I go from hence, let this be my parting word'—and when his pocket book came back to me—I found these words written in his dear writing—with your name beneath. Would it be asking too much of you, to tell me what book I should find the whole poem in?

The letter was a long one, signed by Susan H. Owen, the mother of Wilfred Owen, who, Susan informed, was killed a week before the awful fighting was over. Wilfred was twenty-five at that time. Chatto & Windus later proposed to bring out a book of verse by Wilfred. His mother asked Tagore if she could send him a copy.

Susan must have been informed of the book (*Gitanjali*, no. 96) in which she would find the poem:

When I go from hence let this be my parting word, that what I have seen is unsurpassable.

I have tasted of the hidden honey of this lotus that expands on the ocean of light, and thus I am blessed—let this be my parting word.

In this playhouse of infinite forms I have had my play and here have I caught sight of him that is formless.

My whole body and my limbs have thrilled with his touch who is beyond touch; and if the end comes here, let it come—let this be my parting word.

Left: The Poet in England when he received the letter from Wilfred Owen's mother.
Facing page
Left: The Poet is taken away from Santiniketan, 1941.
Right: The last journey, 7 August 1941.

GENEALOGY

- **DWARKANATH TAGORE** (1794–1846)
  - **DEVENDRANATH** (1817–1905)
    - A daughter who died in infancy
    - Dwijendranath (1840–1926)
    - Satyendranath (1842–1923)
    - Hemendranath (1844–1884)
    - Birendranath (1845–1915)
    - Saudamini (1847–1920)
    - Jyotirindranath (1848–1925)
    - Sukumari (1849–1864)
    - Punyendranath (1850–1851)
    - Saratkumari (1854–1920)
    - Swarnakumari (1855–1932)
    - Barnakumari (1857–1948)
    - Somendranath (1860–1928)
    - **RABINDRANATH** (1861–1941)
      - Madhurilata (1886–1918)
      - Rathindranath (1888–1961)
      - Renuka (1890–1904)
      - Mira (1892–1969)
        - Nitindranath (1911–1932)
        - Nandita (1916–1967)
      - Samindranath (1894–1907)
    - Budhendranath (1863–1864)
  - Girindranath (1820–1854)
    - Ganendranath (1841–1869)
    - Gunendranath (1847–1881)
      - Gagendranath (1867–1938)
      - Samarendranath (Born 1870)
      - Abanindranath (Born 1871)
  - Nagendranath (1829–1858)

Bibliography

Adhikari, Sachindranath. 1974. *Silaidaha O Rabindranath*. Calcutta: Jijnasa .

Bhattacharya, Sabyasachi. 1997. *The Mahatma and the Poet*. Delhi: National Book Trust.

Bhowmik, Samar. 1997. *Ranu Mukhopadhyayer Jibanalekhya*. Calcutta: Unique Book Centre.

Bhowmik, Someswar. 'Likhan tomar helay'. In *Autumn Annual* 2005-2006. Kolkata: Presidency College Alumni Association.

Chakrabarti, Ajitkumar. 2007. 'Bhakta O Kabi'. In *Rabindranath Tagore Patrabali*, edited by Rudraprasad Chakrabarti. Kolkata: Paschimbanga Bangla Akademi.

Chakrabarti, Rama. 2001. *Bhara Thak Smritisudhay*. Kolkata: Tagore Research Institute.

Chakrabarti. Rudra Prasad. 1995. *Rangamancha O Rabindranath*. Calcutta: Ananda.

Chakrabarti, Gautam and Subhash Chaudhuri. 1972. *Surendranath Thakur—A Centenary Compilation*. Calcutta: Surendranath Thakur Janma Satabarshik Samiti.

Chakravarty, Bikash (ed.). 1998. *Poets to a Poet*. Calcutta: Visva-Bharati.

Chanda, Rani. 1983. *Alapchari Rabindranath*. Calcutta: Visva-Bharati.

——. 2000 (edn). *Gurudeb. Calcutta*: Visva-Bharati.

Chatterjee, Rimi B. 2001. 'Canon without Consensus: Rabindranath Tagore and the Oxford Book of Bengali Verse'. In *Book History*, Vol. 4. University Park: The Pennsylvania State University Press.

Chatterji, Ramananda (ed.). 1931. *The Golden Book of Tagore*. The Golden Book of Tagore Committee.

Chaudhuri, Amitabha. 2002. *Rabikahini*. Delhi: National Book Trust.

Das, Sajanikanta. 1960. *Rabindranath: Jiban O Sahitya*. Calcutta.

Dasgupta, Uma (ed.). 2003. *A Difficult Friendship: Letters of Edward Thompson and Rabindranath Tagore*. Delhi: Oxford University Press.

Datta, Krishna and Andrew Robinson (eds.). 1991. *Purabi. A Miscellany in Memory of Rabindranath Tagore*. UK: The Tagore Centre.

Deb, Chitra. 1985. *Analochita Rabindra Prasanga*. Calcutta: Modern Column.

Debi, Maitreyi. 1979 (edn.). *Mangpute Rabindranath*. Calcutta: Prima Publications.

——. 1999 (edn.). *Svarger Kachakachi*. Calcutta: Prima Publication.

Debi, Mira. 2001 (edn.). *Smritikatha*. Calcutta: Visva-Bharati.

Debi, Sita. 1964 (edn.). *Punyasmriti*. Calcutta: Maitri.

Devichaudhurani, Sarala. 1945. *Jibaner Jharapata*. Calcutta: Rupa.

Dey, Abhik Kumar. 2006. *Smritir Chhabi: Rabindranath Thakur*. Kolkata: Punascha.

Dutta, Krishna and Andrew Robinson (eds.). 2005. *Selected Letters of Rabindranath Tagore*. Cambridge: Cambridge University Press.

——. 2000. *Rabindranath Tagore: The Myriad–Minded Man*. Calcutta: Rupa.

Dyson, Ketaki Kushari. 1988. *In Your Blossoming Flower-Garden Rabindranath Tagore and Victoria Ocampo*. New Delhi:Sahitya Akademi.

Elmhirst, Leonard K. 1975. *Poet and Plowman*. Calcutta: Visva-Bharati.

Espmark, Kjell. 1991. *The Nobel Prize in Literature: A Study of the Criteria behind the Choices*. Boston.

Forster, E. M. 1936. *Abinger Harvest*. UK. Arnold.

——. 1962. *Two Cheers for Democracy*. UK: Harvest Book.

Gandhi, Gopalkrishna (ed.). 2007. *A Frank Friendship: Gandhi and Bengal: A Descriptive Chronology*. Kolkata: Seagull.

Ghosh, Aurobindo. 1973. *Bande Mataram: Early Political Writings*. Pondicherry: Sri Aurobindo Ashram.

Guha, Chinmoy (ed. and trans.). 1996. *The Tower and the Sea: Romain Rolland—Kalidas Nag Correspondence*. Calcutta: Papyrus.

Hay, Stephen N. 1970. *Asian Ideas of East and West: Tagore and His Critics in Japan, China and Asia*. Massachusetts: Cambridge Press.

Kar, Sudhir Chandra. 1960. *Rabindra Aloke Rabindra Parichay*. Calcutta: Nabajug Prakasani.

Kripalani, Krishna. 1980 (edn.). *Rabindranath Tagore: A Biography*. Calcutta: Visva-Bharati.

Kundu, Kalyan, Sakti Bhattacharya and Kalyan Sircar (comp. and ed.). 2000. *Imagining Tagore: Rabindranath Tagore and the British Press 1912–1941*. Kolkata: Sahitya Sansad.

Lago, Mary M (ed.).1972. *Imperfect Encounter: Letters of William Rothenstein and Rabindranath Tagore 1911–1941*. Massachusetts: Cambridge Press.

Macmillan. 1936. *Collected Poems and Plays*. UK.

Mahalanobis. Nirmal Kumari. 1970. *Kabir Sange Europe*. Calcutta: Mitra O Ghosh.

— —. 1988 (edn.). *Baise Sravan*. Calcutta: Mitra O Ghosh.

Majumdar, Lila. 1971 (edn.). *Ar Konokhane*. Calcutta: Mitra O Ghosh.

Majumdar, Nepal. 1980. *Bharate Jatiyata O Antarjatikata Ebang Rabindranath Vol. 6*. Calcutta: Chatushkon.

Majumdar, Sailajaranjan. 1989 (edn.). *Yatrapathe Anandagan*. Calcutta: Ananda.

Mukherjee, Sujit. 1964. *Passage to America*. Calcutta: Bookland.

Mukhopadhyay, Bandana (ed.). 1999. *Facets of a Genius*. New Delhi:Akashvani and Visva-Bharati.

Mukhopadhyay, Prabhat Kumar. *Rabindrajibani O Rabindrasahitya—Prabesak*. Vol. 1 (1970), Vol. 2 (1977), Vol. 3 (1990) and Vol. 4 (1964). Calcutta: Visva-Bharati.

The Nobel Foundation Directory. 1991–92. Stockholm: Nobel Foundation.

Paul, Prasanta Kumar. *Rabijibani*. Vol. 1 (1982) and Vol.2 (1984). Calcutta: Bhurjapatra.

— —. Vol. 3 (1987), Vol.4 (1988), Vol.5 (1990), Vol.6 (1993), Vol.7 (1997), Vol.8 (2001) and Vol.9 (2003). Calcutta: Ananda.

— —. (ed.). 2005. *Kalyaniyeshu Prasanta. Rabindranath–Prasantachandra Mahalanobis Patrabinimoy*. Kolkata: Paschimbanga Bangla Akademi.

Rabindra Bharati University. 2009. *Rabindranath Tagore: A Journey through the lenses*. Kolkata.

Ratray, John W. 1962. 'I shall stand'. In the *Visva-Bharati Quarterly: Tagore Centenary*. Calcutta.

Ray, Jayanti (ed.). 1975. *Nobel Puraskar O Rabindra Sangbardhana*. Kolkata: Tagore Research Institute.

Rhys, Ernest. 1915. *Rabindranath Tagore: A Biographical Study*. UK: Everyman Library.

Rothenstein, William. 1934. *Men and Memories*. Vol. 2. New York: Coward-McCann.

Sahitya Akademi. *The English Writings of Rabindranath Tagore*. Vol. 1 (1994), Vol. 2 (1996), Vol. 3 (1996), Vol. 4 (2007). New Delhi.

Sanyal, Abanti Kumar. 1976. *Bharatbarsha* (translation of *Inde* by Romain Rolland). Calcutta: Radical Book Club.

Sarkar, Sumit. 1973 (stet.). *The Swadeshi Movement in Bengal 1903–08*. New Delhi: People's Publishing House.

Sen, Amita. 2002. *Santiniketaner Asram Kanya*. Kolkata: Tagore Research Institute.

Sen, Prabodhchandra. 1972. *India's National Anthem*. Calcutta: Visva-Bharati.

Tagore. Surendranath (transl.). 1921. *Glimpses of Bengal*. UK: Macmillan.

Thompson, Dr. Edward J. 1921. *Rabindranath Tagore: His Life and Work*. Calcutta: YMCA Publishing House.

Thompson, E.P. 1988. *Alien Homage*. Delhi: Oxford University Press.

Visva-Bharati. 1980. *Pathe O Pather Prante*. Calcutta: (Letters from Rabindranath Tagore to Nirmalkumari Mahalanobis)

— —. *Rabindra Rachanabali*. 33 Vols (1935–2000). Calcutta.

— —. 1942–2004. *Chithipatra*, 19 Vols. Calcutta.

— —.1970 (edn.). *Gitabitan*. Calcutta.

— —. *Rabindra-Viksha*. 50 Vols. (1976–2009). Calcutta.

— —. 1981 (edn.). *On the Edges of Time*. Calcutta.

— —. 2002 (edn.). *Chhinnapatrabali*. Calcutta.

Wojtilla, Gyula. 1983. *Rabindranath Tagore in Hungary*. New Delhi: Hungarian Information and Cultural Centre.

Acknowledgements

I have known Nirmal Bhattacharya for a long time, since his days with Sahitya Akademi and National Book Trust. It was kind of him to suggest my name to Niyogi Books of Delhi for writing this book. It was a sheer pleasure to come into contact with this charming couple, Bikash and Tultul, who were as excited as I was to plan and execute this engrossing job. Chinmoy Dey, my neighbour and friend, gladly typeset the first draft of the manuscript. Madhuparna Banerjee edited the text with great care. Partha Sengupta scanned the photographs used in this book and gave a presentable form to the published photographs which were not of ideal quality. I have mentioned all the books, on which I depended for the text and photographs, in the Bibliography.

Index

Note: Page numbers with *f* indicate photographs.

NIYOGI BOOKS
on
Rabindranath Tagore

- Tagore's Paintings: Versification in Line
  by Sovon Som

- Architecture of Santiniketan
  & Tagore's Concept of Space
  by Samit Das

- Tagore's Mystique of Dance
  by Utpal K. Banerjee

- Selected Essays, Speeches, Letters of
  Rabindranath Tagore
  Compiled, Translated and Edited by Subhrangshu Maitra

- Symbols and Songs:
  A Study of Leitmotif in Tagore Songs
  by Kishore Chatterjee

- The Four Quartets
  Translation of Chaturanga by Nirmal Kanti Bhattacharjee

- The Inverted Mirror:
  Cartoons on Rabindranath Tagore
  by Sushovon Adhikari

- King of the Dark Chamber
  Translation of Raja by Rabindranath Tagore

- Rabindranath Tagore: His World of Art
  by Supriya Roy and Sushovan Adhikari